COMIC BOOK
CRIME

NICKIE D. PHILLIPS AND STACI STROBL

COMIC BOOK CRIME

TRUTH, JUSTICE, AND THE AMERICAN WAY

NEW
YORK
UNIVERSITY
PRESS

New York and London

NEW YORK UNIVERSITY PRESS
New York and London
www.nyupress.org

References to Internet websites (URLs) were accurate at the time of writing.
Neither the author nor New York University Press is responsible for URLs that
may have expired or changed since the manuscript was prepared.

LIBRARY OF CONGRESS CATALOGING-IN-PUBLICATION DATA
Phillips, Nickie D.
Comic Book Crime : Truth, Justice, and the American Way / Nickie D. Phillips and Staci
Strobl.
pages cm. — (Alternative Criminology Series)
Includes bibliographical references and index.
ISBN 978-0-8147-6787-0 (cl : acid-free paper)
ISBN 978-0-8147-6788-7 (pb   )
1. Comic books, strips, etc.—History and criticism. 2. Crime in literature. 3. Justice in
literature. 4. Social values in literature. 5. Literature and society—United States—History. I.
Strobl, Staci. II. Title.
PN6725.P48 2013
741.5'973—dc23
2012050855

New York University Press books

Manufactured in the United States of America
10 9 8 7 6 5 4 3 2 1

CONTENTS

ACKNOWLEDGMENTS

Some books write themselves. This was not one of them, and so we wish to thank everyone who helped us along the way. Our hard work would have been futile without the guidance and support of many people. In particular we would like to thank Dr. Jeff Ferrell, of Texas Christian University and the University of Kent, and Dr. Mark Hamm, of Indiana State University, who "discovered" our first comic book project and provided the encouragement and inspiration without which none of our subsequent research would have happened. While some scholars we knew looked askance at us early-career criminologists focusing on comic books, Ferrell and Hamm saved us from internalizing too much of that judgment and doubt. We also profusely thank our editor, Ilene Kalish, New York University Press, for helping us shape our big idea into something that other people might want to read, Emily Wright, our copyeditor, and Despina Papazoglou Gimbel for their help, particularly in organizing the comic book images and finalizing the manuscript.

We also want to acknowledge Dr. Franklin Wilson, of Indiana State University, for tirelessly organizing the International Crime, Media, and Popular Culture Studies Conference so that we had a safe haven to retreat to each year to take comic books, and other popular cultural artifacts, very, very seriously. The Professional Staff Congress for the City University of New York provided grant money for our research on Arab Americans in comic books, and Provost Timothy J. Houlihan, Director of Media Relations Richard Relkin, and others at St. Francis College offered resources and encouragement at key moments. Dr. Maki Haberfeld, John Jay College, has always supported our diverse and sometimes odd interests, in addition to being a close friend.

We also would like to call out to several comic book fans and retailers who kept us well stocked and answered our industry questions, big and small: David Cruz, Muhammed Nashir, and Tom Lupo at Galaxy Comics (Brooklyn), the crew at Jim Hanley's Universe and in particular the Speak On It! group (Manhattan), Forbidden Planet (Manhattan), Bergen Comics (Brooklyn), and Al Mejias (the New York Manga & Comics meet-up).

Special thanks also go out to Dr. Mary Tabakow, American University at Dubai, and Chad Denton, University of Missouri at Columbia, for reading early drafts of the book and providing comments, and to comics scholar Dr. Jonathan Gray, John Jay College, for liking our work enough to include it in his popular comic book course. Comics writer Greg Rucka kindly read a draft of an early article of ours and helped to fine-tune our thinking in preparation for writing this book. Communications scholar Dr. Patrick Collins had encouraging words along the way, accompanied by clips of interesting comic book articles. Jose Rivera was a steadfast companion at many a comic book convention. And, the Reynolds House Inn in Roscoe, New York, provided the perfect lodging for a marathon revision retreat.

Freelance journalist Karen Iris Tucker selflessly read and improved our grammar and style so that we did not embarrass ourselves too badly along the way. Professor Matt Michaels, John Jay College of Criminal Justice, helped orchestrate our sampling and otherwise provided much-needed methodological assistance. In addition, Tucker's and Michaels's emotional support along the way was unsurpassed, and we cannot acknowledge them enough in these pages.

Finally, we must thank our friends and family, particularly our parents, for believing that we really were writing a book and that it would eventually be published. Our refrains of "sometime next year" did not grow as old as they should have.

1

HOLY CRIMINOLOGY, BATMAN!

COMICS AND CONSTRUCTIONS
OF CRIME AND JUSTICE

Comic book readers around the world know that the medium's unforgetta-ble heroes and villains are capable of leaping out of their pages and into our lives. Upholding "truth, justice, and the American way" with super-powered strength and agility that is "faster than a speeding bullet," Superman emerged from his Kryptonian rocket ship and onto the American cultural landscape, an origin story told and retold countless times to no less fanfare. Iconic Spider-Man inspired a generation of youths who related to his soft-spoken geekiness, yet reveled in the "great power" he gained from a spider bite—also saddling him with the proverbial "great responsibility." Wonder Woman's golden "lasso of truth," originally forged from the magic girdle of Aphrodite, gave the world a woman super-empowered to squeeze the truth out of even the toughest villain. Captain America, Batman, and Green Lantern: the list goes on, and yet so many have become mainstays in American popular cul-ture, nearly universally recognizable and often deeply loved.

Comic book lore inspired generations of readers—even members of the criminal justice community who work with real-life criminal offend-ers. Such was the case with Judge Jack Love of Albuquerque, New Mex-ico. Judge Love sentenced the very first offender to electronic monitoring after reading a Spider-Man story in which the superhero is tagged with a device that tracks his movements. Judge Love saw the potential for such a device to keep tabs on probationers and developed electronic monitoring, now commonly used in community corrections across the country.[1]

Although comic books are far from manuals for how to run the criminal justice system, we can learn much about American society by interrogating the ways in which cultural meanings about crime and justice are negotiated and contested within them. In this context, comic books offer expressions of contemporary life that tap into our hopes, fears, personal insecurities, and uncertainties about the future, as do popular media in general. Comic books, particularly those of the superhero genre, are replete with themes of crime and justice, yet are frequently ignored by criminologists.[2] We explore the ways in which meanings about crime and justice are negotiated and contested in comic books and the way these imaginings form part of a broader cultural context in which readers absorb, reproduce, and resist notions of justice.

We examine comic books in terms of what criminologist Stephanie Kane described as an "experimental ethnographic space," a place occupied by characters as its virtual inhabitants.[3] Indeed, the world of Superman drops the reader into a kind of alternate America, where Smallville and Metropolis act as proxies for real American towns and cities. Batman invites us into a dark and dystopic Gotham where we meet the Riddler and the Penguin and get lost in the dark passageways of Wayne Manor or vicariously play with the technological gadgetry of a reclusive and crime-obsessed millionaire. Through extended virtual visits to these imaginary worlds, we paid attention to both the visuals and the text—the juxtaposition of which provides a wealth of opportunities for interpretation.

"[C]omics are more flexible than theater, deeper than cinema," explains Pulitzer Prize–winning comic creator Art Spiegelman in a 1991 *New York Times* interview.[4] Comic creator Scott McCloud states that the "heart of comics lies in the space *between* the panels—where the reader's imagination makes still pictures come alive!"[5] Unlike other mediums such as film or television, comic books rely much more heavily on the reader as participant—to use his or her imagination to fill in "the gutter," or space between the panels. McCloud further explains that the more abstract the artistic rendering, the more the reader fills in, or creates his or her own level of detail. Comic books then provide a means for exploring images of villains, heroes, and notions of justice in a participatory and fluid medium.[6]

Like other scholars who have investigated the relationship between cultural artifacts and fandom, our approach also considers the plurality of the audience and explores the ways in which devoted readers, sometimes colloquially referred to as "fanboys," not only absorb comic book narratives but also may actively negotiate and shape the narratives themselves.[7] At times, readers have directly influenced plot lines, such as in DC Comics' decision to let voters decide whether the second Batman sidekick Robin (a.k.a. Jason Todd) lives or dies at the hand of the Joker in *A Death in the Family* (1988). Invited to call a hotline, over ten thousand readers voted by a narrow margin for Robin to meet his demise.[8] Readers may also influence the storylines in a more subtle process, by using their economic power to purchase one comic book over another.

As anthropologist Matthew Wolf-Meyer points out, fans communicate through specific language and inside knowledge that is indicative of cultural importance while serving to distinguish them from outsiders.[9] More casual readers are easily recognized by their inability to communicate this insider knowledge. Fans, on the other hand, submerge themselves in the minutiae. There are voluminous weekly podcasts available online, many with related forums drawing thousands of members, devoted to discussion and commentary on each week's comic book releases. At a New York City–based comic book and graphic novel meet-up, group members described their consumption of comic books and graphic novels in an indulgent, pleasure-oriented way, planning their next purchase and reveling in the "first time" they read a certain comic book or graphic novel.

The format of the comic books, the seductive illustrations coupled with captivating dialogue boxes, draws in readers, who then encounter the medium's dominant themes and messages. We suggest that the repetition of cultural meanings in comic book narratives often reinforces particular notions of justice, especially the punishment philosophies of retributive justice and incapacitation. Further, we argue that these types of punishments are meted out by crime-fighting heroes and superheroes who are depicted as predominantly white males defending a nostalgic American way of life. These particularities of the comic book formula, which we describe in this book, are important to explore and interrogate. Like most other popular culture artifacts, they contribute to the retributive discourse that legal studies scholar David Garland points out dominates our social responses to crime.[10]

To bolster our analysis of crime-and-justice content, we conducted focus groups with a purposive sample of comic readers in order to understand the intensity of the connection between the readers and their participation in the world of comic books, both inside and outside the text. By "outside the text," we mean that we will situate comic books within the larger environment of popular cultural fandom. As participant observers over a period of several years, we spent hours in comic books stores, attended comic book conventions, conferences, reading groups, and book signings, monitored relevant online discussion boards and Twitter feeds, and listened to weekly comic book–focused podcasts.

Realizing that comic books continue to reflect the social environment from which they emerge, we began our sampling after the terrorist events of September 11, 2001.[11] In particular, themes related to global terrorist threats have proliferated, and the "death" of Captain America has been analyzed as commentary on the ineffectiveness of patriotic American superheroes to fight for justice in our multicultural and morally vague postmodern world.[12] Over the past several years, more diverse, complex characters have appeared. For example, in pre-9/11 comic books, whenever Arabs and Muslims were depicted, they were almost always villains, whereas since 2001, heroic Arabs and Muslims have been depicted in such best-selling books as *X-Men: Messiah Complex* and *The Losers*.[13] Notably, after 9/11 comic books created a space for a new characterization of Arabs, possibly as a counter-reaction to more stereotypical constructions in media discourse. Although the fundamental formula in many comic books, which we will discuss in the following chapters, remains identifiable, we believe that contemporary comic books are best understood in terms of this post-9/11 shift in plots and characters.

Throughout the book, we will refer to a cross-section of two hundred contemporary American comic books, published from 2001 until 2010, which includes icons such as *Batman, Captain America, Spider-Man, Wonder Woman,* and *Superman* (see appendix A).[14] The vast majority of the comic books we consider were published by DC or Marvel, which together comprise approximately 70 percent of the annual market share (see table 1.1).[15] Most of the books in our sample belong to the superhero genre. Unlike other mediums such as movies, television, and video games, the superhero genre dominates the landscape of comic books, perhaps because it is the originator of most of the superhero characters that remain influential today. Yet, this has occurred despite many examples of notable non-superhero comics (e.g., *Maus, Persepolis, Optic Nerve,* etc.) that have achieved critical acclaim. Regardless, non-superhero titles are poor sellers relative to the superhero genre and do not drive monthly sales, according to the comic book distributors' monthly sales data.

We allowed the lived experience to dictate our methods and subject material by tapping into both best-selling comic books and those that have achieved critical acclaim or are considered important by readers themselves. Based on our ethnographic engagement with the world of comics, we paid particular attention to the books that bloggers, message boards, forums, focus groups, and members of the comic book community identified as important, controversial, popular, influential, or otherwise interesting.

Next, we ensured that our sample is representative of what sells best, making the assumption that popularity is a reasonable proxy for cultural influence. We based our sample on the monthly comic books distribution rankings using the ICv2 (Internal Correspondence version 2), which provides a ranking of direct market sales to comic book stores although it does not compile data on sales from "big box" stores like Barnes & Noble. Using their website, we accessed sales data for the time period between March 2003 and August 2009. Our sample included dozens of the one hundred most popular comic book series and many of the one hundred most popular graphic novels based on a popularity index (see appendix A for more information about our popularity index).[16] Through our popularity index we confirmed that our purposive sample tapped into the content that an allegedly objective measure of popularity—sales—would have also suggested. In addition, we read several more titles, bringing our total sample to nearly two hundred.

Cultural Criminology and Comic Books

In analyzing contemporary comic books, we employ a cultural criminological framework, suggesting that the cultural meaning and symbolic importance of comic books represents a viable area of exploration for criminologists. Cultural criminology is an evolving theoretical perspective influenced by various critical approaches such as labeling theory, postmodernist analysis, social constructionism, and critical criminology, among others.[17] Cultural criminologists describe the contemporary media environment as "an infinite hall of mediated mirrors" in which fast-paced packages of information and entertainment are constantly produced and reproduced, resulting in "a circulating cultural fluidity that overwhelms any certain distinction between an event and its representation."[18] This connects to notions described by theorists as "postmodern" or "late modern," in which "popular cultural signs and media images increasingly dominate our sense of reality and the way we define ourselves and the world around us."[19] In postmodern thought, images of reality increasingly constitute reality itself. Or, as Jean Baudrillard theorized, society exists in the hyperreal; images of images of images begin to replace the original until all that resonates and contains cultural meaning is the facsimile.[20]

Accordingly, there is an increasing convergence of fiction and nonfiction in our everyday lives. For example, entertainment is fused with news, news commentary is often indistinguishable from news reporting, and prime-time entertainment has increasingly turned to crime-related "reality" shows packaged and sold as raw and unfiltered reality (e.g. *COPS* and the *SWAT* franchises).[21] Here, we are not suggesting that one is unable to distinguish between fiction and reality, but rather recognizing that, as cultural studies scholar John Storey points out, "the distinction between the two has become less and less important."[22] In this context of the blurring between fact and fiction and the increasing significance of popular culture on public discourse, it is no longer advisable for criminologists to ignore what Nicole Rafter calls "popular criminology," or the criminological imaginings that lie at the intersection of academic criminology and popular culture.[23]

Our interest lies in exploring how the portrayal of crime and justice in comic books contributes to conceptions of when, where, and against whom violence is appropriate and to the intensity with which readers connect to the reading experience portraying that violence. As criminologist Jock Young states, the mass media "does not cause aggression so much as provide a script or narrative which suggests when violence is appropriate, against whom, for what reasons and with what effects, together with images of those against whom violence is permitted and prohibited."[24]

Consumption of comic books is a rich and meaningful experience for readers. Comic books (the most impactful, at least) connect with readers at a visceral level—evoking emotional responses that we link to criminologist Jack Katz's concept of engagement in a "ritual moral exercise."[25] In his analysis of news media, Katz is suggesting that readers do not seek out crime news to get to the "truth" of any matter. Instead they seek to confront moral concerns. The consumption of news stories is a way for readers to work out their moral anxieties. Katz writes, "Although each may read in isolation, phenomenologically the experience may be a collective, emotional 'effervescence' of moral indignation."[26] In a similar fashion, we suggest that comic books, with their recurring themes of crime and punishment, provide a means for readers to work through moral dilemmas. Even as heroes often show restraint, the violent graphics and extended fight scenes have a retributive emotional resonance. David Garland describes this engagement, pointing out that punishment evokes a range of emotions, from resentment, defined as moving "the 'indifferent bystander' to feel strongly that action must be taken to put right the injustice" to an even more base sentiment of sadistic gratification in the suffering of others inflicted through punitive power.[27]

Reading comic books is a way of experiencing and expressing retribution and vengeance that is short-lived and contained within the context of "fantasy" (i.e., there's a time and place for vengeance).[28] Such real-life violence perpetrated in a civilized society would be deemed at the very least unacceptable, if not criminal. In fact, at the moment of consumption, readers themselves express a visceral, emotional desire to engage violently with the bad guys. For example, during the course of our study, we found several readers expressing sentiments such as, "[S]ometimes bad people deserve a beating" and "just need to be throttled" or, more succinctly, "[W]e want blood." At the same time, they are careful to highlight that the comic book universe is not "our reality" and that to engage in "the real world" as a "superhero" would be foolhardy if not suicidal.[29]

Insofar as comic books primarily consist of narratives of violence, crime, and justice, reading them is itself a transgression. Readers express this notion by stating, "All justice is based somewhat on revenge" and "It feels good to punish."[30] One comic book fan even likened the comic book world to the "porn world" for having a formula with a similar teaser style, a hyperreality of violence that often culminates in virtual "blood on our claws."[31] Put even more starkly, one blogger wrote in regard to his love of the *Moon Knight* series, "I gotta' say, it feels sick of me to think it, but I love reading *Moon Knight*, because deep down I know his moral compass, his concept of justice, are both totally fucking *wrong*."[32]

Through our analysis and exploration of the way fans receive these comic books messages, we offer an explanation for how comic books contribute to and reflect a larger popular discourse on crime and justice in America. Within the comic book narratives come ideological moments frequently representing American-style apocalyptic justice. We explore superheroes as they navigate paths to justice that operate outside the rule of law. Here, we find that in administering extralegal justice, heroes make "deathworthiness" calculations along the way, deciding whether to kill villains or let them live. We center this discussion in the context of legal proceedings regarding death-eligiblity decisions made by prosecutors, noting that comic books explore deathworthiness in fictional contexts free from legal constraints, but ripe with emotional satisfaction for readers. Not all villains or characters are deathworthy. It is through these deliberations of deathworthiness that we find the notion of contextual justice. Rather than deathworthiness decisions being made solely on the basis of the legal culpability of the offender, we find that such decisions hinge on the intrinsic nature of the hero him/herself. Readers judge the heroes' actions through the lens of contextual justice. Whether the actions of the hero are accepted as legitimate or not by the readers rests largely on the character traits of the hero rather than the nature of the crime.

We also find that comic books frequently engage in a retributive tease—a reliance on retributive, get-tough rhetoric that is fashioned as messianic. Yet, the action often falls short of the promise of retribution and instead relies on incapacitation as the preferred path to justice. We refer to this as "apocalyptic incapacitation," or incapacitation that occurs in the context of retributive rhetoric and posturing. For many, it is among the more satisfying elements of comic book consumption.

The reliance on incapacitation, administered rhetorically as retribution and most often by a white male hero, is undoubtedly a product of the formulaic nature of the medium and its dependence on recirculating popular characters through the years. These stories must ratchet up the action without necessarily disrupting the comic book world's basic social landscape. This is not necessarily surprising, as many have interpreted superheroes as keepers of the status quo. Most famously, Umberto Eco argued that the comic book medium itself leaves no room for counterhegemonic ideology.[33] However, we suggest that, at times, there are expressions of resistance to be found, particularly at the intersection of race, gender, sexual orientation, and heroism in a post-9/11 context. Our findings are similar to those of popular culture scholar Jeff Williams, who acknowledges that most of mainstream comics reinforce the status quo while independently published books are more likely to challenge the current social order and raise ideological questions that confront the prevailing paradigm.[34]

Comic Book Culture

Fans of comic books are far removed from the persistent loner-geek stereotype. In fact, the consumption of comic books and comic-inspired media is far from an isolated, solitary act. We found that fans are quite eager to share their impressions and understandings with other like-minded individuals as part of a larger subcultural community. As John Fiske suggests in *Understanding Popular Culture,* texts (or film, video games, television, or any other form of entertainment media) are not, in and of themselves, meaningful. He states, "Popular texts are to be used, consumed, and discarded, for they function only as agents in the social circulation of meaning and pleasure; as objects they are impoverished."[35]

Over the years, comic book fans have developed a thriving community. In the 1960s fans assembled for their own comic "cons," or conventions. Today, these conventions rank among the most popular destinations for comic book fans around the country, including cities such as Chicago, Philadelphia, and Seattle. When first launched in 1970, the San Diego comic book convention attracted about three hundred fans, yet more recently annual comic book conventions have drawn tens of thousands of fans and are now held in several major cities, with the largest cons operating on both coasts. For example, a recent San Diego Comic Con attracted a crowd of at least 130,000, and the New York Comic Con attendance has more than quadrupled from approximately 20,000 at its 2006 revival to approximately 95,000 in 2010.[36] Here, at these multimedia extravaganzas, fans relish the opportunity to meet face to face with creators and artists, often requesting autographs or pitching their own story ideas or artwork.

In his study of the social significance of the fan subcultural community, researcher and professor of communication, journalism, and cinematic

The New York City Comic Con, 2011. The popularity of comic book conventions, known as "cons," grew significantly after they were reinvented as popular culture, multimedia extravaganzas. (Photo: Nickie D. Phillips)

A fan dressed as Superman poses at San Diego Comic Con, 2009. (Photo: Nickie D. Phillips)

arts Henry Jenkins describes fans not as mere consumers but as "active social producers and manipulators of meaning."[37] He writes,

> Viewed in this fashion, fans become a model of the type of textual "poaching." . . . Their activities pose important questions about the ability of media producers to constrain the creation and circulation of meanings. Fans construct their cultural and social identity through borrowing and inflecting mass culture images, articulating concerns which often go unvoiced within the dominant media.[38]

Similarly, a study of the comic book fan culture finds that readers are active participants in the medium and may, at times, influence the direction of the storylines.[39] Beginning in the 1950s, many comic books actively encouraged participation of the fans by allowing feedback in the ever-popular letters pages commonly found in the back of monthly issues.[40] Recognizing the significance of reader contributions, the letters pages were a way to form a sense of community among the readers and creators. The letters serve as a place for readers to express admiration for the heroes, to condemn the current story trajectory, or to offer suggestions for future directions.[41] While many mainstream comic books have eliminated pages for printing fan letters, contributing to the letters pages continues to remain a badge of honor, with comic book fans bragging that "my letter" was printed in past issues and noting that names and addresses were routinely printed in the letters pages.[42] The sense of community that was forged with the letters pages continues to evolve on the Internet, where comic fan pages are numerous and readers post (frequently anonymous) comments and reviews on various blogs, forums, and web pages.

During the 1990s and early 2000s, as long-term comic book fans came of age, many transitioned from fan to creator.[43] Creators and writers such as Joss Whedon (*Buffy the Vampire Slayer, Angel, Serenity,* and *Dollhouse*), Kevin Smith (*Daredevil: Guardian Devil, Daredevil: Daredevil ½, Spider-Man/Black Cat: The Evil That Men Do, Batman: Cacophony*), Brian K. Vaughn (*Y The Last Man, Ex Machina*) and J. M. Straczynski (*Amazing Spider-Man, Fantastic Four, Silver Surfer: Requiem, The Brave and the Bold*) are among the most successful "fanboy creators."[44] These writers often transition to a variety of other mediums and back, from comic books to television to film. Similarly, Valerie D'Orazio, who wrote *Emma Frost Origins*, sent in her first pitch for a

Punisher storyline at age thirteen, and Greg Pak, who has written *Magneto: Testament* and *Planet Hulk,* among other critically acclaimed books, was a comics fan as a youth. Fans who had previously contributed to letters pages and followed storylines for years were now in the position of creator, shaping narratives and contributing to the mythology of the heroes they had grown to love and the villains they despised.

The Mainstream

Although "comic book culture" (i.e., annual comic cons and myriad cultural artifacts pertaining to comic books and superheroes) remains vibrant, over-all, sales of monthly comic books have declined over the past several years. In fact, without merchandising and wildly successful movie franchises, the state of the comic *book* industry is somewhat tenuous.[45] The cultural influence is vast, but since the mid-twentieth century, actual readership has declined precipitously and now exists as a subculture.

Although estimated readership in the United States is disputed, the comic book industry reports a total of $681 million in comic book and graphic novel sales in 2009, down 5 percent from 2008.[46] Most recently, an increasing number of titles have become available in electronic and online formats in the hopes of attracting new readers.[47] It is too early to retrieve accurate sales numbers on comic books sold in digital form. However, it is clear that Marvel and DC consistently top the list of publishers by sales earnings, trailed by independent publishers.[48] Additionally, comic book–related merchandise brings in significant revenue. Marvel earned $15 million from licensed merchandise in 1995.[49]

Die-hard fans follow monthly installments of a title in the form of "flop-pies" (or "issues") with stapled bindings. These story arcs are frequently collected into books and marketed as "trade paperbacks" or "graphic novels."[50] Occasionally, self-contained works exist from the start as graphic novels. A number of genres populate comic books (e.g., romance, horror, crime, war, autobiographical, westerns, etc.), as well as hybrids.[51] For example, many superhero comics may include characteristics of the romance genre and/or the horror genre. However, in terms of sales, the overwhelmingly predominant genre is that of the superhero.[52] In fact, Henry Jenkins documents that the superhero genre has become so accepted as the dominant paradigm

The Rockville, Maryland, public library encouraged visitors to check out a graphic novel during the summer of 2008. (Photo: Staci Strobl)

that when creators attempt to push boundaries within the genre, for example, offering different structure and aesthetics than the traditional fare, fans frequently express their rancor.[53]

We find that across the various types of comics, themes of crime and justice abound, acting as a connecting thread throughout the medium. However, we acknowledge that the creative content of the books is somewhat constrained in the following ways: through editorial control, by virtue of successful spin-offs into other media, and because of the formulaic nature of the genre and readers' expectations of continuity. These categories are not exhaustive, but are presented to give some idea of how the content, including themes of crime and justice, is at times influenced by concerns other than the creative imaginations of the writers, artists, pencillers, colorists, and letterers.

Editorial Control and Technological Advancements

Historically, mainstream comic book content was, to a large extent, a product of self-censorship based on criteria outlined in the Comics Code. The Comics Code was developed as a reaction to public and political outcry against

*Table 1.1. Market Shares of the Top Five Comic Book Publishers
(Based on Total Unit Sales of Comic Books and Graphic Novels in 2009)*

PUBLISHER	QUANTITY SHARE	DOLLAR SHARE
MARVEL COMICS	45.63%	40.47%
DC COMICS	32.22%	29.28%
DARK HORSE COMICS	4.05%	5.16%
IDW PUBLISHING	3.49%	4.17%
IMAGE COMICS	3.25%	3.67%
ALL OTHERS	11.36%	17.25%

Source: Diamond Publishers, 2010.
http://www.diamondcomics.com/public/default.asp?t=1&m=1&c=3&s=5&ai=90742

graphic depictions of violence and other abhorrent behavior appearing in comic books during the late 1940s and 1950s. Though the indignation was primarily directed toward comics in the crime and horror genres (as opposed to the superhero books), nearly every publisher voluntarily submitted to the Code to maintain sales. Throughout the next several decades, the Code was subject to revisions and eventually abandoned. Currently, Marvel and DC implement their own internal standards dictating content. (See chapter 2 for a more in-depth discussion of the significance of the Comics Code.)

Story arcs are as much driven by the editors as by the creators, if not more so. Since profit motives drive the industry, publishers and editors have an incentive to provide content that they believe will be most attractive to the consumer. At times, this undoubtedly influences the ways in which crime and violence are portrayed. On her *Occasional Superheroine* blog, Valerie D'Orazio describes her experiences working on the editorial team at one of the major comic book corporations (presumed to be DC Comics) and meetings where concern for sales drove decisions to move the stories to a more violent, gritty edge. She relates an interesting, and perhaps outrageous, account of editorial influence. She writes, "So our books *changed.* There was rape, and murder, torture, death, and mutilation. Superheroes did amoral or outright evil things and the line between good and bad was blurred."[54] In her post, she expresses her discomfort with one particular storyline and the decision to victimize "the most innocent, virginal, good-natured 'nice' character they could find and ravage her not once but *twice*." Most disturbingly, she recalls the enthusiasm with which the editors embraced the violence: "It started with my associate editor running gleefully into our boss's office, several boards of art in his hand. 'The rape pages are in!'"

The appearance of more graphic violence and sexual content over the past several years has partly been attributed to the "aging" comic book fans and their desire for more mature material. As readers age, the editors find themselves in the position of offering content that appeals to the older base as well as attracting new, younger readers. We suggest that the content of the books reflects the larger, white male heteronormative social context from which these books emerge. Most editors and creators of the titles in our sample are white men, and it is through this patriarchal lens that justice is served.

Spin-Offs

Whereas the contemporary comic book industry may target a subcultural niche, the mythology of superheroes reverberates throughout society and spins off into toys, video games, movies, and television shows. Since 1990, the number of commercially successful movies inspired by comic books or superhero tales has grown substantially.[55] The two top-grossing films released in the United States in 2008 were comic book inspired—*The Dark Knight* and *Iron Man*. In fact, only a few weeks after the DVD release, *The Dark Knight* soared to number two on the all-time domestic box office gross.[56] In addition, both Marvel and DC have released several motion comics, a combination of art and dialogue from the comic book pages with animated transitions between panels and voiceover, compatible for computers and mobile devices. These releases include titles such as Marvel's *Spider-Woman*, *Iron Man: Extremis*, and *Astonishing X-Men* and DC's *Superman: Red Son* and *Batgirl: Year One*. Moreover, video games are a 37-billion-dollar industry worldwide, with a portion of the comic book–inspired games selling several million copies per title.[57] Other, unforeseeable changes in content and distribution are probably on the horizon due to the corporate restructuring of DC Comics into DC Entertainment and the acquisition of Marvel Entertainment by Walt Disney Co. in 2009.

While the popularity of comic book–inspired media attests to the broad cultural impact of these characters, there is concern among comic book fans that the motion picture and video game industries wield influence on the development of the characters and the direction of the story arcs in the comic books rather than the other way around. Comic book publishers may devote titles to single characters or teams, not because they believe the characters necessarily appeal to readers but because they believe the characters will transition well to major motion pictures. Here, comic books are less the creative genesis and more a supplement to licensed material produced and marketed in other formats. The mythology bounces from medium to medium and back again, transforming cultural meanings of crime and justice. For example, the transformation of Nick Fury from a white hero to an African American hero in *The Ultimates* comic book originated with the hopes of casting the immensely popular Samuel L. Jackson in the *Iron Man* movies.[58] Ultimately, heroes and villains are recast and reimagined through these various mediums, influencing popular conceptions of heroism, villainy, and paths to justice.

Formulaic Nature of the Superhero Genre and Continuity

The formulaic constraints on mainstream superhero comic books affect the content, including the portrayals of crime and justice. For example, we found that peacemaking was an unlikely path to justice for superheroes due to the constraints of the medium. Alternatives to retributive justice are occasionally sought among superheroes, but usually only if the series is short-lived and not part of a larger, mainstream continuity.

Though superhero comics may be consumed as free-standing, individual works, the vast majority of these story arcs fit into a larger, ongoing super-plot, referred to as "continuity." For example, most DC comics take place in the context of the "DC Universe," and therefore comics relate to each other and establish an overarching continuity. Within this universe, there may be multiple appearances of the same heroes and villains in co-occurring titles (e.g., Superman may simultaneously appear in the *Superman* title as well as in *Justice League of America* and *Action Comics*). At times, a single narrative event may occur as a limited-run title (e.g., DC's *Blackest Night* and *Brightest Day*, and Marvel's *Civil War* or *Secret Invasion*) that unites the heroes and villains into what is known as a "crossover event." The repercussions of a crossover event often impact characters in the decades that follow. Author and cultural commentator Roz Kaveney writes that by the 1960s and '70s, single-issue stories gave way to longer, more complex tales, with characters appearing and reappearing. In fact, by the 1980s, they were less "about individual fine issues of comics or even one good issue after another, but about runs of comics where a long game was played, or special short runs when a writer and artist were allowed to do something remarkable."[59] Because continuity for many characters has existed over decades, liberties have been taken to reimagine and reset characters, and so the continuity is not logical in all cases. In some cases, when continuity becomes too complex and convoluted, it must be reset, or "retconned." Through retcon, or "retroactive continuity," characters may be updated and plots may be revised to allow forward momentum. For example, the acclaimed DC Comics' 1985 series *Crisis on Infinite Earths* was an effort by the editors to revamp and simplify their multiple universes, which had become unwieldy, and to allow new readers a "jumping on" point.

To further complicate matters, some storylines involve DC or Marvel universe characters acting in arcs labeled as "noncontinuity." These stories may involve the same characters and settings, but for the most part do not impact the larger continuity. Overall, this state of affairs may make it difficult for casual readers to find a comfortable point of entry and may further create a sense of subcultural insularity that is hard to penetrate if one is not fully immersed as a long-standing and faithful reader. The comic book impenetrability is similar to that of other popular culture niches such as Dungeons & Dragons role-playing games, Magic: The Gathering card games, and daytime television soap operas. However, to a greater extent than with these previous examples, comic book insularity spawns an external pantheon of entertainment products that go well beyond the subculture. The importance of this study is that we explore the insular nature of the medium's crime and justice themes, as well as follow its ripple effects into the larger cultural constructions of crime and justice.

What follows is a study of an oft-neglected cultural artifact in criminology: the comic book. Our sample suggests that comic books, although diverse, most often reflect an ideological orientation that reinforces the dominant notions of retributive justice in American culture and celebrates nostalgic ideas about community through apocalyptic plots. Ironically, our sample also shows that retribution plays out as an incomplete project, leaving readers teased as to how violent a hero will be in pursuing justice during the battle between good and evil. This tease, though ideologically short of the promise of retribution underlying many of the storylines, nonetheless provides emotional satisfaction in the spectacularly violent and graphic ways in which restraint is ultimately accomplished.

The following two chapters provide a backdrop for our analysis. Although it is beyond the scope of our book to write a comprehensive history of crime and justice in comic books, chapters 2 and 3 offer a brief history for the purpose of providing some historical context to our analysis. We show that depictions of heroes and villains in comic books are a product of their social context and that much of the content is driven by industry concerns rather than the singular imaginings of any given creators. We specifically address the influence of the Comics Code and note how the industry's self-censorship impacted the portrayals of crime and justice. In chapter 3, we show how the events of 9/11 reverberate in comic books by ushering in a reconsideration of the concept of heroism and serving as a cultural resource for dealing with anxieties in an era of uncertainty surrounding public safety. We also explore the shift in depictions of Arab and Muslim characters since 9/11. Together, chapters 2 and 3 set the stage for our analysis, which considers a wide range of comic books published after 9/11.

The remaining chapters of our book are devoted to the way the crime narrative generally plays out in contemporary best-selling comic books. We suggest that, like many popular cultural artifacts, comic books contribute to the larger discourse about crime and justice in America. We organize our analysis along the common narrative formula presented in these books; each of our chapters is a step along the "path to justice." Our trajectory takes us from the crime problem, often imagined as apocalyptic in nature, to the villains as the embodiment of evil to the heroes and their portrayed racial, ethnic, and gender identities and sexual orientation to the various paths to justice they follow and ultimately to the criminal justice policy implications inherent in these stories. Along the way, we take account of the ways in which the meanings surrounding crime and justice circulate, giving special consideration to how these stories ultimately reinforce dominant notions of justice, portraying when, against whom, and in what context violence is appropriate. Throughout our analysis, we consider how the consumption of comic books serves as a vicarious transgression for readers. In this way, we engage with the readers to explore how these books serve as a way of confronting moral concerns and working out anxieties about fear of crime.

In chapter 4, we explore the crime problem as an apocalyptic crisis, noting that often comic books drop the reader into a catastrophic criminal event that threatens an idyllic social order. Heroes find themselves nostalgic for a more peaceful past as the world around them falls into a landscape of dystopic criminality and social disorder. The desire for the return to a better world drives the heroes' utopian quests for justice. Understanding that criminal justice is itself a process, the purpose of these chapters is to uncover the circulating meanings surrounding the paths to justice in this common narrative formula.

Part of the importance of these circulating meanings lies in the power of media—including that of popular culture—to reflect and shape what type of person is considered a threat to the social order and what type of person may be considered heroic. In chapter 5, we examine the portrayal of those who threaten the social order, comic book villains, as characters with individual problems and pathologies. Comic books as a visual medium often portray villains as the embodiment of evil with their crooked faces and ugly exteriors.

On the flip side, in chapter 6, in our exploration of the hero, we explore vigilantism and the violent means through which heroes navigate their paths to justice. In chapters 7 and 8, we analyze how race, ethnicity, gender, and sexual orientation are used to construct difference for both the heroes and the villains in ways that at times reinforce and reproduce stereotypes and at times recognize and reflect the diversity of the readers. We point out how the books portray a narrow notion of who and what type of person may be considered heroic. Rather than interrogate whether the books accurately reflect the "reality" of crime and justice in America, we suggest that the myths contained in these stories, specifically as they relate to heroes of difference, reverberate throughout the subculture and ultimately shape a larger cultural discourse.

Finally, in chapter 9 we confront the policy messages readers may take from comic books as part of an overall consumption of popular culture in a postmodern mediated environment. We show how retribution and incapacitation fare well in comic books, while calls for the rehabilitation of villains are conspicuously absent. Our goal is for the following chapters to provide information about the impact of popular culture in late modernity and, most importantly, about what we have come to expect from our heroes, ways in which we comprehend evil, and the strong cultural embrace of retributive justice.

"CRIME DOESN'T PAY"

A BRIEF HISTORY OF CRIME
AND JUSTICE THEMES IN COMIC BOOKS

Dan Richards graduates last in his class at the police academy, but his talent for fighting crime outshines even the "honor man" among the graduates. During his academy days, Richards had secretly built an extensive file of known criminal personalities. When a Mafia thug frames him and a classmate for the murder of his rival, corrupt politician Al Armaud, Richards uses the file to track down the culprit—a man who uttered the odd catch phrase "tickle the stars" during the commission of the crime. According to Richards's file, "tickle the stars" is the hallmark utterance of Johnny Consentino, also described as head of a protection racket, who has a "dark moustache" and is a "loud dresser." Now acting as a vigilante, Richards dons a black mask and hunts for Consentino with his fierce and trusty black dog, Thor. Finding Consentino's hideout, Richards and Thor ambush Consentino and his associates. "Who . . . who's dat guy!?" one associate calls out in the scuffle. On the fly, Richards replies, "Manhunter!!" thereby christening his alter ego.

This story, published in 1942 in *Police Comics* #8, introduces readers to "Manhunter," a character who has since been reimagined in the DC Universe and lives on in many crime-fighting adventures. Manhunter represents an early American comic book vigilante who acts as an adjunct to law enforcement and, indeed, serves as an official member of law enforcement himself when not his alter ego. In the early 1940s, comic books featuring such vigilante superheroes as Manhunter had significant impact on the public imagination. They set the tone for a medium that would often be a vehicle for law-and-order messages throughout its history.

During World War II, titles like *Captain America* that depicted heroes battling foreign enemies riveted readers at home and servicemen abroad, selling nearly a million copies a month.[1] After the war, however, attention turned instead to a type of comics that featured grisly tales of misdeeds. This crime genre involved twisted tales of suspense inspired by true-life events. Yet, as with the superhero titles, these comics also possessed a bias toward plots that ultimately extolled law and order.

Sales of these gory comics eventually took a dip due to public resistance to the graphic depictions of violence and wickedness. Ultimately, super-hero comic books reemerged in the mid-1950s, becoming the best-selling genre in the comic book industry that it still is today. This chapter provides a brief history of comic books, focusing on the emergence of superheroes, the rise and fall of the crime genre, and the shift in depictions of heroes from defenders of the status quo to figures that are capable of challenging the dominant rules of society.

The War on Crime Begins

Many of the first comic books were reprints of newspaper comic strips and panels.[2] Crime-related strips during the 1930s, such as *Dick Tracy, Detective Dan,* and *Secret Agent X-9,* featured plainclothes detectives and investiga-tors determined to stamp out crime. Among these hard-boiled characters, Dick Tracy is considered by comic historian Mike Benton to be the first "crime-fighting detective" in comic strips and the first "to introduce brutal-ity, gun play, and torture to the comic page."[3] According to Benton, strips such as these capitalized on the public's anticrime sentiment in the 1930s and coincided with the rising popularity of G-Men as heroic crime fighters. J. Edgar Hoover, then director of the Federal Bureau of Investigation, was so convinced of the importance of crafting a positive media image of the FBI that he consulted with a journalist to craft a comic strip based on real-life FBI cases, titled *War on Crime. War on Crime,* like virtually all of the 1930s crime-related comics, focused on crime fighters as moral role models who "show readers why 'crime does not pay.'"[4]

The 1930s also ushered in the popularity of lurid and thrilling tales known as "pulps." For example, *Detective Comics*, published in 1937, featured pulp-inspired characters and was one of the first titles to focus on crime fighting. The following year Superman was introduced in *Action Comics*.[5] Superman emerged as a savior figure for Americans fighting social injustices beyond mere crime-fighting. In his cultural history of comic books, Bradford Wright contextualizes the emergence of Superman during the Great Depression, describing him as a progressive "super-reformer" who advocates for "social reform and government assistance to the poor," a hero protecting the average citizen from social and economic ills.[6] Similarly, Superman, the "Champion of the Oppressed," is described by journalism professor David Hajdu as embodying "the Roosevelt-era ideal of power employed for the public good."[7] Wright notes that in the 1930s, comic books "rarely, if ever, questioned the integrity of the federal government or national political leaders" and frequently advocated for government regulation on businesses.[8] In early *Action Comics*, Superman, with an emphasis on social reform, fought against organized crime, white collar criminals, and corrupt city authorities.

Shortly after the inception of Superman, Bob Kane and Bill Finger created the character of Batman, who first appeared in *Detective Comics* in 1939. Conceived as a darker, more brooding crime fighter than Superman, Batman was born from the tragedy experienced by young Bruce Wayne. One night Bruce leaves the theater with his parents only to witness them be mugged and murdered by a street criminal in an alley. Deeply aggrieved, a young Bruce vows to avenge the crime. Taking their cue from the violent seminal storyline, early Batman stories were described as grim detective tales, with "most adversaries meeting a brutal demise."[9] In their battles for justice during this era, both Superman and Batman were generally averse to killing; however, early comics showed that both occasionally killed enemies and Batman was at times portrayed using guns.[10]

Many comics readers refer to the period from the late 1930s through the early 1950s as the Golden Age of comics, a time when numerous well-known superheroes were first introduced, including the Flash (1940), Green Lantern (1940), Wonder Woman (1941), Green Arrow (1941), and Captain America (1941).[11] *All-Star Comics* introduced the Justice Society of America, which highlighted a team of superheroes including the Flash, Green Lantern, Hawkman, Hourman, and Atom, among others. Comic books were popular among young people, as well as those serving in the U.S. armed services.[12] Wright describes comic books during World War II as heavily propagandistic, with the superhero books of the era championing "a loosely defined Americanism synonymous with lofty ideals like democracy, liberty, and freedom from oppression."[13]

Comic creators used the character of Hitler as a frequent foe of superheroes during the war, and fascism was commonly criticized. One of the more famous images—that of Captain America punching Hitler—appeared on the cover of Timely's *Captain America Comics* #1, published prior to the United States entering the war. Similarly, Daredevil, along with a team of heroes, battles Hitler in Lev Gleason's *Daredevil*, released in 1941. Its cover reads, "The most terrifying battle ever waged—Hitler stacked the cards against humanity—But—Daredevil deals the ace of death to the mad merchant of hate!" Before the bombing of Pearl Harbor, Wright notes, comic books "featured Nazi villains far more frequently than they did Japanese villains." But soon, the Japanese were regularly portrayed as "sinister, ugly, subhuman creature[s]."[14] For example, *Action Comics* #58 portrayed Superman alongside a poster with the slogan, "You can slap a Jap."[15]

Superhero comic books tackling the "godless Communists" during the Cold War were not as successful as those attacking the Axis powers from World War II, though the newer enemy was often portrayed just as crudely. For example, in *Captain America*, Wright notes, the Communists were portrayed as "evil, overweight, and poor dressers."[16] In addition to battling foreign enemies, superheroes often advocated service and sacrifice from the readers at home, providing both a symbolic and a literal means of participation in the war effort. During World War II, readers were encouraged to donate to charities, purchase war stamps and bonds, and collect scrap metal, paper, and glass.[17]

In the 1940s, comic books were a major form of entertainment for youth, permeating nearly every home in America and selling as many as eighty to one hundred million copies a week.[18] In addition to the superhero genre, popular genres ranged from romance, western, and war to teen, funny animals, and humor.[19] The largest portion of comic book readers was comprised of children who shared the comics, reading and rereading the pages of the books "until they were virtually destroyed."[20] After the Allies won the war, however, sales of superhero comics experienced a decline and publishers responded by expanding their offerings into other genres.

In post–World War II America, while sales of superhero comics began to decline, interest in the crime and horror genre increased. Initially catering to mature youth, titles such as *Crime Does Not Pay* (first published in 1942), *Lawbreakers Always Lose, Law against Crime,* and *Crime and Punishment* were filled with sordid tales of crime and violence. By 1948 one of the most popular titles inspired by true crime events, *Crime Does Not Pay,* was selling over a million copies a month.[21] According to Hajdu, crime comics jumped from merely 3 percent of all comics in 1946 to 14 percent by 1948, and "by the end of 1952, nearly one-third of all the comics on the newsstands were devoted to the macabre."[22] Wright describes these various crime comics as containing "beatings, shootings, stabbings, burning bodies, gruesome torture, and sickening varieties of dismemberment" and as being riddled with misogyny.[23] The front page of one story, titled "The Wild Spree of the Laughing Sadist—Herman Duker," features a woman held at gunpoint, with a blackened eye and blood dripping down her chin. Duker, a psychopath, leads a particularly deranged life of crime. He gains pleasure in torturing animals as a child, frequently attacks his peers, burns a cat alive, runs away from home, kills a shopkeeper and a milkman for money, and, as a result, is electrocuted. Motion lines in the panel accentuate the electrical charges surging through his body. His last words are pleas for help and a second chance. Despite the depravity depicted in these books, the criminal always meets his or her comeuppance. The retribution, though, is described by Wright as an afterthought, saved for the very end of the story. The majority of the narrative remained focused on the graphic, grisly misdeeds of the protagonist.[24]

In the early 1950s, Entertaining Comics (EC), headed by William Gaines (later publisher of *MAD* magazine), published top horror, science fiction, and suspense titles such as *The Haunt of Fear, Shock SuspenStories, Weird Fantasy,* and *Vault of Horror.* These titles feature tales of graphic violence, including the popular EC title *Crime SuspenStories,* which relies on twists of fate that lead those who cheat, lie, and kill to a grim fate. For example, in "Dead-ringer" a man realizes that he bears an uncanny physical resemblance to a millionaire amnesiac in a local insane asylum. The man decides to kill the millionaire and assume his identity. The plan is successful until the impersonator learns that the millionaire was a much-hated husband and business partner who cheated innocent people out of their life's savings. The imposter meets his fate one day when three men accost him and reveal that their father committed suicide as a result of the millionaire's scams. Ignoring pleas that he was not the real millionaire, the men shoot the imposter in cold blood. In another tale titled "High Tide" a prisoner escapes an Alcatraz-type island and poses as the skipper on a mailboat bound for the mainland. Not realizing which among them is the escaped convict, the passengers attack each other in a frenzy. After fooling the other passengers, the escaped convict is seemingly destined for freedom until his plan is thwarted by the high tide and he drowns while swimming to shore.[25]

"In Every Instance Good Shall Triumph over Evil"

Ultimately, the crime-and-violence-saturated comics were met with resistance by parents, religious groups, and policymakers. Believed to contribute to a downward spiral of depravity and juvenile delinquency, comic books published during the 1940s and 1950s were subject to an onslaught of attacks most notoriously led by child psychiatrist Fredric Wertham. In his book *Seduction of the Innocent*, Wertham argued that the graphic depictions of violence and sexualized content in comic books actually contributed to juvenile delinquency.[26] Wertham had a long history as a respected clinical psychiatrist and was particularly interested in the plight of disadvantaged minority youth. In his study on comic books, Wertham based his conclusions on anecdotal evidence gathered through years of experience working with juveniles. Hajdu notes that while Wertham was not the first to criticize the presumed harmful content of comic books, he was the first to give the topic book-length treatment and to generate widespread national attention.[27] In addition to his book, Wertham's ideas regarding the link between comic book reading and juvenile delinquency were disseminated in various newspapers and magazines, and members of the public began to take note.[28]

At the time, much like today, the public was concerned with the effects of the mass media on childhood development. And, despite the lack of empirical research indicating a causal relationship between the consumption of mass media and delinquency, many community groups and religious organizations, such as the National Organization for Decent Literature, organized by the Catholic Church, worked to condemn the content in comic books and urged the prohibition of their sale to minors.[29]

Among the first to recommend legislation prohibiting the sale of comic books to minors, Wertham energized critics with his scathing rebukes. In

1948, as a result of the mounting criticism against the comics, the Association of Comics Magazine Publishers implemented a code that "forbade depiction of sex or sadistic torture, the use of vulgar and obscene language, the ridicule of religious and racial groups, and the humorous treatment of divorce."[30] The Code was an effort to reaffirm the status quo and explicitly stated that "policemen, judges, Government officials, and respected institutions should not be portrayed as stupid or ineffective, or represented in such a way as to weaken respect for established authority."[31] The Code was among the first efforts to regulate content by relying on voluntary participation by the publishers. However, due to the difficulty of enforcement and reluctance of publishers to participate, over the next few years the Code was virtually abandoned.

Despite the failure of the Code, critics remained steadfast. Legislation was proposed in various states to prohibit the sale of comic books. The public rallied with comic book burnings, and newspaper editorials reflected debates about free speech. In turn, the industry began to reel from the onslaught of resistance.[32] The crusade against comic books culminated in dramatic testimony at the 1954 congressional hearings held by the Senate Subcommittee to Investigate Juvenile Delinquency.[33] The committee was convened to study the causes and extent of juvenile delinquency, including attention to the effects of the mass media on juveniles. The segments of the hearings—chaired by Senator Robert Hendrickson—that gained the most publicity were those that focused on the influence of comic books. Various witnesses, representatives of the comic book industry, and experts testified at the hearings, including Wertham and EC publisher William Gaines.[34] Examples of macabre crime stories and horror comics were displayed before the committee, and Wertham presented detailed anecdotal evidence regarding the evils of comic books, suggesting that the books were a leading cause of juvenile delinquency.[35]

Wertham's methodology was heavily criticized, notably by sociologist Frederic Thrasher.[36] Thrasher argued that no media studies to date had found a direct connection between media consumption and behavior. He maintained that if there was any effect, it would be more subtle and part of a multifactorial set of other social issues. Wertham's findings were based on anecdotal evidence, and he frequently made sweeping generalizations about the effects of all comics, including superhero titles, on childhood development. Nonetheless, his testimony was convincing, and as Hajdu notes, "[T]he core idea that comic books were insidious seemed beyond dispute."[37] Gaines put forth his best effort to defend the industry, but by all accounts was ineffective. Defending the depiction of parricide, severed heads, asphyxiation, and various grisly murders proved daunting even if the implicit, and explicit, social message of the comics was that crime does not, in fact, pay.

As a result of the Senate hearings, the comics industry formed the Comics Magazine Association of America, which produced a code modeled after the Film Production Code of the 1930s, thereby imposing its own form of self-censorship.[38] The association's approval led to a literal stamp that was displayed on comic books covers and was designed to signal to parents that the comic was decent entertainment for children. Wright describes the Code as "far more extensive, precise, and restrictive than the publishers' 1948 code."[39] Unlike with the previous code, most publishers participated and submitted their comics for review. Gaines initially refused to participate in the Code and, as a result, ceased publication of his once extremely popular horror and crime titles.

The Code outlined restrictions in several areas, including, among others, dialogue, religion, costumes, marriage and sex, and advertising. Generally, the Code forbade using the terms "horror" or "terror" in the title, gruesome illustrations, the depiction of sympathetic criminals, excessive violence, details and methods of crimes, as well as profanity and obscenity. The Code was explicit in its desire to uphold the status quo and declared that "policemen, judges, government officials and respected institutions shall never be presented in such a way as to create disrespect for established authority" and that "in every instance good shall triumph over evil and the criminal [be] punished for his misdeeds."[40] The Code ensured that comic book content would thereafter perpetuate the interests of the ruling class and reaffirm stereotypical ideas about gender, race, and sexuality, in particular emphasizing a physical, muscular, and emotionless masculinity.

To the extent that creativity was encouraged by the publishers, creators were stifled by the implementation of the Code. Yet after the hearings, the crusade against comics was not over. As a result of the hearings, sales of comic books in major cities and several states were prohibited or limited.[41] The comics industry was irreparably damaged as the publication of comics titles decreased dramatically, closely followed by readership.[42] According to Hajdu, in 1952, there were approximately 650 comic book titles published per month; however, by 1956, the number of titles per month dropped to about 250.[43]

Ultimately, mounting pressure from the government and moralists, along with other changes in the entertainment industry, cemented the decline of the comic book industry as the most popular form of entertainment among youth. However, the appeal of entertainment that pushed boundaries, challenged authority, and engaged young minds was not quashed altogether in comic books; rather, it proliferated in films, paperback novels, and television.[44]

Though the comic books were "cleaned up," the Comics Code had further ramifications for the industry. Journalism professor Amy Kiste Nyberg suggests that most significantly, the Comics Code helped solidify the "superhero comic as the dominant genre in the years following the code's adoption."[45] In fact, during the 1960s the comic book industry ushered in a revitalization of comic book superheroes. This era, also commonly known as the Silver Age, saw the reimagining of characters popular during the 1940s and the creation of new superheroes that have become mainstays in American popular culture.

The Silver Age and the Status Quo

Under the leadership of editor Julius "Julie" Schwartz, various DC characters were successfully revamped and the Justice Society of America was revived and teamed with superheroes in the Justice League of America.[46] Mainstream comics in the Silver Age were in compliance with the Code, and Wright documents that the narratives of these stories published by DC "aligned its superheroes squarely on the side of established authority, with which it naturally equated the best interests of American citizens."[47] He further describes a few important themes common in the books of the era, which emphasized responsibility to the community over individualism, presented the role of the heroes as helping humanity, and "hail[ed] science as a progressive force in the service of humankind."[48]

In this context, the development of the Comics Code represents a reinforcement of the hegemonic order.[49] Wright adds that the comic books of the era, such as those published by DC, Dell, and Charlton, "all affirmed the basic assumptions of an American Cold War consensus. All conformed nicely with the Comics Code, and none questioned the state of American society or the meaningful place of individuals within it."[50] There were, however, pockets of resistance to be found in the superhero genre. During the 1960s, Marvel introduced Rawhide Kid (1960), the Fantastic Four (1961), Spider-Man (1962), the Hulk (1962), Thor (1962), and Iron Man (1963). Through these Marvel characters, Wright finds occasional narratives expressing "the rejection of consensus and conformity" with an undercurrent of anxieties permeating society in the Cold War era. For example, by the late 1960s, Iron Man transitioned from being a "strident cold warrior" to opposing involvement in the Vietnam War.[51]

Many of the Marvel characters were considered revolutionary in that they introduced moral complexities, insecurities, and flaws, prompting introspection by the heroes themselves.[52] For example, the Fantastic Four were introduced as a tight-knit, family-like unit engaged in a quest to beat the "commies" in the race into space. Brilliant scientist and engineer Reed Richards, his fiancée Susan Storm, her brother Johnny, and their friend Ben Grimm blasted into orbit only to be hit with cosmic rays that bestowed each with unique superpowers. According to *Marvel Chronicle*, the creators Stan Lee and Jack Kirby "wanted their new heroes to be real people who argued among themselves, made mistakes, and had feet of clay."[53] With such a unique focus on character development, the series helped reinvigorate the popularity of superheroes.

The End of Innocence

In line with the social and political landscape of the day, mainstream comic books in the late 1960s and early 1970s presented social commentary and at times overt political messages. In the first few pages of *Green Lantern/Green Arrow* #71, published in 1970, Green Arrow invites Green Lantern to take a broader look at "how the other half lives . . . if you can call it living." Green Arrow points out that the disadvantaged living in Star City must cope with economic stress due to costs in caring for elderly relatives, eviction notices from "fat cat landlords," and racial discrimination. Once enlightened, Green Lantern realizes that "evil was all around me . . . disguised as familiar, everyday persons and places! I've lived this long without learning that *bad* doesn't have to be a bug-eyed monster or a mad scientist."

Green Arrow shows Green Lantern the struggles of the poor and disenfranchised in the inner city. (*Green Lantern/Green Arrow: The Collection*, volume 1, Dennis O'Niel and Neal Adams, DC, 2004)

Likewise, in a 1971 *Time* magazine article, journalist Gerald Clarke writes of the shift toward social concerns in comic books,

> The comics' caped crusaders have become as outraged about racial injustice as the Congressional Black Caucus and as worried about pollution as the Sierra Club. Archfiends with memorable names like the Hulk and Dr. Doom are still around, but they are often pushed off the page by such new villains as air pollution and social injustice.[54]

Still, the Comics Code held sway over the mainstream publishers and limited the extent to which superheroes challenged the status quo, particularly with regard to crime and justice. Such was the case until 1971, when the government actually sought out the use of comics as a means for alerting the public about the evils of drugs.

That year, the U.S. Department of Health, Education, and Welfare contacted Stan Lee to write a Spider-Man storyline condemning the use of drugs.[55] Lee agreed and produced a story that, though unambiguously antidrug, was in clear violation of the Comics Code, which forbade mention of drug use.[56] He portrayed drug use as an inevitable downward spiral, a social problem affecting all races and classes. The story begins with Spider-Man (a.k.a. Peter Parker) rescuing a young African American man who is teetering on a rooftop "stoned out of his mind," chanting, "I can float—fly like a bird." After the rescue, Peter finds that the drug problem plaguing the city strikes a bit closer to home, as it is later explained at the Daily Bugle that "drugs aren't just a ghetto hang up! They hit the rich—same as poor."

Pining over his deteriorating relationship with his girlfriend, Harry, Peter's best friend, suddenly spirals into drug abuse. Harry "pops pills" and is driven into a "total clinical psychosis. What a layman would call schizophrenic." In a hallucinogenic state, Harry describes the drugs' effects: "It's like—I'm drowning—falling—dying inside! Nothing seems real—nothing hangs together—The pills! . . . They're driving me—out of my mind!" In a street corner drug buy, Harry vows that he is not hooked, with this buy being the "first time—and the last" fix that he will need. The drug seller replies mockingly, "yeah—that's what they say." Peter strives to save Harry while simultaneously fighting his villainous father, Green Goblin, who is determined to destroy Spider-Man.

Because the comic book mentioned the forbidden topic of drug use, the Comics Code authority refused to give approval and the book became the first mainstream comic to be published without the Comics Code stamp.[57] With the success of this particular Spider-Man arc, the Comics Code was revised "to meet contemporary standards of conduct and morality."[58] The revised code provided for the inclusion of drugs and drug use in comic book story arcs, but only if such portrayals vilified its use. Nyberg notes that once the Code was revised, Marvel agreed to publish future issues in accordance with it. The Code continued, however, to forbid portrayals that promoted distrust of the forces of law and justice.[59]

During the early 1970s, *The Amazing Spider-Man* was also credited with affecting monumental change in the comic book world with a shocking plot twist: the murder of Peter Parker's girlfriend, Gwen Stacy. In a battle with the supervillain Green Goblin, Gwen was thrust off a New York City bridge. As she falls, Spider-Man propels a web to catch her, suspending her in midair. However, when Spider-Man reaches her side, she is already dead. In the aftermath, Spider-Man is tortured by the thought that the discharge

Peter Parker's friend Harry is portrayed as a drug addict. The book stresses that anyone of any race or class may be afflicted. (*The Amazing Spider-Man: The Death of Gwen Stacy*, Stan Lee and Gil Kane, 1999, originally published 1971, 1973)

of his web while trying to save Gwen actually inflicted the damage that caused her death. The ambiguous nature of the art and graphics on the page, that is, the "SWIK!" of his web, followed by a "SNAP," leave the reader uncertain as to whether the fall or the attempted rescue actually caused her demise. While such a turn of events may seem like a commonplace literary device to a contemporary reader, at the time, it was considered a major turning point in comic book narratives. It was unusual for super-hero comic books to wade into such emotionally traumatic territory. Fans were shocked at the loss of a character with which they felt intimately connected. In fact, many comic book enthusiasts have considered the "death of Gwen Stacy" story arc the end of the Silver Age of comics—the end of innocence.[60]

Nearly forty years later, comic book fans credit the storyline with being a "game changer," a story with such emotional resonance that it felt like a "punch in the gut."[61] Yet, the emotional impact was only part of the significance of the story. A former Marvel editor commented that for the first time, a death in comic books "felt entirely real, and occurred on camera."[62] The story provided an opening for realism that had been sorely missing in comics because of the restrictions of the Code. The death of Gwen Stacy paved the way for the possibility of other, significant characters meeting the same fate.

After the "Game Changer"

Throughout the 1970s, roughly considered the Bronze Era, comic books began to see a small but notable increase in the racial and ethnic diversity of their characters.[63] For example, when *X-Men* reemerged in 1975, it included multiracial and multinational messages of tolerance. The new team consisted of members of African, Russian, German, Japanese, and Canadian descent and soon became a fan favorite. Several black superheroes appeared in the 1970s, including Marvel's first African superhero, Black Panther (a.k.a. T'Challa), a descendant from the fictional African nation Wakanda appearing in *Fantastic Four* (#52, 1966). Marvel also introduced its first black American superhero, the Falcon (1969, in *Captain America* #117). The Falcon had been a criminal until he partnered with Captain America, and later protected the people of Harlem. In 1972 Marvel introduced its first African American superhero title, *Luke Cage: Hero for Hire*. In this title, inspired by the popular "blaxploitation" films, Cage was an innocent man framed and incarcerated for a drug crime. In a deal struck so that he could gain early parole, Cage agrees to participate in a chemical experiment. As the experiment goes awry, Cage gains super-strength and escapes prison. On the outside, Cage serves as a "hero for hire."[64]

Over the next decade, comic books took a darker, grittier turn into the Modern Age. During this time, many books began to exhibit a heightened level of maturity and increasingly gained literary respectability.[65] By the 1980s, publishers were beginning to find it economically viable to publish some titles outside the constraints of the Code. The changes in the distribution of comic books from newsstands to the direct market and the increase in independent publishers ultimately led to a revision in the Code. The major publishers, including DC and Marvel, appointed "an editorial task force of industry insiders" to rewrite the Code, and the revised version was adopted in 1989.[66] Most importantly, Nyberg writes, "By sidestepping the

Code, publishers have acknowledged for the first time that comic books are not just for children."[67]

Several titles contributed to the increasing literary sophistication of comic books, including superhero titles such as *Batman: The Killing Joke* (1988), *Daredevil: Born Again* (1986), and *American Flagg!* (1983), as well as to the rise of non-superhero titles such as *The Sandman* (1989) and graphic novel titles such as *Maus* (1986).[68] Importantly, Alan Moore's *Watchmen* and Frank Miller's *Batman: The Dark Knight Returns* have been credited with ushering in a more mature level of complexity and sophistication in storytelling, with a focus on the conflicts inherent in heroism and with a "darker, morally ambiguous narrative."[69] Simultaneously, with the waning influence of the Comics Code, books contained increasingly violent and sexually explicit material.

During the 1980s, comic books began to examine the consequences of absolute power as the role of superheroes in a democratic society was questioned by the public, the media, and at times the heroes themselves.[70] Several scholars have noted that superhero comics advance ideological notions of law in various ways. For example, journalism and media studies scholar Jason Bainbridge notes that as of the 1980s superheroes began to operate in a more proactive manner, frequently questioning themselves and their responsibilities in an ever-changing world.[71] The narratives themselves frequently suggest that there are no longer two sides to each issue; rather, there are a multiplicity of perspectives, thus creating a space for the negotiation of themes of crime and justice.

The transition in comic book content and tone during the 1980s has been attributed to a changing social environment characterized by rising crime rates and the corresponding increased fear of drug-related crime and violence, as well as a general sense of increased cynicism among readers.[72] Whatever the cause, the readers fully embraced stories and illustrations that pushed them beyond their comfort zones and were eager to explore new (re)imaginings of their favorite superheroes and villains. In his exploration of the origin of the superhero genre, Peter Coogan suggests that the traditional superhero conventions were no longer sufficient for either the creators or the audience. For Coogan, "[T]he superhero's selflessness becomes problematic. Heroes either move 'up' into governance or 'down' out of superheroing."[73] These stories began to explore the significance of the superhero in society and the consequences of absolute power in refreshing ways that shook up the industry.

For example, although Batman (a.k.a. the Dark Knight) has always been a more shadowy figure compared to Superman, it is the Batman with a decidedly darker edge that continues to resonate in popular culture today.[74] Notably, *Batman: The Dark Knight Returns* was released as a four-issue miniseries featuring an older, retired Batman, described by Wright as a "slightly mad right-wing moralist" who returns to action as Gotham City is descending into chaos as a result of gang violence.[75] Playing with "fascist iconography," Miller shows Batman as authoritarian, seizing power and torturing suspects in a society presided over by a Reaganesque president and a pundit-dominated infotainment media.[76]

The comic book is significant for its recasting of Batman (as a radical revolutionary) and Robin (reimagined for the first time as a female), and for its scathing critique of media in contemporary society. English professor Graham Murphy argues that in *Batman: The Dark Knight Returns,* Batman represents the possibility of social reform, fighting toward a potential utopia, in contrast to Superman, who serves as merely an extension of the government, representing "social retrenchment . . . defending current conditions rather than inspiring or embodying any oppositional energy."[77] While Superman works to maintain the status quo in a society plagued by the threat of nuclear annihilation, Batman is wholly devoted to fighting social injustice and recruits his own underground army to "bring sense to a world plagued by worse than thieves and murderers."

The attempt to make sense out of a senseless world is also a prominent theme in Alan Moore's *Batman: The Killing Joke.* This story offers a potential origin story for the Joker and explores the symbiotic nature of the relationship between Batman and the Joker—showing that very little separates the psyche of the villain from that of the hero. Here, misfortune indiscriminately strikes, leaving the downtrodden to make a choice between succumbing to hopelessness or being willing to find some meaning in a life that has been met with tragic circumstances. A struggling, down-on-his-luck stand-up comedian desperate to support his pregnant wife turns to crime. The comedian is persuaded by a group of criminals to participate in a robbery at his former workplace, a chemical plant. On the eve of the heist, the comedian is informed that his wife has died in an accident. Though distraught, the comedian proceeds with the plan. The heist goes bad, and Batman confronts the comedian. To avoid capture, the comedian jumps into a vat full of toxic chemicals. As he emerges from the vat, he

The Dark Knight Returns, along with *Watchmen*, are frequently considered turning points in the comic industry, leading to darker, grittier material. Here, the underground army assembles under Batman to fight for social justice at any cost. (*Batman: The Dark Knight Returns*, Frank Miller, Klaus Janson, and Lyn Varley, DC, 1997)

discovers that not only his appearance has changed (a powder white face and green hair) but also his personality—he has become the Joker.

The Joker is portrayed convincingly as a scary and menacing threat. Gone is the colorful, clownish, eccentric buffoon often portrayed in the comics and television during the 1950s and 1960s. Rather, a more sinister "Joker" emerges from the vat; a psychopath who tortures a caged, naked Police Commissioner Gordon and paralyzes his daughter, Barbara, by shooting her in the stomach, rupturing her spine. The vivid artwork by Brian Bolland portrays arresting images of the sexually assaulted victim as her clothes are stripped and photos taken of her as she writhes in pain. The Joker uses the photos to taunt Commissioner Gordon to prove that any man can be driven to insanity. In a world described by the Joker as a "black, awful joke," the Joker has been driven "crazy" by his life circumstances. Acknowledging the random injustices of life, the Joker quips, "[I]t's all a joke! Everything anybody ever valued or struggled for . . . it's all a monstrous, demented gag! So why can't you see the funny side?" Refusing a chance at rehabilitation, the Joker matches wits with Batman in a conclusion that leaves open the possibility that Batman has, once and for all, silenced the Joker.

Though *Batman: The Killing Joke* was released as an "out-of-continuity" graphic novel in 1988, it was so well received that the events portrayed impacted the DC Universe for years to come. For example, although the injuries Barbara Gordon sustained left her paralyzed from the waist down, she lived on to fight crime as *The Oracle,* a wheelchair-bound surveillance/computer expert and skilled martial artist on call to assist the superheroes. The story is a powerful meditation on crime causation, showing that we are driven to crime by circumstances beyond our control and that there is only a fine line between a good person and an evil person.

Both *Batman: The Dark Knight Returns* and *Batman: The Killing Joke* remain critical and commercial successes that continue to influence writers and artists today. However, it was Alan Moore's work published in 1986, *Watchmen,* that many regard as having the strongest impact on superhero comics. *Watchmen*, an out-of-continuity DC title, introduced two generations of superheroes and deconstructed the genre in such a way as to question the very notion of goodness and altruism. The book disrupts the concept of the superhero, revealing instead frailties, temperamental shortcomings, psychopathic tendencies, and ultimately the dangers of all-encompassing power. The book asks resolutely, "Who watches the watchmen?"

Popular culture scholar Roz Kaveney refers to *Watchmen* as a "thick text," a nuclear cautionary tale featuring many themes, including the corruption of absolute power, the role of superheroes in a democracy, collateral destruction left in the wake of superheroes' actions, the use of deadly force by heroes, and the public's paranoia about heroes. Kaveney writes of *Watchmen,*

To describe it as the most profound of meditations on the world with superheroes in it is to limit a work that has many other meanings and many other axes to grind; it is nonetheless true. "Who watches the watchmen?" the tag asks, and there is no ultimate answer; themselves, each other, the mundane world, the reader. No one, the anarchist Moore reminds us, is good enough to be another person's master.[78]

With the publication of *Watchmen*, readers were forced to confront the legitimacy of heroism in ways that were not demanded of them before. This reimagining of justice shatters any simplistic notion of good versus evil. Unfortunately, in the decade that followed, few titles received the kind of accolades heaped upon the books written by Alan Moore and Frank Miller in the late 1980s. In a lament to the quality of work that followed, Moore has stated that while he had hoped *Watchmen* would "unlock a lot of potential creativity" among writers, instead, "it doomed the mainstream comic industry to about 20 years of very grim and often pretentious stories that seemed to be unable to get around the massive psychological stumbling block that *Watchmen* had turned out to be, although that had never been my intention with the work."[79]

A few years later, DC would engage in what many called a publicity stunt by publishing *Superman* #75. The "death of Superman" story arc finds Superman defeated at the hands of Doomsday in a splashy, battle-saturated comic at the end of which both Doomsday and Superman lie "dead."[80] The deaths gained much media attention and sold millions of copies. Despite this best-selling story, many comic book enthusiasts describe the 1990s as the nadir of comic books in terms of content from the mainstream publishers. The diminishing comic book readership flocked instead to new alternatives and creator-owned content like Image Comics' *Spawn* and its dark and cynical protagonist. Like Superman and Doomsday, superheroes appeared to be in their death throes, and the comic book industry in general suffered declining sales. Since the late 1990s, superheroes have had their largest cultural impact in the area of motion pictures. The comic book industry continues to struggle with declines in sales and finds itself in the precarious position of trying to attract new, younger readers with fresh material while still maintaining the aging loyalists who have grown accustomed to the more adult-focused storytelling and pulling in the jaded readers who quickly tire of the been-there-done-that formula. However, changes in the social and cultural landscapes inspire new calls for superheroes. In particular, the events of 9/11 set in motion a reconsideration of heroism in an age of anxiety about terrorism.

Throughout this chapter, we have suggested that among the greatest attractions of comic books through the decades are the explicit themes of crime and justice. For the most part, these inspiring tales feature heroes that serve to reaffirm the status quo, with little room for counternarratives. These tales frequently serve as metaphors for existential anxieties and fears present in a given social context. These themes resonate through various genres, but have had the most impact in the superhero genre and the crime genre. Due to various public interest groups and the corresponding constraints of the Comics Code, the crime genre has yet to reemerge with the same level of popularity as it reached in the late 1940s. Today, it is the superhero genre that dominates the industry. We have shown that comic book content, particularly that of crime and punishment, is impacted by the formulaic nature of the superhero genre, as well as by influences in the industry that are beyond the control of the creators. The Comics Code stifled the expression of any nonnormative portrayals. Once it was challenged and loosened, readers began to see stories portraying superheroes in a different light, confronting social ills that had previously gone unmentioned, and bringing their own flaws and fallibilities to light. Stories emerging from the loosened Code also highlighted the antidemocratic nature of all-encompassing power. Fans witnessed the reflexive nature of superheroes as they began to question their proper role in the world.

3

THE WORLD IS SHIFTING

TERRORISM, XENOPHOBIA,
AND COMIC BOOKS AFTER 9/11

The post-9/11 age of comics is devastatingly crystallized in the graphic novel *Shooting War,* which is deeply informed by real-life events on the ground, as well as by the ways in which digital technology and blog journalism have transformed the coverage of world events. Rogue journalist Jimmy Burns blows open the story on American military war crimes through the release of his video clip of a lieutenant executing an elderly Iraqi. The video shows a woman in traditional Iraqi garb being shot in the head at close range, her blood splattering, and framed by the familiar YouTube tool bar and logo.

Shooting War is one of many graphic novels that explicitly tackled the events of 9/11, challenging our ideas about heroism, the concept of evil, and responses to criminal threats such as terrorism. Though comic book narratives were saturated with crime-and-justice themes before the attacks, this chapter illustrates the unique ways in which post-9/11 comic books deal with threats of terrorism as a signpost of the age. Terrorism fits comfortably within the prototypical comic book plot formula.

This is not the first time comic book writers have modeled their storylines on wartime hardships as they unfolded in real life. During World War II, for example, Superman valiantly fought crime alongside patriotic Americans. Yet there are distinct differences to be found in the ways in which comic book writers after 9/11 shaped their plots. For example, how in the

Many post-9/11 comic books explicitly feature the global war on terror. Here, a YouTube video shows an American soldier shooting an Iraqi woman at close range in *Shooting War*, a post-9/11 graphic novel. (*Shooting War*, Anthony Lappé and Dan Goldman, Grand Central Publishing, 2007)

aftermath of 9/11, the comic book industry began to rethink the relevance of comic book superheroes, often portraying the characters as deferring to the real-life heroism of police officers and firefighters. In contrast to the unwavering patriotic fervor found in comic books during World War II, comic books in the post-9/11 era are more varied in their political leanings. They are, at times, reactionary and jingoistic, while at other times they are not afraid to address the perceived controversial tactics employed by then-president George W. Bush and his administration during the so-called war on terror. We contend that these comic books resonate in a political climate polarized by ideology and are important cultural expressions of an American society caught off guard and struggling to make sense of an uncertain future.

The events of 9/11 also created an opening for mainstream comic books to experiment with weaving into their plots Muslim and Arab heroes. We consider how the Arab and Muslim world began constructing its own mass-marketed comic book heroes. Although it is too early to entirely assess the era's impact, it appears that the post-9/11 age in comic books is a bipolar moment of both reactionary formulas and new, 9/11-related innovations in storylines and characters.

Notable post-9/11 innovations include Sid Jacobson and Ernie Colón's *9/11 Report: A Graphic Adaptation*. This book represents the first time an actual government report—in this case the report by Thomas Kean's 9/11 Commission—was recreated in graphic novel style, allowing Americans to engage in a more readable version of the results of the extensive investigation into the causes of the attacks. As Kean explained in the preface, the commission "hope[s] that this graphic version will encourage our fellow citizens to study, reflect—and act."[1] The hope that readers would engage in a public discourse about 9/11 in response to a graphic novel shows how the medium had become respected enough to carry important, nonfictional, government-generated information. It also suggests that the meaning of this comic, or any other, rests in the ways in which the text is used. Several college courses incorporated it, including a graduate class in policy analysis at John Jay College of Criminal Justice and an English class called "Literature and Culture after 9/11" taught by James Mulholland at Wheaton College. In online discussion forums, the graphic novel received mixed reviews as to whether a graphic version of a government report of real events was appropriate. As Mulholland explained about his class discussions,

> Our discussion of the graphic adaptation focused a great deal on what the formal and generic transformation meant for the information in the report. . . . Many felt like it was exploitative and utilized too many of the features of action cartoons. Others argued that visual drawings, rather than printed text, put us in the position to imagine that which we did not want to imagine—to visualize the final moments on the plane for example.[2]

The creators followed up their *9/11 Report* with another graphic novel titled *After 9/11: America's War on Terror (2001–)*, which draws from international news reports to depict the critical events, decision makers, and consequences of America's war on terror, as well as the context in which the war began and unfolded. The publication of these graphic novels is one of many indicators that comic books changed in the years following the attacks, both in the kinds of messages that could be conveyed and in their purpose.

Our findings indicate that the following themes are writ large in the post-9/11 comic book landscape: a redefinition of the role of heroes, anxieties about America's role in the world, and a preoccupation with Middle Eastern settings and Arab and Muslim characters. Taken together, these elements add a new twist to a crime plot formula that has long featured paranoia about mass casualty events involving an identifiable "other" (whether an ethnic other or an intergalactic one) and that necessitates heroic action. An upheaval such as 9/11 plays into the apocalyptic fantasy of mainstream comic books, especially when the perpetrators are conveniently ideologically and culturally distinct from mainstream America. At the same time, this xenophobic tendency shows signs of deterioration as creators attempt to imbue the formula with alternative constructions, such as the counternarrative in Art Spiegelman's *In the Shadow of No Towers,* a memoir of the terrorist attacks juxtaposed with early-twentieth-century cartoon strips. Spiegelman challenges the retributive and anti-Arab and anti-Muslim reactions some Americans had after the attacks, placing such anxieties into a particular historical context via a selection of vintage cartoons.

Heroism in an Age of Anxiety

Comic books published immediately after 9/11 reflected changing sensibilities about the role of heroes. As journalist Susan Faludi describes in her nonfiction book *The Terror Dream: Fear and Fantasy in Post-9/11 America,* Americans' sense of control over their own security was blown apart by the terrorist attacks.[3] This ushered in a new era of relating to heroes in popular culture, including superheroes in comic books. For the comic book industry, the attacks of 9/11 required a reexamination of the concept of heroism and, more specifically, a reexamination of "America's place in the world."[4]

A number of comic books were released commemorating the newly minted heroes of the event—police, firefighters, and other first responders—representing one way in which the medium became a means of directly addressing the attacks.[5] Marvel comics released an oversized comic book called *Heroes* celebrating the first responders of 9/11 with images featuring firemen carrying injured women from the ruins of the World Trade Center towers. Other commemorative comic books included *Comics' 9-11: Artists Respond, 411, The World's Finest Comic Books Writers and Artists Tell Stories to Remember, 9-11 Emergency Relief, A Moment of Silence,* and *The Call of Duty: The Brotherhood.*[6] According to criminologist Jared Lovell, the in-the-flesh, first-responder heroes left the fictitious superheroes without a job to do. In his analysis of post-9/11 comic books, he writes, "Today, it is America that is all-powerful while Superman is weak."[7]

Some tribute books portray the frustration that superheroes are unable to leap out of the pages of Marvel and DC to respond to the terrorist attacks. In *9-11 Emergency Relief*, Danny Donovan's autobiographical character rails,

> I damn them for not being real. For not being there for me. I was there for them—when their wedding was crashed by the villain, when their secret identity was compromised. When they went crazy, got cloned, died and came back as anti-heroes. I was there. Why weren't they?[8]

Neil Kleid's protagonist asks a similar question in his contribution to *9-11 Emergency Relief*, responding with, "And then it hits me. They're right there." A stoic portrait of a fireman accompanies the text, American flag in the background.

One comic that captured the hero obsession of the post-9/11 world was Vertigo's *Human Target*, which efficiently weaved the terrorist attacks into the fabric of its more general crime-fighting plot. *Human Target*, which inspired a television show on the Fox network in 2010, chronicles the adventures of Christopher Chance, who impersonates his clients in order to save them from criminal exploitation. In "The Unshreddable Man" story arc, Chance impersonates John Matthews, an accountant who fakes his own death by disappearing on 9/11 and thereby running away from pending investigations by the Securities and Exchange Commission. His employer and family assume he died in the terrorist attacks because he worked in New York's financial district and was unaccounted for. But when he seeks revenge on his corrupt employer through an extortion plot, Chance convinces him to redeem himself and go to the authorities to rat out his former boss instead. In an ironic moment, however, Matthews's wife is vehemently against his returning to his life,

> John Matthews, you've become some sort of hero to the kids. We made up these stories . . . about how you must have died when you went back inside to help others. That's their Daddy. Their Daddy was a good man who died on nine-eleven. And he's fucking staying dead, understand? You made your choice. You're stuck with it.

Ultimately Matthews does not return to his life before 9/11 and as a result, the story arc draws attention to the mythic proportions of accounts of the

9/11 heroes. In face of the fact that Matthews was actually a self-serving coward using the attacks to go underground, his wife prefers the fictional account because it better conforms to the overwhelming mythology of the time: that good people lost their lives in the World Trade Center helping others to escape. In addition, the story arc speaks to the plethora of conspiracy theories that 9/11 sparked about whether those whose remains were never found were truly dead.

Human Target is a significant post-9/11 landmark because nearly every story arc in it contains explicit reference to how the world of crime fighting has changed since 9/11. In a story arc about the mysterious death of a New York professional baseball player, the owner of the team explains to Chance the importance of New York baseball after 9/11: "This is more than just baseball. After nine-eleven . . . we came to represent New York's fighting spirit. If there's something dirty going on . . . I want it stopped." And in another storyline about the trafficking of children across the Mexican-American border, Chance's paramour explains that since 9/11, immigration controls have gotten tougher, causing parents to take increased risks to bring their children into the United States from Latin America. In a plot about a modern messiah figure who starts his own cult, Chance thinks about the reasons such a figure would be a comfort given the times, saying, "Al Qaeda. Terrorism. The war against terrorism. The threat of a real draft. Ineffectual government, and of course that old favorite mortality, no one's safe." Similarly, in *Ultimates: Super-Human*, the anxiety of the post-9/11 world acts as the lens through which crime of all stripes is filtered and ultimately understood. S.H.I.E.L.D. Agent Nick Fury talks to Bruce Banner (a.k.a. Hulk) at a posh lunch establishment in a skyscraper overlooking the Manhattan cityscape and states, "[W]e're living in crazy times, Doctor. Crime is becoming super-crime. Terrorism is becoming super-terrorism. Even the fattest, most stupid politician on Capitol Hill realizes that Son of Star Wars is going to be useless against the kind of problems America's really facing."[9]

Similarly, *Ex Machina*, a comic book about Mitchell Hundred, a man who has the power to communicate with and control machines, was an early mainstream comic to incorporate 9/11 in its plot. Hundred used his abilities to respond to the terrorist attacks and saved the second tower of the World Trade Center from collapse. However, he harbors extreme guilt over not having prevented the destruction of the first tower. He goes into public service, and the events of the comic book follow his tenure as mayor of New York City in a world described as overreliant on heroes to solve all of society's problems. Such a public orientation creates psychological stress on Hundred throughout the series. Other, more mainstream superheroes use 9/11 as justification for their activities, including *The Punisher*, who explains in one story arc that the "stricken horror of innocence killed stone dead" is seared into his memory (*The Punisher* #37).

Graphic Political Wranglings

After 9/11, publishers released comic books that contained ideologically diverse material that represented both reactionary and progressive responses to the tragedy. Media scholar Henry Jenkins notes that 9/11 offered the chance for countercultural messages in comic books to inspire new readers.[10] For Jenkins, mainstream 9/11-themed comic books indicated a shift toward a more global perspective, reflecting the dissatisfaction with corporate-manip-ulated globalism that perpetuates inequalities and "toward more metaphori-cal or utopian modes of expression"—a cultural space for imaginings of a better tomorrow.[11] Reactionary comic book narratives exist alongside those that challenge patriotic jingoism. In his article for *The American Prospect*, author Julian Sanchez also notices the more complex, and often seemingly contradictory, narratives emerging in post-9/11 comic books. He writes,

> [T]he politically inspired stories of the "War on Terror" era have been remarkable not only for their ubiquity and sophistication, but also in the way they have exposed—and sometimes exploded—the political ideas embedded in the superhero genre itself. . . . But the efforts of comics writ-ers to grapple with current events raise a corollary question: Is the super-hero a natural neocon?[12]

As Sanchez's question suggests, in one sense Superman celebrates total power in a rather fascistic manner, often breaching legal and ethical boundaries for the greater good in a largely uncontested political con-text.[13] The neoconservative notion of using authoritative power to maintain a certain cultural, social, and political status quo is certainly a dominant part of many superhero comic books. Marvel's crossover event *Siege*, for

Ground Zero's iconic illumination sets the stage for a post-9/11 New York storyline. (*Ex Machina* #1, Brian K. Vaughn and Tony Harris, Wildstorm, 2004)

example, revolves around the Iron Patriot (a.k.a. Norman Osborn) and his leadership of a national peacekeeping task force—a force that is reimagining America as a police state and doing so in the name of national security. Although the plot ultimately leaves Osborn without his police state, the need for an ultra-secret, pro-American strike force with little regulatory or legal oversight is not significantly questioned.

On the other hand, Marvel's successful *Civil War* series examined the extent to which American civil liberties should be curtailed for the sake of national security. The plot line asks that question alongside political ruminations about the Bush administration's response to 9/11. The series describes the fallout that occurs when the government rules that superheroes are weapons of mass destruction (WMDs) and must be registered in order to operate legally. Some heroes register and others resist the government. The political split threatens the unity of the Marvel superhero world.[14] Later, in *Siege*, the Mighty Avenger known as Stature (a.k.a. Cassie Long) reveals that she witnessed her team members torturing Loki, a villain, for information: "I couldn't believe it! We're Avengers for crying out loud, when did torture become an option?" This plot detail recalls the debate surrounding the Bush administration's use of waterboarding as a common interrogation technique used on terrorists. It also suggests that comic books are capable of questioning the political status quo at times, or at least on some discrete points.

Similarly, in *Captain America: New Deal*, the superhero questions America's participation in post-9/11 wars that may hold nations accountable for what individual terrorists have perpetrated.[15] Notably, Captain America became more popular among comic book fans after 9/11. The World War II–era "super-soldier" struck a chord with readers caught up in the surge of patriotism after the attacks.[16] Despite the patriotic fervor it sated, post-9/11 Captain America can actually be read as a critique of the reactionary war on terror the attacks spawned, so much so that a *National Review* film critic felt the need to weigh in on the cultural threat the storyline posed. In a white paper distributed by the Foundation for the Defense of Democracies, Michael Medved and coauthor Michael Lackner write,

> We might expect such blame-America logic from Hollywood activists, academic apologists, or the angry protesters who regularly fill the streets of European capitals (and many major American cities). When such

sentiments turn up, however, hidden within star-spangled, nostalgic pack-aging of comic books aimed at kids, we need to confront the deep cultural malaise afflicting the nation on the eve of war.[17]

In his column for Frontpagemag.com, Michael Lackner further lambasts Marvel's vigilante Punisher for becoming "a radical." He writes of the dangers of ignoring the anti-American sentiment in comic books,

> It appears that [comic writer Garth] Ennis and Marvel prefer to live in a vulgar world of leftist fantasy, where an evil American government allied with greedy multinational corporations is the enemy of humanity. If such self-hating beliefs are allowed to permeate the popular culture unchal-lenged, if our strength of will is sapped before we defeat our real enemies, our very survival may be jeopardized.[18]

Critics overly concerned with the "blame America" sentiment in comics were no doubt assuaged with the release of one of the highest-grossing movies of all time, the comic-book-inspired film *The Dark Knight,* featuring one of America's most iconic superheroes, Batman. Various conservative commentators hailed the film as vindication of former President Bush's war on terror strategies, including the subversion of constitutional procedure, coercive interrogation, and unrestricted domestic surveillance.[19] For example, Andrew Klavan wrote in the *Wall Street Journal,* "There seems to me no question that the Batman film *The Dark Knight,* currently breaking every box office record in history, is at some level a paean of praise to the fortitude and moral courage that has been shown by George W. Bush in this time of terror and war."[20] These critics may also find solace in a subsequent DC comic book, *Justice,* which also contains a conservative, self-reliant message. The villains in this storyline, who include Lex Luthor, Poison Ivy, the Rid-dler, and Black Manta, challenge the Justice League of America (JLA), com-posed of Wonder Woman, Superman, Batman, Aquaman, the Flash, Green Lantern, and Martian Manhunter, among others. The villains purport to be fighting against the heroes because they consistently fail to prevent societal ills, such as curing the sick and disabled and feeding the hungry. Instead, Lex Luthor opines, the superheroes' role in society appears reactive and ineffec-tive in stopping the cycle of suffering. Lex Luthor and his ilk devise a secret plan to solve various social problems in order to gain support from the public, and ultimately rid the world of its least desirable members: "Don't you see? Mankind could have been free from its predisposition to care for its weaker element. It would no longer be measured according to the lowest common denominator." The heroes reject the false utopia engineered by the villains and instead view the illnesses, droughts, poverty, and other hardships that individuals endure as making them stronger. In a close parallel to the conservative American narrative of self-reliance and individual choice, the villains and their social-justice agenda are defeated in favor of individual-based criminal justice emphasizing moral accountability. In *Justice*, Batman states, "[W]e have all been changed by our tragedies, no matter how much we have tried, and *should* try to avert them. No matter what cures we seek, or whom we seek them from. These challenges have given us a desire for justice." Therefore, in the post-9/11 age, superheroes may be resonating with readers who are experiencing political frustration at the pervading worldview of fear and of the perceived need to protect only oneself, at the expense of the collective. The vigilantes in *Justice* indeed lend themselves well to contemporary notions of self-deputizing aggression against those labeled as evildoers. They in effect leave behind notions of altruism and peacemaking that could hypothetically be the response to crimes of global proportions. The pursuit of justice as an abstract and seemingly pure concept in *Justice* helps to set aside the moral responsibility for others, devaluing their suffering, in favor of a very narrow, self-serving mission.

Arabs and Muslims in Comics: Villains and Beyond

Even as comic book creators stick to the apocalyptic and justice-oriented plot formulas, a primary shift in the comic book landscape in the post-9/11 age is the expanded portrayal of Arabs and Muslims. In the past, Arabs and Muslims were almost unanimously depicted as terrorists and bandits. More recently, however, they have been reimagined as heroes and superheroes, revealing the changing sensibilities of the medium. Originally, Arabs and Muslims in comic books were documented by communications scholar Jack Shaheen.[21] Besides Shaheen's work, little academic scholarship has focused on Arabs and Muslims in comic books.

Historically, an overwhelming majority of comic book portrayals of Arabs and Muslims construed them as villains acting as outsiders and "others" to heroic protagonists. Until recent years, Joe Sacco's *Palestine* remained one of the only comic book counternarratives regarding Arabs and Muslims. A type of journalism in graphic novel form, the work depicted Sacco's observations from the front lines of the West Bank and Gaza Strip during the early 1990s, showing the day-to-day indignities and suffering of the Palestinian people under occupation. Groundbreaking and critically acclaimed, the comic book sounded a nearly lone voice in presenting Arabs and Muslims in a humanistic light.

More typical of mainstream comic book fare pre-9/11 is Batman villain Ra's al Ghul, who has an Arabic-inspired name meaning "the demon's head." Another Batman villain, Ibn Al-Xu'ffasch, has a name meaning "son of the bat." Numerous mummy-type villains also appear in comics, drawing on ancient Egyptian lore. *Terra Obscura*, for example, showcases Mystico, a mummy recalled to life by a mad scientist.

In his pre-9/11 analysis of Arabs in comic books, Shaheen analyzed 215 comic books published from 1950 through 1994. He found that Arabs, when primary characters, were most often portrayed as villains, falling into one of three categories: the repulsive terrorist, the sinister sheikh, or the rapacious bandit.[22] The depiction of an Arab as a terrorist hell-bent on opposing the Western world appears in the best-selling comic book *Batman: A Death in the Family* (1988). In it, the Joker is found selling a nuclear Cruise missile to Jamal, a terrorist leader. A similar depiction occurs in *The Punisher: Nuclear Terrorists over Time Square* (1987), in which a group of Arabs steals a kilo of plutonium hoping to target New York City. In both these books, 1980s Cold War paranoia is fused with the construction of the Arab villain. Arabs as sinister sheikhs are constructed as headdress-wearing malevolents hoping for world domination through corrupt business and dirty politics. For example, in *Moon Knight: Fist of Konshu* (1985), Sheikh Ahmed Aziz is obsessed with restoring the ancient Egyptian empire. Finally, Arabs as bandits are represented in comics as bands of killers; for example, in *Sgt. Rock: Traitor's Blood!* Shaheen provides a number of reasons why these constructions of Arabs have predominated. He explains that the average American knows little about Arabs and that there are relatively few Arab Americans as compared with other American ethnic groups. As a result, negative portrayals often go unquestioned and Arabs become convenient villains, a portrayal shored up by similarly biased news coverage.

For example, in *Vigilante*, published in 1986, a crowd at a local bar watches news footage of a terrorist attack on Manhattan. The Middle Eastern terrorists are willing to die as martyrs and proclaim that they "shall be grateful for the chance to die in the name of Allah." At the bar, the citizens cry, "[O]ughta shoot 'em all . . . only good Arab is a dead Arab. . . . If I were there, I'd kill those bloodless bastards!" Reeling from the threat of terrorism, the American citizens are driven by vengeance. In Queens, groups of armed men, clad in face masks, proclaim, "We've been lettin' those damn Arabs and foreigners run roughshod over us too friggin' long! We're all Americans . . . we got to protect our families against those freaks . . . all them Arabs and Chinks and Russians takin' over businesses from us!" Meanwhile, Peacemaker, a super-powered soldier allegedly battling for peace, declares, "This is America . . . and we're under attack from an enemy called terrorism." The threat is neutralized when Vigilante, along with Peacemaker, kills most of the terrorists through a barrage of gunfire. The two heroes find themselves in a confrontation with a lone terrorist. Vigilante and Peacemaker battle each other to determine who gets to kill the now unarmed enemy. In the melee, Vigilante shoots the terrorist, Jahmed, in the back—problem solved.

The proliferation of post-9/11 comic books with Arabs or Muslim characters includes *411*, released in 2003 by Marvel. It portrays an Israeli avenging the death of his daughter at the hands of Palestinian extremists. Yet unlike most comic plots, which focus on retribution, the overall message points to nonviolence as the preferred response. The 2003 English translation of Marjane Satrapi's non-superhero autobiographical graphic novel *Persepolis* generated a significant amount of media attention, most likely due to post-9/11 curiosity about the Muslim world.[23] In addition, both *Superman* and *Captain America* serials portrayed their heroes wrestling with the events of 9/11.[24] Terrorism in the Middle East also surfaced in the plots of *Queen & Country*, *Justice League of America*, and *Human Target*. And, Tashkeel Publications unveiled *The 99* in 2006—a comic book that depicts a series of heroes who each embody one of the ninety-nine names (such as "generosity" and "wisdom") of Allah.[25] In 2010, *The 99* teamed up with the Justice League of America (JLA) in a crossover event (*JLA/The 99*). The crossover never explicitly mentions Muslim identity, but placing the two teams together in a plot to protect the world from terrorism depicts cooperation between Muslims and non-Muslims.[26] As a testament to the popularity of *The 99* in the Arab world, for example, the first of five 99-based theme parks opened in Kuwait in March of 2009.[27]

After 9/11, the Middle East was more frequently used as the setting for comic books. The terrorist attacks, in conjunction with the Second Intifada, a Palestinian uprising that began in 2000, were influential in bringing this region to the fore in both superhero and non-superhero genres.[28] *Cairo* portrays an adventure involving a group of American, Arab, and Israeli friends in Egypt, and *Pride of Baghdad* follows a pack of lions wrestling with their freedom after escaping from the Baghdad Zoo during U.S. military operations. In the superhero genre, comic books such as *Superman: For Tomorrow* includes a Palestine-like location in the Middle East as the source of a high-tech weapon that caused people to vanish en masse. Superman explains that the weapon was triggered on "[a] piece of earth that's known for war. . . . Some might say . . . life, civilization, faith [started here]. . . . A region, a desert, where blood flows more freely than water."

We found crime plots involving Muslims or Arabs or Middle Eastern locations in books such as *Batman Detective Comics*, *Ultimates 2*, *Captain America: The Chosen*, *X-Men: The Messiah Complex*, and *52*. In addition to the increasing appearance of Muslims and Arabs as heroic figures, our analysis revealed other themes, including a lack of understanding of the people of the Middle East, amalgamation of Eastern philosophy and spiritualism, the presence of fake Middle Eastern locations, and the need for ethnic and religious tolerance. One of the dominant themes observed was recognition that the West is ill equipped to understand the diverse peoples of the Middle East. Flat characters of Middle Eastern origin emerged, much as in the pre-9/11 analysis by Shaheen. Afghani Muslim villains acted as the backdrop to *Captain America: The Chosen*. These foes are shown as angry, wearing turbans, and engaging in suicide bombing missions, with little character development and scant information as to their motivations. Important, however, is the presence throughout the book of a new awareness of the superficiality of the American experience with Arab and Muslim people. For example, Captain America laments that it is hard to tell friend from foe in Afghanistan because they all look the same. He says, "How can I help anybody if everybody looks the same . . . if I can't tell the people I want to help from the people I need to fight." Despite this awareness, however, the story arc reveals little by way of a solution to the problem.

Another construction across the titles was the merging of Muslim spirituality and Arab ethnic identity into a muddled package of otherness in
which these identities are blended with other Eastern ones. Although Batman villain Ra's al Ghul hails from a nomadic tribe in Arabia, further back
his ancestry is Chinese. His father, a martial arts expert, has a Japanese-style
name, Sensei. Ra's al Ghul is known for using the regenerative Lazarus Pits
to regenerate his injured or near-death physical body, and recently he has
been resurrected in the body of a Nanda Prabat (Himalayan) monk. Since
then, Ra's al Ghul has practiced Buddhist rituals and chants associated with
Tibetan or Nepali traditions. In another example, Black Adam, despite being
an implicitly Muslim character and ruler of the nation of Kahndaq, derives
powers from ancient Egyptian gods that hold the key to immortality. This
represents a conflation of Islam and pre-Islam (*jahaliya*) in the Middle East
that would be unlikely to be allied in the same individual.

The spiritual otherness of Arabs and Muslims and the danger they represent is found in stories in which magic is being unleashed in the Middle
East. In *Cinderella: From Fabletown with Love*, secret agent Cinderella follows the flow of dangerous magical items being leaked from the Middle
Eastern fable world to the "mundy" or mundane Middle Eastern world. As
Aladdin, a spy for the Middle Eastern fable world, explains, "The situation in that already unstable region has only worsened, threatening the
true Baghdad itself." And, Cinderella narrates, "I mean, this is a part of the
world where billionaires build artificial islands in the shape of things. All
they need is a death ray or two and they will be ready to take over the
world." *Cinderella* involves the construction of a "Middle Eastern" fable
world separate from the Western one depicted in the popular *Fables* series.
Using the role of women as a symbol of the differences between the two
fable worlds, Aladdin and Cinderella travel to an oil rig in the North Sea
where three "harem sisters" are trading in arms and magic in order to earn
enough money to found their own kingdom—so they will never be harem
slaves in Sinbad's court again. In front of a billboard advertising prostitution, these harem women explain that the freedom they obtained in the
mundane West was only an illusion because "[t]here may be no harems in
this mundane world, no eunuch guards and high impassable walls, but we
soon learned that women here wear chains of a different sort." Comic book
universes have long contained fake towns and countries, including those
representing the Middle East and Islam. Sometimes they are seemingly

inconsequential asides, like the reference to Bahraqistan, in a comic short in *Girl Comics* (#1, 2010) or "Dubai, Saudi Arabia" in *X-Men: Psylocke.* (Dubai is not located in Saudi Arabia, but in United Arab Emirates.) They are also more substantial settings that are fictional Middle Eastern countries such as Kahndaq and Bialya, featured in 52. Frequently, in these depictions, a "monster society" lives where war, pestilence, and death abound.

Notably, these faux Middle Eastern locales are portrayed as requiring the intervention of Western powers, and their superheroes, to assist them in building democracy and containing threats. In *Justice League of America's* "Extinction" storyline (#91, #92), the league gives a visiting alien a tour of Earth, including a place in the Middle East called Minglia where "people like their religion" and it is "full of men with guns," insurgents and suicide bombers. While there, Green Lantern intercepts and safely detonates a truck bomb headed for a school. Also in the DC Universe, the fictional country of Qurac, located on the Persian Gulf south of Iraq, has historically acted as a stand-in for a Middle Eastern terrorist state. It features a metahuman mercenary strike force headed by a group called the Jihad. The attitude of DC heroes to this location has historically been one of disdain. The mockery of Qurac is exemplified in the Joker having been the U.S. ambassador to the country. Cheshire's decision to explode a nuclear missile over the country in a 1993 issue of *Deathstroke* made sense to her because no one else in the DC Universe would care about any casualties there. In an alternative construction of Qurac, the country features an oil-rich sultan and a large harem for the ruling class, a reference to a stereotypical Gulf oil state. Whether a terrorist haven or a decadent oil monarchy, Qurac contributes to a larger media context in which shorthand, knee-jerk, and reactionary portrayals of Arab and Muslim countries is common.

A contrast to the reactionary portrayal of Muslims and Arabs in these books is a dominant theme of the need for tolerance. Main staples like the *X-Men* series incorporated Muslims as mutant heroes. For example, Soraya Qadir, a veiled Afghan student, studies at the Xavier Institute, where mutants are trained to understand and use their powers. Code named "Dust," Soraya possesses the power to turn herself into sand so she can penetrate places unseen or create diversionary dust storms. Central to the plot in *X-Men: Messiah Complex* is the relationship between Soraya and her Japanese roommate, who believes the veil is about subservience and shame. Soraya tells her it is really about modesty and is central to her culture. She says, "I do not judge the way you dress. I ask that you do the same for me."

Religious tolerance is at times highlighted in these books. The most counterhegemonic of the books, *Jalila*, depicts the adventures of an Arab female superhero and nuclear scientist. Jalila states often that she is motivated by a desire for people of the three monotheisms to find peace with each other. The comic book, originally from Egypt and in Arabic, was released in English in 2007. Ayman Kandeel, who created the character of Jalila, told the press that he wanted to depict Muslims, Christians, and Jews living together peacefully, confronting the mutual threats of organized crime, evil robots, and aliens.[29] Likewise, *The 99* creator Naif al-Mutawa, in an open letter to his sons published by the BBC, wrote about why he created his comic book: "I told the writers of the animation that only when Jewish kids think that *The 99* characters are Jewish, and Christian kids think they're Christian, and Muslim kids think they are Muslim, and Hindu kids think they are Hindu, that I will consider my vision as having been executed."[30] The mission to have universal appeal, it should be noted, is no less than the marketing strategies of DC and Marvel, who have worldwide audiences and often see the comic book world as one that transcends culture despite its American origins.

Many depictions of female Arabs and Muslims as crime-fighting protagonists contribute to a shift in comic books that also involves gender. A character like Jalila is constructed as both traditional and modern. She is committed to family honor, for as a single female she lives with her two brothers. Jalila takes the lead in avenging her parents' death, a path of revenge that would traditionally be in the hands of males in her family. Her brothers, however, are otherwise disposed, one struggling with drug addiction and the other a terrorist. In this way, she appeals to independent women as well as more conservative ones. Jalila's assertiveness can be read as entirely honorable to traditional Arab sensibilities because it is born out of necessity, given the death of her parents and her brothers' criminal lifestyles.

Taken all together, the dominant themes identified suggest a bipolar moment in regards to Arab and Muslim characters in comic books. The crisis of 9/11 provided an opening for a discourse change, but at the same time, the continued villainization of Arabs and Muslim also was detectable in comic books. Mainstream comics entertained the possibility of heroic

Jalila, an Arab superheroine, uses her scientific training to fight terrorists. (*Jalila* #1, Ayman Kandeel, and Allan Goldman, AK Comics, 2006)

Arabs such as Soraya. The Arab and Muslim world began constructing their own heroes in comic book form through such projects as *The 99* and *Jalila*. In postcolonial theory, this is known as writing "back to the center."[31] Formerly colonized people, who have been educated by colonists in the English language and literature, and exposed to English-language cultural artifacts such as American comic books, seek to create their own from their perspective. AK Comics (publisher of *Jalila*) is explicitly engaged in this project. In 2005, its managing director and editor, Marwan Nashar, told the press, "I grew up reading 'Spider-Man' and I loved him. But I couldn't get into Peter Parker. I mean, he lived in New York. I always wondered why there weren't any Arabs leaping off buildings."[32] Although writing "back to the center" in the world of comics remains in its infancy, *The 99* and *Jalila* are early successes. In 2005, AK comics, publisher of *Jalila*, as well as *Zein* and *Aya*, reported that they sold approximately forty-five hundred copies of each issue of their comics released in United States.[33] And five hundred thousand copies of *The 99* are sold each year worldwide.[34]

Writing (and Drawing) Back to the Center

One of the goals of postcolonial theory, in its challenge to racist and imperial texts, is to encourage the opening up of discourses to multiple voices. Postcolonial literature has often been described as involving "hybridity" or "creolity" in that imperial culture had differential impact on the people in colonized spaces, creating a mixed cultural heritage that is both imperial and local.[35] Among post-9/11 graphic novels, Toufic El Rassi's *Arab in America* presents the personal story of an Arab American coping with anti-Arab sentiment in the midst of the war on terror. He wrestles with his Lebanese identity even though he has spent most of his life in the United States and is a naturalized citizen. The hybridity of his identity creates a neither-here-nor-there creolity through which he attempts to make sense of his place in American society in the grips of post-9/11 trauma. He writes, "All these memories and feelings bubbled up in me after the [9/11] attacks. . . . I felt like I should hide or apologize or something. I don't know why, but I felt guilty. . . . Every time I saw a policeman I felt an icy shiver down my back." Acting as a primer on events in the Middle East since the Lebanese civil war of the early 1980s, the autobiographical graphic novel links the personal with the political, exposing the everyday indignities of comments about his identity that friends and acquaintances have made over the years, everything from "towel-head" to "sand nigger." The pages of graphically represented Middle Eastern history suggest that increased education and awareness about Arabs is one step forward in creating tolerance in a mixed-up postcolonial and post-9/11 world. In this sense, the post-9/11 "writing back to the center" has expanded on Sacco's *Palestine,* which, in retrospect, was ahead of its time as a work that deconstructed the postcolonial Middle East. In a preface to the 2001 collected edition, Edward Said, preeminent postcolonial scholar and author of the landmark text on the subject, *Orientalism,* pays homage to Sacco.

[Sacco] is drawn to [Palestine] partly because of his Maltese family background . . . partly because the postmodern world is so accessible to the young and curious American, partly because like Joseph Conrad's Marlow, he is tugged at by the forgotten places and people of the world, those who don't make it on the television screens, or if they do, who are regularly portrayed as marginal, unimportant, perhaps even negligible if it was not for their nuisance value which, like Palestinians, seems impossible to get rid of.[36]

The nuisance value of Arabs and Muslims in the eyes of mainstream America reached critical mass after 9/11, creating a market for the increasingly curious. As a result, the dominant narrative and its critique shared shelf space in the years after 9/11. Despite the inroads made by Arab and Muslim creators in opening up storylines to nonvillain portrayals, comic books remained a reactionary touchstone for xenophobia in books such as *JLA* and *Captain America: The Chosen,* in which Arabs and Muslims are villainous backdrops. The amalgamation of Eastern religious spirituality into one package of otherness also represents a less than progressive understanding of the nuances of peoples who identify as Arab or Muslim.

Shadows and Towers

The iconic exploration of the way comic representations relate to the 9/11 attacks remains *In the Shadow of No Towers.* The Pulitzer Prize–winning comic writer and artist Art Spiegelman created a unique dramatic work that acts as a memoir of the attacks—which he witnessed—and an exploration of early-twentieth-century cartoon strips. Spiegelman told the press that he returned to the old comic strips in the days after 9/11 for comfort. The book includes the strip "Little Nemo in Slumberland" by Winsor McCay, in which the main protagonist dreams that he is ten stories tall, but still lost in the metropolitan canyons on Manhattan. Critical theorist Kristaan Versluys explains that the book is an attempt to sort out a "limit event," an event whose trauma was so great that it is difficult to make sense of it in any of the normal cognitive and cultural ways.[37] A similar theme surfaces in the graphic novel *Waltz with Bashir* (2009), which is the chilling account of a former Israeli soldier regaining a long-suppressed memory of the war in Lebanon in

1982. In *Waltz with Bashir*, the image of dogs with glowing eyes is repeated as the protagonist begins to confront the unthinkable, lying in waiting in the deepest realms of his subconscious. Similarly, Layla Lawlor's contribution in *9/11 Emergency Relief* used the metaphor of a shattered fractal for trying to understand the events of 9/11 that were "too big to be taken in all at once."[38] And, Alissa Torres's *American Widow* chronicles the slow healing process after she lost her husband, one of the many individuals who jumped from the upper floors of the World Trade Center. The unthinkable fact of her husband's death plays itself out in disturbing dreams and paralyzing depression, made all the more surreal by well-intentioned charities bombarding her with bureaucracy.

In Spiegelman's graphic novel, the repeated image of a bright and burning tower represents a holding on to the trauma and a refusal to succumb to rash or easy responses. The use of old comic strips has the effect of creating distance from the event and juxtaposing the hopefulness of the strips with the despair of the attacks. Versluys suggests that the result is a "screwball effect" that also points to Spiegelman's confessedly severe posttraumatic stress.[39] The book is rendered in a variety of different graphic styles infused with the apocalyptic 9/11 refrain "THE SKY IS FALLING!"

Spiegelman's work acts as a reverie on the perceptions of the loss of safety and security that the attacks generated, as well as a scathing critique of the war on terror. In one section, Spiegelman's psychological decline is depicted in a vertical display of his face repeated until the last image is of him is as a mouse, a reference to his Pulitzer Prize–winning work about the Holocaust, *Maus*. The caption explains that he is "equally terrorized by Al-Qaeda and his own government." According to Versluys, Spiegelman is asserting that he wants to be left alone in his trauma rather than succumb to the violent responses advocated by the Bush administration behaving in "dystopian Big Brother mode," which "hurtle[s] America into a colonialist adventure in Iraq."[40] Spiegelman's work brings together the comic book's historic obsession with apocalypticism and the more recent contested political landscape generated by the 9/11 attacks.

In *Reframing 9/11: Film, Popular Culture, and the "War on Terror,"* Reza Aslan writes that popular culture both informed our interpretation of the events of 9/11 (i.e., the perception that the attacks were "like a movie") and continues to serve as a cultural space for us to make sense of the attacks— as we continue to craft a narrative that helps us cope "with the chaos and confusion of the past few years."[41] The events of 9/11 continue to be inter-preted and recast in popular culture, including in contemporary Ameri-can comic books. We found that many comic books published in the after-math of 9/11 explored and confronted the role of American heroes that find themselves in an age of anxiety surrounded by potential terrorist-centered criminal and global threats of epic proportions. The debate on whether heroes serve as "natural neocons" or as left-wing apologists extends far beyond the confines of a narrow comic book culture fandom and attests to the power of our national mythology expressed in comic books. Although superhero comic books generally continue to operate in a fairly formulaic manner—including within a heteronormative context—the events of 9/11 created a space for resistance to the hegemonic dominance of white, male, hypermasculine heroes and a more nuanced portrayal of villains.

A BETTER TOMORROW

APOCALYPSE, UTOPIA, AND THE CRIME PROBLEM

In the opening pages of *Coup d'Etat*, published in 2004 by DC imprint Wildstorm, the state of Florida suffers destruction and mass casualties brought on by aliens who attack its residents, and whose motives remain elusive.[1] The series occurs in a separate universe that features the Authority, a team of superheroes that works toward saving the world from various threats, both on and off the planet. In this particular storyline, attacking aliens are juxtaposed with talking heads on television who are outraged that this crisis is unfolding in a normally peaceful place: "[A]s night falls on what was once the great state of Florida, America mourns its lost and displaced." A serene sun dipping into the Gulf of Mexico, punctuated only by the dark silhouettes of palm trees, provides the backdrop for a soliloquy by superhero Jack Hawksmoor of the Authority. Hawksmoor, a debonair and red-pupiled noncostumed hero, is the "God of the Cities"—he can immediately tap into the gestalt of any city he finds himself in and has the ability to combat distant threats to it and the planet in general. Hawksmoor laments that the loss of life in Florida was "the straw that broke this planet's back." Partially blaming the crisis on the Florida government, which failed to defend its people, Hawksmoor states,

> They've squandered the opportunity to create a better tomorrow and chosen instead to foolishly risk the lives of everyone on the planet. And if you

think we're going to allow this bullshit to continue then you haven't really been paying attention to who we are. The time for warnings is long past, you've proven you can't be trusted . . . so as of now we're taking over.

In mainstream comic books, a better tomorrow is always on the horizon, but never in the present, typically depicted as in the throes of crisis and despair. That crisis and despair almost always centers on a criminal threat of apocalyptic proportions, whether deep-seated government corruption, entrenched organized crime, terrorism, or even war crimes such as geno-cide. Protagonists, haunted by the way things could be and outraged by the way they are, go to extreme lengths to strive for a utopian future often firmly rooted in the nostalgic past—whether for a Florida before an alien firestorm earlier that day, or for more distant times and even more ide-alized places. Overwhelmingly, nostalgia for a perceived idyllic past is a dominant theme within American comic books and propels characters on quests for a better, safer world.

The Crime Problem as the Apocalyptic Breaking Point

The crime problem in the comic books we studied represents the point of crisis for the given community and necessitates the hero's journey toward achieving apocalyptic justice. Although the crime problem itself may spawn macro-level social, political, and moral chaos and be depicted in dystopic social imagery, the root of the problem is often individualized and pinned on a particular vil-lain or set of villains operating destructively for their own selfish gain.[2]

We found that the dominant crime problems encountered were terror-ism, government corruption, and organized crime, followed by violent street crime. Historically, comic book analysts have found street crime to be the most prevalent crime type.[3] Notably, cultural and economic global-ization and the events of 9/11 are most likely the antecedents of a shift to more transnational, terror-focused crime in more recent comic books, as we described in the previous chapter.

We also found government corruption to be a prevalent theme in comic books. For example, in *The Losers*, a band of rogue CIA agents betrayed by their superiors are left for dead. The group, determined to avenge their abandonment, relive numerous historical events involving U.S. government corruption such as the Vietnam War and the Iran-Contra affair. *Fell*, a comic book with each issue featuring self-contained stories, details detective Richard Fell as he fights crime in a dystopic urban blight known as Snowtown. The series is illustrated by Ben Templesmith, most notable for his dark, haunting imagery. The style lends itself to conveying the horrors and despair in the "Feral City" of Snowtown. In one issue, the government skirts its responsibilities, leading to the social breakdown and crime problems in Snowtown. There are no child welfare services in the city, leaving children at the mercy of abusers and pedophiles. To make matters worse, "dumb" judges grant child custody to convicted felons.

Law enforcement is often incompetent and unable to handle the criminal threat. In *Two-Face: Year One*, Gotham City district attorney Harvey Dent (a.k.a. Two-Face) says to Batman, "This isn't just about me nailing the mob. This isn't even about me proving that I'm not a murderer. This is about showing this city that I—that we—can put the bad guys away by the book." Shortly thereafter, though, a defendant throws acid on Dent, disfiguring his face. As a result of this personal and professional tragedy, Dent resorts to vigilante justice and commences with determining criminals' fates by the flip of a coin.

One of the more frequently occurring crime problems in our sample is terrorism. In *Queen & Country* #21, an MI-6–like operations chief decries "the endless inquiries" that the war on terror has spawned. One image depicts the operations chief swishing his brandy glass in a display of authority and cool sophistication that could only emanate from a veteran of the most clandestine intelligence operations. He says,

> The world is shifting on us Frances and the service is struggling to keep up. This thing in Iraq and the focus on UBL [Usama bin Laden] and his ilk, the endless inquiries into offshore accounts and wire transfers. . . . For all that Sir Wilson was a gifted spymaster, there are a number of my peers in Whitehall that have never fully grasped . . . the more nuanced elements of allied cooperation.

Thus, the portrayal can be read as a post-9/11 comment on how the spy game is increasingly challenged by the subtleties of the new age of terrorism and on how the accepted rules have changed. In *Queen & Country Declassified* (volume 3), a return of Irish separatist violence threatens elections in the county of Armagh, Northern Ireland. The graphic novel features a supplementary glossary of terms in order to explain the many counterterrorism references,

> As part of its emphasis on realism, *Queen & Country* uses many abbreviations, acronyms and terms found in the everyday life of a Government agency. . . . Regular readers have become accustomed to these terms over time, but the unfamiliar setting of *Declassified, Volume III* [Northern Ireland] requires a whole new set of abbreviations and slang.

The desire to reflect real-world government agencies through the correct use of terms and acronyms shows how comic books flirt with reflecting reality, such as the global war on terror, even as they deliver sometimes implausible, but entertaining, storylines.

A less frequent, but still important, crime problem in our sample of contemporary comics is psychopathic criminality. Many story arcs depict a villain whose primary motivation is a psychological fixation or desire to harm others. Many of Batman's foes, from the Joker to Two-Face, suffer from deep personal scars that propel them into psychopathy, obsession, and criminality. The Scarecrow develops his homicidal alter ego after being a long-time victim of child abuse. And, the comic book *Sam & Twitch* shows detectives combating such criminals as pedophile clowns, vengeful "Franken-women" (women created in scientific laboratories), and others described as "monsters." In the same story arc, Twitch's daughter is kidnapped by a criminal targeting Twitch for revenge for a past arrest. The panels depicting the kidnapping evoke every parent's worst fear. Disguised as a helpless elderly lady, the offender lures Twitch's daughter into assisting him. The daughter's attire, a cheerleading skirt and turtleneck, as well as her willingness to assist an old lady, suggests her innocent good nature, all the more tragic as she is violently abducted and forced into the trunk of a car.

Imagining a Better World

Because the crime problems depicted often reach apocalyptic proportions, comic book creators and editors have developed imaginative narratives about creating a better world. Constructions of a better world in comic books take

An MI-6–like master spy swirls and sniffs his brandy while waxing poetic about the emergence of terrorism in the post-911 age. (*Queen & Country: Definitive Edition*, volume 2, Greg Rucka and Mike Hawthorne, Oni Press, 2008)

the form of narrowly construed nationalism or more global imaginings of a peaceful world, or even parallel worlds, in which basic Western values of democracy and human rights are upheld, constructed as a type of future utopia. In Western culture, the concept of utopia has referred to a place that has achieved social, legal, and political perfection. It was first coined as such by Sir Thomas More in his book *Utopia* (1516), reaching its height in literary novels such as H. G. Wells's *A Modern Utopia* (1905) and Aldous Huxley's *Island* (1962). Although the word "utopia" usually refers to a fictional time and place, its meaning often subsumes the more fantastical notion of heterotopia, an imagining of a *possible* perfect world not yet in existence. Both concepts, however, involve a "drive toward totality," meaning the governing of all of life by a particular principle of perfection, often painted as a millennial fantasy of a returning savior in the Christian Humanist tradition or a state of secular, scientific perfection. Literary scholar David Bleich has suggested that these "waking fantasies" allow humans to express fundamental drives and desires such as abundance, safety, healthiness, rural nostalgia, community, and social order.[4]

The readers recognize this yearning as an important attraction of the medium. As one focus group participant explained,

New York was a shit-hole in the 70s. The public perception of this was very exaggerated, but crime has since gone down. Yet crime reporting has gone up. The fear is disproportionate. . . . We feel that there are all these forces out there that are utterly malicious and it's really nice to envision this perfect world where there are defenders . . . that is the mentality that sort of drives this stuff.[5]

Another focus group participant connected the utopian fantasies in comic books to readers' general sense that the world contains "more insecurities and less absolution" than ever before.[6]

Connecting with utopian narratives in comic books is a process by which individuals transcend their particular time and space in order to create new images of themselves and their world.[7] Mike Alsford, theologian and author of *Heroes and Villains*, suggests that pop culture heroes evoke a heightened sense of "coadunacy," or the interconnectedness and interdependence of the individual to the values and needs of the community, society, or, in some cases, humanity.[8] However, in superhero comic narratives, the community itself is never adequate to restore social order or achieve utopia. A hero, or a team of heroes, is necessary to reach beyond the constraints of ordinary mortals and operate outside the boundaries of the justice system ostensibly for the greater good, in essence presenting a powerful mythologized version of American individualism.

In a manner reminiscent of political scientist Benedict Anderson's notion of "imagined communities," comics explore the relationship between nostalgia and the desired utopian social order.[9] Thus, comic books can be seen as ideological tools similar to poetry, myth, and legend, filled with constructions of an idealized past and offering up ideas about community, identity, and belonging. Anderson suggests that the historic rise of print media was vital to bringing notions of community to a wider audience and gave birth to nationalism, connecting people to common cultural artifacts and fostering cohesion among people who would never meet face to face. Cultural anthropologist Arjun Appadurai notes that communications technology such as the Internet has taken this further, connecting people from vast distances and creating communities and national diasporas that further transcend geographical and temporal boundaries.[10]

[H]umans are capable of connecting with communities that lie beyond the local and immediate and that investment in such imagined communities strongly influences identity construction and engagement in learning. . . .

> Our identities must be understood not only in terms of our investment in the "real" world but also in terms of our investment in *possible* worlds.[11]

From this perspective, a nation is an imagined community to all its members, the construct of which is not necessarily the same as the nation itself.

American nationalism and patriotism have figured prominently in the construction of the utopian past in comic books. The premise in Captain America involved his disappointment in not being able to serve in World War II and his subsequent decision to participate in a clandestine military project in which he was scientifically transformed into a super-soldier. Fighting Nazis and Communists who were determined to impose their competing values on the world, Captain America becomes a defender of the American way of life, constructed as a utopia, throughout the twentieth century and until his post-9/11 death and beyond. Notably, the actions of the government in the aftermath of 9/11 propel Captain America to challenge policies believed to violate individual rights, counter blind patriotism, and champion the notion that a better America lies ahead.

American "spirit" is also invoked as heroes work to save New York City from an apocalyptic attack launched in retribution for a "secret war" waged by Nick Fury, head of S.H.I.E.L.D. (*Secret War*).[12] Explosions engulf the city as the heroes indicate that they must move this fight away from populated areas. Villain Lucia Von Bardas appears and reveals that she has orchestrated the grand attack. She quips to the heroes,

> [C]ongratulations on your perseverance and American spirit. Most of you were supposed to be dead by now. . . . [T]his is the day you all pay for your sins. . . . [Y]ou are here to witness the destruction of your people as you tried to destroy mine. The deaths of millions of American souls will be on your head Nick Fury.

It is later revealed that the attack was retaliation for an invasion lead by Nick Fury that ousted Lucia Von Bardas from power in her country of Latveria. Here, the efforts to persevere in the face of evil are construed as evidence of the American spirit, despite the fact that Von Bardas was prompted by Fury's decidedly undemocratic and imperial quest to invade her country, forcibly removing her from power, perhaps echoing real-life American interventionism in the war on Iraq.

In our earlier study into the constructions of a nostalgic past in comic books, a majority of comics referred to a need to maintain American geo-political hegemony and depicted a yearning for America as a bulwark of freedom and democracy as the world's primary superpower.[13] In *Route 666* #19, a Cold War tale, the protagonist exhibits the superhuman ability to see Communists in the form of demons, thus identifying who among the members of society should be feared. The protagonist appeals to the government of Empyrean, a shadow America, to help her prevent the demons from gaining power. As one of her associates states, "If Cassie can make someone see one of these creatures the way she made us see 'em, then maybe we can organize a decent counterattack!"

In "Entertainment and Utopia," film critic Richard Dyer points out that entertainment's central thrust is to offer a utopian sensibility, an emotion or feeling about an idyllic future that relates to real experiences.[14] However, entertainment in this sense is not necessarily presenting narratives that move toward utopia in a linear, progressive fashion; rather, they are recalling the past. Dyer suggests that, "far from pointing forwards, they point back, to a golden age—a reversal of utopianism that is only marginally offset by the narrative motive of recovery of utopia."[15] Patriotism and nationalism are often merged with a nostalgic longing for an America of the past. For example, small-town America is a prominent imagining in comic books, in particular Superman's Smallville. In *Superman: Kansas Sighting*, Superman returns to his midwestern American roots and waxes poetic about the slow pace and social cohesion he remembers. Similarly, in *All-Star Superman*, Clark Kent returns to a Smallville diner, reunited with old friends Pete and Lana. "Look at us! The old gang, all grown up!" Metropolis is "overwhelming" to Clark and he states, "I just don't know if I need to be in the city at all." When Clark expresses skepticism about visitors he has received while in Smallville, Lana asks, "Did the big city make you so cynical already?" Later, Clark remarks, "This soda . . . I'd . . . ah . . . I'd forgotten how *rich* the food was back home."

Small-town America is also visited in *Wolverine: The Brotherhood*. In one scene, Wolverine is depicted sitting in an urban coffee shop reading Thoreau's *Walden*, a classic of American Transcendentalism. He later visits a small-town diner and asks about available pies. Another patron comments on his motorcycle, "Good bike. American." Wolverine is seeking revenge for the murder of a small-town girl who escaped from a terrorist cult (which also serves as a female sex slavery ring) only to be killed by the cult leaders. As Wolverine says to his friend Elf (a.k.a. Nightcrawler), "They were a cult. They'd broken a town. Made it afraid. They kidnapped women. Girls. And they used them up." Wolverine implies that the natural order of a small town is the lack of fear and the expectation of safety.

Similarly, lost in exile in New York City, the characters in *Fables* yearn for their bucolic place of origin, Homeland. Meanwhile, they have established a pseudo-American town featuring free elections and a criminal justice system complete with due process protections. And, Neil Gaiman's *Violent Cases* (2003, first published in 1987) exhibits nostalgia for the old English social order. The main character reminisces about his childhood in Portsmouth, England, recalling custom-fitted tweed jackets, birthday parties at the queen's hotel, and rain-soaked streets. *Violent Cases* concludes with the protagonist observing that "[n]obody seems to wear a hat these days."

Apocalyptic Anxieties Spanning the Past and Future

The contrast between the crime-ridden present and the hope for a better future sets up a fundamental anxiety that mainstream comic books describe and explore. In general, comic book stories are often a moral panic about the decline or complete demise of family, democracy, and freedom. The old order, often depicted as a white, middle-class community with strong family values, enviable social capital, and equality, is put in jeopardy by an over-arching evil taking the form of criminal violence— which has annihilated a peaceful status quo.[16] Existing law enforcement and judicial mechanisms are often depicted as ineffective and broken, a crisis necessitating a superhero.[17] The hero is shown longing for the nostalgic past and fixated on an imagined community within the virtual world of the comic book. That imagined community is one the reader can experience vicariously—and may be little more imaginative than notions of community and nationhood that are experienced in daily life (insofar as community and nationhood are always human constructs, even in their most real-world manifestations).

Within the utopian desire for control is an inherent anxiety about that which must be tamed in a continual process of weeding out evil. In the postmodern sense, this quest for social control is characteristic of what criminologist Jock Young calls a "bulimic society" in which a continued and uncontrolled hunger for the utopian reigns.[18] In later work, Young confronts the fever pitch of anxiety about this dystopic condition, which necessitates hyperbolic responses and reactionary tendencies as part of a mass psychology that is "a mistake in reason" but is not, on a more in-depth level, "a mistake in emotion."[19] Similarly, one can read comic books as a narrative of moral disturbance in which moral panic arises from a crisis in the hegemonic structure.

As an emotional, reactionary hunger for the past, the utopian desire looks toward the future, described by sociologist Daniele Hervieu-Leger as representing a continuity "reaching back further than the one that suits the social conventions of the present . . . with a past that is blessed and beneficent, and which stands in opposition to the misfortunes, the dangers, and the uncertainties of the present."[20] Interestingly, anthropologist Matthew Wolf-Meyer argues that there is a fundamental distinction between the utopian narrative in popular comic books and that of other genres because comic books focus on the process of achieving utopia and typically reveal that it is unattainable, whereas science fiction, for example, is more concerned with the effects of a utopian order.[21]

In *Superman: For Tomorrow*, Superman brings his vision of utopia to fruition. In an effort to accomplish what his father could not, Superman creates "Metropia," his vision of a perfect world. This utopia was designed as a safe haven for all people of Earth. Unlike his father, who was only able to save one lone infant from the planet Krypton's impending doom, Metropia was designed for Superman to save all humanity in the event of Earth's destruction. The first image of this utopia shows a Garden of Eden–style paradise, complete with Lois Lane in a peach tree tasting an unforbidden fruit. Superman describes Metropia as "perfection. Or at least as close to what my idea of perfection can be. Real perfection." However, the perfection is short-lived as villains seek to create their own empire using a vanishing device that spirits humans from Earth to Metropia. Although he realizes that his intentions were pure, Superman feels "ashamed. What I'd done was created what no man—super or otherwise—had any right to create." Ultimately, Superman returns the vanished back to Earth, but only through giving up his Metropia.

Sociologist Zygmunt Bauman describes the contemporary longing for utopia not so much as a "chase after utopia" as a running away from failed utopias. Bauman writes, "In contemporary dreams, however, the image of 'progress' seems to have moved from the discourse of *shared improvement* to that of *individual survival*."[22] The result is a perpetual striving to escape disaster, to eliminate anxiety and fear. We argue that the process of utopian failure becomes a narrative formula in comic books that is manipulated and embellished with exciting characters and storylines but that ultimately lives between success and failure in a perpetual state of yearning and anxiety. Comics being primarily a serial medium, many of the cliffhangers and conclusions (which may not be a conclusion if the series starts up again at a later date) unravel any notion of having achieved utopian perfection and more often than not leave crumbs of failure and continual anxiety in their wake. In *Uncanny X-Men: The Rise and Fall of the Shi'ar Empire*, Vulcan and Deathbird, the villainous threats to the empire, live to fight another day and remain committed to launching future vengeance. This stalemate necessitates an X-Men outpost, led by Havok, on a Shi'ar planet, for ease of future fights for justice. Emma Frost, a telepathic superhero, reflects that as she looks back at her life, she sees the same catastrophes repeat themselves in the perpetual threats and attempts at wiping out the mutant race—and the X-Men must continually address them (*Dark Reign: The Cabal*). In one of the last pages of *The Flash* (#230), the superhero is preparing to retire despite the fact that he has not fully eradicated evil; he surmises that his replacement, who will be the new Flash, will have more to do to make the world safe. And, in *Ra's al Ghul*, the villain Ra's al Ghul has a knife to Batman's throat but lets Batman go after he makes a convincing argument for being spared. Ra's al Ghul says, "I defer to your wishes . . . until the next time we duel, Detective." The villain cannot kill his arch-enemy if the cat-and-mouse game between them is to continue.

Writer and artist of the wildly popular *Spawn* series of the 1990s, Todd McFarlane, explained to a fan publication that the serial nature of the medium propels creators to imagine enduring plots and characters that can continually be reimagined and written into new adventures. "Do I know the end of the story? Yes. Do I hope that I never have to tell it? Yes. I have conceived of the ending of Spawn, but the only way I would tell it is if nobody cared about the character anymore."[23] Still beloved, the series was re-released in 2009 in a collection of graphic novel reprints, suggesting that any nail-in-the-coffin ending to the saga will remain pending.

Enduring Dystopia

Comic book protagonists longing for a utopian world find themselves hopelessly mired in the present crime-ridden and socially disorganized dystopia. In the first issue of *Midnighter Armageddon*, a spin-off of *The Authority*, the story arc is titled "A Failed World." The Midnighter is propelled to the future and experiences the chaos of a postapocalyptic London, where decimation and destruction are the work of evil "intruders" who have destroyed good, civil society. The Midnighter comments facetiously, "Okay I get it. A possible future. Some dystopian world created by a disaster I have to avert." In a subsequent frame he comes across a church in ruins, commenting, "Ah hell, look what they've done to you." In defense of Christian and democratic values, the Authority, Midnighter's superhero team, must fight the destructive intruders in the absence of legitimate law and order. Their methods, ironically, are violent and authoritarian even as they hope to restore safety and democracy in an imagining of a global community based on Western values.[24] These values ultimately emphasize international cooperation and transnational governing bodies, similar to the United Nations. Likewise, in a Justice League of America story (*JLA* #91-93), Superman is summoned from his post as a representative at the United Nations in order to counter, along with his superhero team, an alien invasion. Although *JLA* features an interplanetary setting, the superheroes hope to achieve harmony among nations on planet Earth as a transnational utopia.

Evil looms in this perpetual comic book dystopia.[25] The gritty cityscape in Frank Miller's *Sin City*, expertly captured in the movie adaptation of the comic book, is a modern classic representation of dystopia. The urban space is populated by strippers, gangs, criminals, and corrupt leaders, and the social order has broken down into a dog-eat-dog world. The comic book's noir imagery consists of black and grey shadows in a seemingly perpetual nighttime. One of our focus group participants underscored the importance of the setting in comic books. The urban blight, the participant said, conveys a "dreary sense of crime, this sense of fear, genuine fear."

Themes of the city as dystopia in comics emanate from earlier literary metaphors of the city as a disease to be rejected. As Susan Sontag noted in her book *Illness as Metaphor*, "[T]he city was seen itself as a cancer—a place of abnormal, unnatural growth, and extravagant, devouring, armored passions."[26] Commonly, mainstream comic books relate urban blight to religious notions of hell and suggest that those in it will suffer the spiritual effects of occupying a dark, unhygienic space. In *Final Crisis*, the Justice League, headed by Batman, Superman, and Wonder Woman, must combat the threat of Darkseid—ruler of the planet Apokolips. Apokolips is described as a literal hell, a smoldering, burning global city, or ecumenopolis, whose inhabitants are devoted to the advancement of technology for the purposes of waging war. Only through redemptive violence can Earth endure and the multiple universes be restored—Apokolips reborn as New Genesis.

Meanwhile, *Northlanders: Sven the Returned*, a comic book that takes place in Viking times, involves a protagonist who returns to his home village. Aptly called Grimness, the village is littered with skulls on stakes and the inhabitants appear sad, cold, and eerily quiet. Sven narrates, "This is worse than I remember it. Grimness was hardly beautiful. But it was never a sewer." In *Wolverine Noir*, private investigator Jim Logan, a.k.a. Wolverine, describes the Bowery in the opening page of the comic as "hell,"

> They say this was a classy neighborhood once. Before the elevated railway came in . . . screeching and roaring its way through the sky, blotting out the sun, spittin' red-hot ash and oil on the damned souls below. We all live in the shadow of something. Something big and uncaring and scary as hell. But this place? This is as low as a man can sink.

The destruction and rebirth in *Final Crisis* plays up the apocalyptic possibilities in comic book narratives. (*Final Crisis #7*, Grant Morrison and Doug Mahnke, DC, 2008)

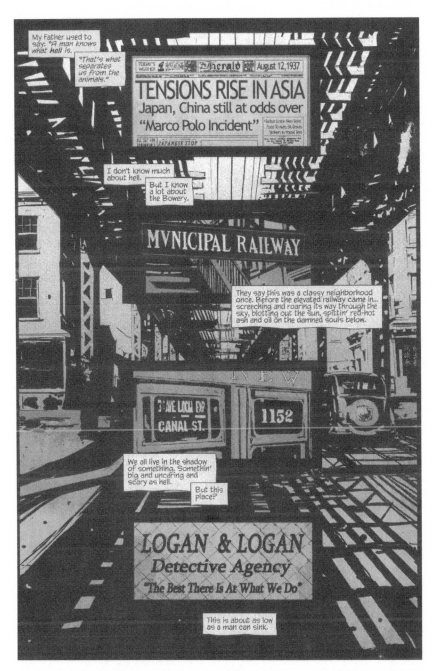

The Bowery lives up to its classic reputation as a dystopic skid row in a noir comic book. (*Wolverine Noir* #1, Stuart Moore and C. P. Smith, Marvel, 2009)

The comic further equates the souls who populate the hellish city with animals. In a dramatic scene, Logan's father, a priest obsessed with the Rapture, explains that "in ancient times, man was the undisputed master of the beasts. Such is the natural order. But today—Ah, my friends, today—man has fallen." Animalistic "man" is the one who gives in to his passions, violent or sexual or both, reflecting Sontag's notion that the city is frequently depicted as bringing out the "abnormal" passions in humans, which are to be feared.

From its first mention in *Batman* #4 to Tim Burton's 1989 surrealist interpretation in the film *Batman* to Christopher Nolan's metropolis landscape influenced by Chicago and New York City, Gotham City has evolved into perhaps the most iconic of urban dystopias. According to architect Jimmy Stamp, "Gotham City has always been a dark place, full of steam and rats and crime. A city of graveyards and gargoyles; alleys and asylums. Gotham is a nightmare, a distorted metropolis that corrupts the souls of good men."[27] Gotham City is featured in *Gotham Gazette*, where the mysterious figure known as the Veil overlooks the city from a rooftop and laments, "Gotham City suffers in seething frustration as it always has." Similarly, in the aftermath of the disappearance (or presumed death) of Batman, Leslie Thompkins, long-time friend of Bruce Wayne's parents and Alfred the butler, returns to Gotham after an extended absence in Africa and finds herself in a city of chaos. A state of emergency is declared as explosions ring through the city streets. Rioting and looting abound as criminal gangs battle over turf and control in the absence of Batman. In her run-in with an escaped inmate from Arkham Asylum, Thomkins wonders if the city is beyond redemption. Witnessing the decay, the Veil questions "[D]oes Gotham City have any hope for salvation?"

Destruction as Restorative Ritual

Is it possible that some cities are "beyond saving"? In his essay on social order in Gotham City, philosopher Brett Chandler Patterson examines human responses in the wake of a breakdown of social order.[28] In the storyline *Cataclysm* (1998), Gotham City is devastated by an earthquake. Patterson describes Gotham City as resorting to "a primitive state" with "people scavenging off

The Veil ruminates about the disintegration of Gotham City in the absence of Batman. (*Gotham Gazette* #1, Fabian Nicieza and Dustin Nguyen, DC, 2009)

the remains of what Gotham once was."[29] Patterson then juxtaposes the dev-astation of Gotham City to that of New Orleans in the aftermath of Hurricane Katrina. Batman begins to restore social order through his leadership, team building with fellow heroes, and negotiating with underground gang leaders. In Gotham, fortunately, nonviolent humanitarians prevail.

Patterson finds similar humanitarian efforts at work in the aftermath of Hurricane Katrina and a long road to restoration. In the world of super-heroes, Batman always finds Gotham City worthy of saving. Unfortu-nately, despite the massive humanitarian efforts of many Americans, New Orleans has not been deemed saveworthy by all. Outspoken former CNN television host Glenn Beck declared, "Tonight, two years since Hurricane Katrina hit New Orleans, and everybody's still talking about rebuilding. I say don't spend one thin dime. . . . How much do I think should be spent rebuilding New Orleans? Zero. Nothing. Not a dime."[30] Though Glenn Beck may be dismissed as a pundit on the "fringe," others in more prominent positions have also expressed resistance to rebuild. On April 24, 2008, *CBS News* reported that former presidential candidate John McCain was "not sure if he would rebuild the lower 9th ward as president." McCain stated, "That is why we need to go back is to have a conversation about what to do—rebuild it, tear it down, you know, whatever it is."[31] The destruction of a major American city by a natural disaster, coupled with incompetent government response, sets the stage for a political debate about the merits of saving a city, putting on full display the tension inherent in enduring the dystopian present to reach a better tomorrow.

"Destroying the village to save it" is a line often used to refer to the United States' involvement in the Vietnam War and the idea that "saving" a village, town, city, or country may come about only by destroying it, wip-ing the slate clean, and starting anew. Nihilistic solutions, such as those perpetuated by comic supervillains, echo the tactics of real-life cults and terrorist groups described by psychologist Robert Lifton in *Destroying the World to Save It*.[32] When Wolverine confronts a band of knife-wielding thugs in *Wolverine Noir*, he reflects, "In the rotting heart of the Bowery—in the shadow of that ancient rage—the knives dance again." The scene sug-gests the cyclical nature of destroying in order to save as a cleansing ritual that must be performed time and time again.

This cycle of cleansing in order to save is reflective of apocalypticism. Moreover, these utopian rememberings of past eras have often taken on a religious sheen, reminiscent of the defense of the chosen people and the promised land in biblical narratives. As author Greg Garrett notes, "[T]he underlying principles of many . . . comic heroes reflect universal principles of morality found in the Hebrew Bible and New Testament but also peculiarly American notions of right and wrong, wrapped in patriotism."[33]

The story arcs in comics are part of the American monomythic retelling of the Judeo-Christian narrative of the redemption of the world from sin. Theologian Robert Jewett and philosopher John Lawrence explore this apocalyptic phenomenon in *Captain America and the Crusade against Evil.* The authors document how policies in the United States have reflected a tendency toward zealous nationalism, accompanied by rhetoric emphasizing the need to eliminate evil enemies and redeem the world through righteous violence.[34] They state,

> It seemed that the United States, when it wished, could be like Captain America himself: strong, capable of acting without consulting or seeking direction, and exercising destructive power with few immediate repercussions. . . . Our conviction is that some of the militant and imprudent aspects of current American behavior are directly related to the increasing predominance of this millenarian outlook, which correlates closely with the secular, apocalyptic, superheroic fantasy.[35]

Lawrence and Jewett argue that in post-9/11 America there is a tension between those who adhere to an ideology seeking "to redeem the world by destroying enemies" and those who disavow such an ideology and would adhere to completely impartial justice that gives no privileged status for anyone.[36] *Irredeemable,* a comic book about the superhero Plutonian, plays on this tension. Plutonian crosses into crime and destruction after experiencing profound discouragement at not being adequately appreciated by the public for the sacrifices he has made as a hero. Horrifically, he executes the genocidal destruction of Sky City, prompting a meeting by the United Nations about how the international body should respond. The general secretary argues for a tight-fisted policy of striking back while many other countries seek an "open hand" in dealing with the superhero, hoping to benefit from, or at least not fall victim to, the kind of destructive power wielded by Plutonian.

Sorting the Wheat from the Chaff

Much as the rapture of American Christian fundamentalism sorts out the deserving souls to be saved from the wicked who will not be saved, comic books also concern themselves with this sorting, and often depict genocidal plots. In a mirror-like way, both antagonists and protagonists wander into genocide. For example, in *Astonishing X-Men: Gifted,* the X-Men must counter a preemptive strike at Earth by the alien villain Ord. It is believed that in three years, a mutant is destined to destroy Ord's home planet, the Breakworld. In an effort to prevent the annihilation, Ord is investigating a "cure" for mutants. If implemented, the cure would effectively wipe out all mutants—or at least their mutant powers. Here, the threat of genocide looms large for both the Breakworld and the mutants.

Usually genocidal violence on the part of the villain is more explicit. For example, in *X-Men: Messiah Complex,* Cooperstown, Alaska, is met with a shocking crisis: "[t]he cold-blooded execution of nearly every child in town. An almost biblical punishment with no discernible motive." In fact, the motive was to kill the last of the mutants—whose special powers land them in the folds of the X-Men. The last mutant was a small child. As X-Man Angel explains, "They killed babies. The sons of bitches killed babies in case one was a mutant."

In *Wonder Woman: The Circle,* Diana Prince's homeland Themyscira is under attack by Captain Nazi and his henchmen. Captain Nazi explains his genocidal plot to Diana: "You see . . . we wanted someplace of our own. A country to remake, in glorious tribute, where our very beliefs are no longer outlawed. . . . [I]magine a world of people like me. . . . [F]or it will be the end of people like you." Captain Nazi orders the killing of all inhabitants of Themyscira. Wonder Woman is subsequently thrust into conflicts in which she must cast her diplomatic tendencies aside in favor of a show of force. In *Elephantmen* (2007), giant anthropomorphic animals bred for war leave corpses of entire species of "weaker creatures" in their wake. Yet, in comics like *Punisher,* the willingness of the hero to kill anyone morally depraved, from a petty criminal and dope fiend to a mass murderer, suggests a genocidal urge to destroy all criminals in an apocalyptic quest to save the world from danger.

Many scholars have pointed out the superhero's messianic role in ushering in a better world and restoring a sense of morality to a world gone bad. Here we argue that this messianism often plays itself out through crime-and-justice-related story arcs and characters.[37] Superman has long been construed as a Jesus figure, particularly since his father Jor-el gave him, his only son, to Earth in order to help humanity and preserve the wisdom and traditions of his home planet. In a particularly explicit reference to Superman as Jesus, the Flash asks himself in encountering a villainous plot in a 2006 storyline, "What would Superman do?" In *All-Star Superman*, Pa Kent, partly tongue-in-cheek, describes his own family situation: "A childless couple, blessed from above with a miracle boy from another world. How does that happen? And not just any boy . . . but the finest young fella I ever met." The messianic figure as the ultimate sorter of the good from the evil is a major theme in *Planetary*. The character of Elijah, an overt reference to the Old Testament prophet who foretells the coming of Jesus, states,

> Imagine a system that selects out the unjustly dead from the past in order to right wrongful deaths. Someone who understands justice. Someone who understands betrayal and loss. Someone who works for an afterlife, who wants all of us to have the best possible chance at fixing the living world.

Comic book heroes evoke messianism in their roles as fighters for justice. They step forward in a time of apocalyptic criminality to usher in a new age of utopia and act as mediator figures between this world and the next.

Although there are exceptions, mainstream comic books follow an apocalyptic formula in presenting themes of crime and justice. The crime problem as crisis and symptom of dystopia highlights the books' reactionary nature as the plot moves toward restoration of a nostalgic status quo rather than seeking a brave new world. The dystopian landscape of the city itself is a virtual character, serving as a visual reminder of the "crime-urban nexus" so prominent in popular imagination.[38]

The striving for a better tomorrow is often cast in religious terms or iconography, symbolizing an ultimate battle between good and evil. The old world is the better world to which comic books typically refer, but in the space between now and then, or now and what will be, the superheroes serve a quasi-messianic role operating on a higher authority. The protagonists rise up, driven by a hunger and yearning for utopia that leads to extreme responses, unafraid of using violence and deception to rid the world of crime—of apocalyptic proportions— and to restore justice.

5

"THAT'S THE TROUBLE WITH A BAD SEED"

VILLAINS AND THE EMBODIMENT
OF EVIL

The story arc in "Dangerous," from *Astonishing X-Men*, heats up when its villain, Danger, threatens the mutant students at the Xavier Institute. She is embodied as a bright blue feminized robot, much like the mechanized gynoids in the classic film *Metropolis* (1928). Danger traps the students in the "Danger Room," a holographic simulation room used for training. While attempting to subdue Danger, the X-Men ask her what she wants. She replies, "The thing I have in common with every dimestore villain these X-Men ever faced. I want to be understood." In seeking to understand villains and their motivations, heroes come face to face with the dark undertow of their worlds. As theologian Mike Alsford explains in his philosophical reverie *Heroes and Villains*, the villain in Western culture is often an exploration of the "beast within," a deviant individual who has selfish motivations and seeks power and control over others and, often, the whole world.[1]

The heroes and villains in the comic book world appear to be stark opposites of each other, yet readers ultimately find themselves immersed in plots that explore the similarities between the two. Like yin and yang, heroes and villains possess a mutual dependence on one another in these ongoing sagas. Both archetypes are psychologically inclined to take bold action and typically have well-developed talents, access to technology, or mystical powers. At their core, however, the elementary difference between the hero and the villain lies in whether his or her engagement in the world is directed toward good or evil. Often, this distinction is tenuous; for example, Wolverine, a mutant X-Men hero, struggles to harness his anger and rage—the very impulses that give him his extraordinary wolf-like powers that can help the world. According to Alsford, Wolverine's popularity stems from the fear he has of his own capabilities and how close he might come to using his powers in ways that are not beneficial to the world.

Like Danger, who calls out in the pages of the *X-Men* for her transgressions to be understood, villains in comic books are often quite verbose in describing their evil designs. In DC's *Identity Crisis*, the villains ruminate at length among themselves about their own iniquity, revealing a range of motivations and a hierarchy of respect for each other: "Luthor and Grodd do it for power . . . Cheetah and Sivana do it for kicks . . . and the bat-villains, well they're just fried to begin with . . . but there are a few of us who are more . . . professional in nature." In the apocalyptic struggle for power and control—even world or universal domination—villains communicate their motivations, giving insight into the grand question that preoccupies the study of criminology: why do individuals commit crimes?

Our exploration of how the medium conveys criminality is grounded in cultural criminology. Although comic book villains exist only in the fantastical pages of comic books, their adventures communicate powerful messages about what motivates crime, at least in their world. Given the omnipresence of superheroes and other comic book characters spun off into Hollywood movies and video games, these villains become important cultural artifacts in understanding popular ideas about why individuals engage in criminal behavior. Given that most people in the world do not become experts in criminal behavior and criminology, popular media representations about the causes of criminal behavior become important possible influences on the public's attitudes about criminal offending.

Part of the appeal for readers of comic books is the intensity with which they connect to the narratives and imagery. Representations of crime and violence can be particularly seductive for their entertainment value. In *Cultural Criminology and the Carnival of Crime*, criminologist Mike Presdee points out that there is pleasure in both engaging in transgressive acts such as crime and violence and merely consuming transgressive acts as entertainment. Similarly, there is pleasure in meting out punishment to those perceived as deserving. He notes,

Put simply, transgressing and doing wrong are for many an exciting and pleasurable experience. For others to be involved in some way in the act of transgression as a voyeur is pleasure enough. *To watch, to be there yet absent, is enough.* We know that to watch and enjoy pain, violence, cruelty and crime, is transgressing in itself and produces both pleasure and guilt.[2]

Readers are quick to point out the transgressive pleasure in consuming comics, particularly as it relates to the villains. In one of our focus groups, the transgressive pleasure of experiencing the Joker's psychoticism emerges from the discussion: "If you read the Joker and you understand the Joker—I know this sounds horrible but—you understand when he does something. You're like 'oh, of course,' And then you're like 'Oh man, I'm horrible!'"[3] Readers tend to be self-reflective, recognizing and commenting on their own discomfort at identifying with the villains and enjoying antisocial behavior. Others note that connecting with malevolent characters proves a psychologically satisfying experience for the reader. A respondent explains, "[The Joker] is pure id . . . it's really cathartic to watch him get into mischief. Honestly, there's nothing more interesting than that."[4] Here, the pleasure of the reading experience is connected to the Joker's instinctual drive to seek pleasure at the expense of others. Reading serves as a form of vicarious pleasure for the reader and itself becomes a transgression.

We suggest that the causes and implications of criminal behavior featured in comic books ultimately reinforce retribution in our culture as a dominant philosophical approach to criminal justice policy. There is a conspicuous disconnect between the nature of crime causation and the implied policy messages found in the books. Comic books tend to frame crime as rooted deeply within the individual, to the neglect of social, economic, or political causes. In particular, psychopathological causes of crime are often explicitly depicted, yet calls for retributive forms of justice often follow. Conversely, in criminological theory, the policy response to psychopathological crime most often relates to rehabilitation or incapacitation—not retribution. In later chapters, we explore more fully the heroes' paths to justice in neutralizing the threats posed by the villains. Here, we suggest that to understand the rhetoric of retributive justice, we must first take account of the portrayals of crime causation itself.

This chapter examines the criminological theories implied by depictions of villains and the cultural meanings surrounding their behavior.

Criminologists have amassed a wide range of theoretical possibilities that have been applied to empirical data on crime with varying degrees of success. If the pages of comic books—as cultural artifacts that may reflect and shape ideas about crime in our culture—were to become the empirical data set, what criminological theories would be best supported?

Criminological theories speak to the potential biological, social, and psychological root causes of crime. Many center on highly complex and seemingly incidental background variables that are not immediately apparent at the discrete moment of the commission of a crime. Similarly, contemporary comic books feature many characters with long and complicated histories and background stories the reader often needs to absorb and understand in order to get the most out of a particular comic book issue. The obsession comic book fans have with origin stories makes any exploration of etiology quite rich, and provides a framework for understanding the development of the villain and his or her moral conscience.

What Is a Villain?

In his analysis of the superhero genre, comics scholar Peter Coogan defines a supervillain as "a villain who is super, that is, someone who commits villainous or evil acts and does so in a way superior to ordinary criminals or at a magnified level," as manifest in the villain's mission, powers, and identity.[5] Supervillains thus present a threat that is greater than the capabilities and constraints of traditional law enforcement mechanisms. For example, in *Batman: Battle for the Cowl*, Batman's sidekick, Robin, contemplates the crime-ridden conditions in Gotham City after a supervillain breakout from Arkham Asylum. Reflecting on the criminal mastermind responsible, he states, "I'm talking about someone good. Someone with experience. Maybe even someone we know . . . so whoever this guy is, he's no ordinary citizen." Later, Commissioner Gordon similarly reflects, "[W]e're not dealing with garden variety criminal masterminds here." A superhero with superpowers (or at least someone who is willing to go beyond the law) is required to neutralize a threat of such magnitude.

The idea that Gotham City is facing a heightened level of threat, with an even more insidious kind of criminal waiting to prey on innocents, has much resonance in a post-9/11 America. Shortly after the terrorist attacks of 9/11, Americans were warned that the country was facing a "new kind of evil."[6] As Vice President Dick Cheney stated rather succinctly on the television news program *Meet the Press* in September 2003, "9/11 changed everything."[7] Media accounts parroting such sound bites from the Bush administration suggested that we were faced with a new enemy, one necessitating responses with new tactics and strategies. On September 12, a day after the attacks, President Bush framed the conflict in cosmic proportions: "This will be a monumental struggle of good versus evil, but good will prevail."[8] Bush cautioned the world citizens that in this cosmic battle, there were only two sides: "You're either with us or against us."[9] For the Bush administration, the enemies in the war on terror were not mere criminals but evildoers "attacking our way of life," putting our very civilization at stake.[10] In essence, they were supervillains.

Bush's invocation of "evildoers" and the reliance on the "good versus evil" dichotomy have brought age-old villainous descriptors to contemporary conflict. If criminal threats are portrayed as so extreme, even apocalyptic in nature, the case can then be made for extreme measures of social control to neutralize the threat.[11]

Criminologists have noted that fictional media portrayals of offenders (and victims) frequently fail to reflect what we know about offenders in the "real" world. Complex motivations of human behavior are often reduced to simplistic, superficial explanations, while social influences on behavior are ignored in favor of individualistic explanations. For example, in his analysis of media portrayals of offenders, criminologist Ray Surette finds that most often criminals are portrayed as psychopathic killers although most criminals are not murderers and few who murder are serial killers.[12]

In her analysis of serial killers in fictional media, Su Epstein points out that they are often depicted as demonic, monstrous, and possessing "superhuman abilities."[13] In cinema, the serial killer is often portrayed as able to withstand numerous assaults and cheat death. Portraying the serial killer as a "mythic monster" allows the viewer to comprehend and cope with the threat of the brutal, immoral behavior of serial killers in the real world—the enemy is not "like us" but is a fundamentally different creature. Further, Epstein notes that media depictions have at times influenced the ways in which law enforcement officers respond to suspects.[14] For example, police investigations may be hindered by erroneous expectations that suspects match a particular media-perpetuated stereotype or profile. This includes the myth that serial killers are always dysfunctional loners, or that they are geniuses. Epstein writes, "[P]olice have been known to release serial killers because they did not fit the mythic persona created by the media."[15] In late modernity, public attitudes and policy responses to crime are increasingly entangled with media representations.[16]

Embodiment of Evil

Villainous icons are frequently used as representations of those considered the most vile and threatening among us. When *New York Magazine* opted to run a cover story on Bernie Madoff, convicted in 2009 of orchestrating the "biggest financial swindle in history," the magazine published an illustration of Madoff's face, Joker-style, with white, pasty makeup, blackened eyes, greenish hair, and blood-red elongated and grinning lips. A similar image of President Barack Obama was widely circulated when protest groups decried his "socialist"-inspired policies. Proving that Joker images are ideologically diverse, a 2004 *Vanity Fair* article depicted former president George W. Bush as the Joker. Grotesque at a glance, these illustrations serve to elicit emotional responses from audiences that tap into popular conceptions of evil.

Graphic representations of villains in comic books often involve physical anomalies that are similar to seminal criminologist Cesare Lombroso's idea of "atavistic stigmata," or markers that symbolize the evil embodied.[17] Born in Italy in 1835 and known as the father of criminology, Lombroso measured physical attributes such as the skulls and facial features of convicts, military personnel, and others and then compared them to that of the general public. He claimed that characteristics such as protruding foreheads, thick lips, wrinkled skin, and asymmetrical facial features were more prevalent in convict populations. Lombroso stated that "while offenders may not look fierce, there is nearly always something strange about their appearance."[18] Drawing on the newly popularized theories of evolution developed by Darwin, he surmised that these convicts must be atavistic, or throwbacks to earlier evolutionary stages in the development of humankind.[19] Positivism, as heralded by Lombroso, is "founded upon techniques of representation," of making visible the criminal.[20] Lombroso's crude assumptions about the nature of criminal behavior are now considered pseudo-science and his findings are widely discredited. However, the

Bernie Madoff, infamous Ponzi schemer, gets a Joker makeover on this cover of *New York Magazine*. (New York Media, March 2, 2009)

idea that criminals may be distinguished from noncriminals by their physical features remains an appealing notion to some today. In fact, the practice of racial profiling—roundly condemned in the late 1990s when perpetrated against racial minorities but revived after 9/11 particularly when directed toward ethnic and religious minorities—is based on the assumption that physical characteristics are indicators of criminal tendencies.

Comic books have long provided visual representations of the villainous other—making criminality visible through physical characteristics designed to reveal their "true nature." This is exemplified, for example, in the case of the Batman villain Harvey Dent, who was once an angelic-looking and upstanding district attorney. However, Dent is disfigured by a defendant who throws acid on his face during a trial. He subsequently goes insane and becomes corrupt. Known as "Two-Face" after the left side of his face is horrendously scarred, Dent becomes the physical embodiment of good versus evil. His face represents asymmetry—one side skinless and scarred, indicating moral depravity, and the other side handsome and whole. Thereafter, Dent determines the fate of his adversaries by the toss of a coin—one side pristine and the other blemished and scarred.

The disfigured and grotesque features of comic book villains are visual depictions of their level of moral depravity and misdeeds. The Joker's

Two-Face's disfigurement represents the duality of good versus evil. (*Two-Face: Year One* #2, Mark Sable and Jesus Saiz, DC, 2008)

mental instability, or "craziness," is written, or scrawled, on his face in the form of the haphazard application of white make-up, greenish hair, and red lips. In *Fantastic Four: Foes*, the villain Threska appears as a blonde beauty to her brainwashed husband, but her "true" face is a skinless, bug-eyed, and brain-exposed skull. So too with the Red Skull, whose head is a literal red skull with deep-set eye sockets and red "skin." He emerged as an agent of Hitler during the 1940s and has remained a long-time enemy of Captain America. Initially, the Red Skull wore a mask given him by Hitler. In a failed effort to poison Captain America with the "dust of death" (designed to kill victims and cause their heads to turn to red, shrunken skulls), the Red Skull's facial features became permanent.[21]

Red Skull fathered a daughter named Synthia Schmidt (a.k.a. Sin, Mother Superior). In *Captain America: Reborn*, Sin is recruited by Norman Osborn to help bring Captain America under his control for his team of villains, Dark Avengers. The Red Skull's brain (or consciousness) has been trapped inside a robotic body. Sin arrives and Red Skull is ashamed of his appearance. Sin brings her father a red skull mask to wear until he gets a "real body." In a botched attempt to transplant the Red Skull into Captain America's body, Sin's face is disfigured in an explosion. Sin is now a mirror image of her father, her face a skinless, crimson skull.

Marked by his heinous deeds, Vandal Savage represents an ancient form of evil as he has inherited the mark of Cain. Savage is described as immortal, with "superhuman intellect, strength, and endurance, and the ability to access other dimensions."[22] In the apocalyptic story arc *Final Crisis: Revelations,* Vandal Savage is stabbed with the spear of destiny, thus receiving the mark of Cain. The mark is a burning cross between his eyes, with flames stretching across his forehead and cheeks. Savage later appears in *The Question: Pipeline (Detective Comics* #863) to coerce the Question and the Huntress to "take away" his mark of Cain. Savage confesses that his global empire of "selling sin" is at risk because the mark forces him to work "in the shadows." In *Arkham Reborn,* the main protagonist, Dr. Jeremiah Arkham, head of an asylum for the criminally insane, introduces readers to the inmates who are dearest to his heart, including the psychopathic killer Victor Zsasz. Covered with self-inflicted scars, Zsasz commemorates every murder he commits with a stitched-up gash on his body. The plethora of scars graphically shows his prolific nature as a killer.

Unlike popular conceptions of criminality in contemporary society, comic books do not seem to rely on race as a marker of evil among supervillains. Phillip Cunningham notes that black supervillains are few and far between and the ones that do appear are "limited in terms of power and purpose."[23] Often situated in the "ghetto," black supervillains are portrayed as hypermasculine, with either great intellect or power, but rarely both simultaneously. Cunningham suggests that increased representation of supervillains of color could provide an avenue of discourse that challenges stereotypes by creating more "complex, contemplative, and powerful black supervillains."[24] The invisibility of black supervillains is likely a reflection of the white, patriarchal world of the medium. People of color are rarely represented as heroes or villains. When they appear, they are frequently one-dimensional, race being the attribute that most often defines them, to the exclusion of their particular superpowers or other personality characteristics. (See chapter 8 for a more in-depth discussion of race/ethnicity and crime.)

Sin gives her father a mask while explaining that it will better represent his true nature. (*Captain America: Reborn* #3, Ed Brubaker, Bryan Hitch, and Butch Guice, Marvel, 2009)

Sin, an attractive red-headed villain, is transformed into the mirror image of her evil father, Red Skull. (*Captain America: Reborn* #4, Ed Brubaker, Bryan Hitch, and Butch Guice, Marvel, 2009)

The Cycle of Violence

The opening page of *Daredevil: Return of the Kingpin* (#116) shows a young Wilson Fisk and his sister witnessing the brutal attack of their mother at the hands of their father. Wilson cries out, "You leave her alone!" His father is shown removing his belt, shouting, "[L]ittle bastard!" Bright red blood splatters on each of the panels. The following page shows an adult Wilson Fisk, kneeling with bloody hands over a female body. From the early abuse and mistreatment at the hands of his father, Wilson Fisk has matured into the Kingpin, the organized criminal mastermind and overlord of the underground in New York City. Even as he struggles to turn from his life of crime, he finds that he is continually pulled back in, and remains helpless to change. The narrator states, "[Y]ou have a disease . . . a virus. And you've been a carrier all your life, even when you didn't realize it. Violence, blood, screaming . . . those are all the symptoms. But you carry death, Kingpin . . . and everyone you touch is infected." Our research found that comic books are replete with childhood traumas and brain impairment, which affect the characters in their ability and desire to conform to the rule of law. Trauma is portrayed as critical to the development of a villain's abilities and motivations. For example, in *Scarecrow: Year One*, long-time Batman villain Jonathan Crane (a.k.a. Scarecrow) was an unwanted, abused child, taunted by his grandmother for his academic pursuits, sadistically punished, and locked in a dark room where crows would fly in and pluck at him. Crane was abandoned by his father and repeatedly traumatized by classmates. As an adult, he felt he was wrongfully terminated from his job as a professor after conducting an in-class experiment using a firearm loaded with blanks. It is then that he became the Scarecrow, scaring victims to death with fear-inducing powder.

In combating Scarecrow, Batman recognizes the similarities between his childhood and that of Scarecrow. They both suffered trauma (as a young man, Batman saw his parents murdered before his eyes), yet Batman channels his rage toward the common good, while Scarecrow turns his hostility toward others. Batman recognizes that the origins of this villain's antisocial behavior are clearly rooted in his childhood. Of Scarecrow, Batman declares, "[I]t's not about the killing. Guy dresses up in something horrific, goes out into the night and terrifies his enemies. He's acting out . . . from deep, visceral trauma . . . probably childhood." Even Scarecrow recognizes and resents the cycle of violence. On the trail of a wife batterer, Scarecrow sprinkles a fear-inducing substance on a baby crib and states, "[T]hat's the trouble with a bad seed, isn't it mother? . . . [I]t just grows on and on."

There are copious other examples of childhood trauma shaping villains in comic books. In *Arkham Reborn*, inmate Raggedy Man is driven insane during childhood by his parents, who keep him trapped in a basement with his survival dependent on a can opener and cans of peaches. In the same book, Alessio Morandi, also known as No Face, was raised in a wealthy Venetian family that was physically and emotionally abusive. When, as a young boy, Alessio realized that he could never measure up to the standards of his family, he took a mask from the wall and glued it to his face. His father laughed mockingly and then ripped off the mask with such force that Alessio's face was irreparably damaged.

Childhood taunts were also instrumental in the development of Professor Pyg. In *Batman and Robin*, Professor Pyg develops an aerosol narcotic and is on a rampage to infect the residents of Gotham City by distributing it through the underground Russian criminal network. Part of his plan involves using the narcotic to control his victims, deemed Dollotrons. Pyg uses a circular saw and drill to transplant the faces of his victims, making them "perfect." As Pyg is transplanting faces through his crude surgical procedure, he reveals that he has been taunted all his life: "[Y]ou can do better . . . you can do better! Nothing's good enough! Nothing's ever good enough!" Similarly, Dark Wolverine develops into a villain who joins Norman Osborn's Dark Avengers after a childhood spent in Japan, during which he was teased for being a "mongrel," half-American and half-Japanese. He blames his father, Wolverine, for his mother's death at the hands of another, an obsession that consumes him into adulthood and leads to his alliance with Wolverine's nemesis, Romulus.

Childhood abuse and neglect shape the lives of myriad types of villains across the comic book universe. In *Catwoman: When in Rome*, the sometimes villain Catwoman learns that she was an unwanted child. Her father did not want a baby girl and wanted to dispose of her but her mother insisted that she be sent to America and put up for adoption. In *Wonder Woman: The Circle*, Wonder Woman battles Captain Nazi, who is determined to take over Wonder Woman's homeland, Themyscira. Under the power of Wonder Woman's lasso, Captain Nazi's abusive past is revealed; his father pimped out his mother and eventually murdered her "over a stack of stolen groceries." In *X-Men: Magneto Testament*, X-Men villain Magneto's past as a nine-year-old victim of Nazi persecution in World War II paints a compelling portrait of childhood trauma involving the horrors of Kristallnacht, the Warsaw Ghetto, and Auschwitz.

In his book on the origins of the superhero genre, Peter Coogan describes this sense of victimhood for the villain as "the wound." He states, "[T]his grandiose self-aggrandizement arises from a sense of victimhood, originating in a wound that the supervillain never recovers from." This operates as a "defense mechanism to make up for feelings of inferiority and inadequacy that arose from maltreatment received when he was younger."[25] Though the implication is that criminals are products of their experiences, the message is also clear that both the righteous Batman *and* the evil Scarecrow were exposed to childhood trauma. There is at times a fine line between the hero and the villain—with only the hero having the strength and will power to rise above past experiences.

Childhood trauma as a root cause is encompassed in a number of positivist criminological theories—those that center on the use of the scientific method to gain knowledge about the world. Positivism aims to link causes to their effects, or, in the case of social science as a "soft science," to find antecedents that correlate to certain outcomes. Positivist criminologists see crime as correlated to factors that can be empirically observed. The idea that a person's behavior is influenced by external factors beyond the individual's control, as opposed to the exercise of free will, is known as determinism.

In a significant minority of the comic books we sampled, trauma-induced brain impairments also led to criminality. Spider-Man villain Doctor Octopus acquired brain damage and a thirst for crime after a radiation accident, which also caused four mechanical arms to fuse into his body (which he was able to control through his mind). Although the arms were surgically removed, making them an optional accessory for this villain, his brain damage could not be reversed and he was relegated to a life of crime.

Similarly, the villain Legion developed Dissociative Identity Disorder (formerly know as Multiple Personality Disorder) after being caught in a violent terrorist attack, during which his brain absorbed the mind of the terrorist. He continued to incorporate the minds of anyone who died near him, causing a multitude of personalities to take root in his brain. He is named after a similarly afflicted demon in the Bible: "And He (Jesus) asked him (the man), 'What is thy name?' And he answered, saying, 'My name is Legion: for we are many'" (Mark 5: 10). In *Batman and Robin*, the villain Flamingo was once an honorable man who fought the mob until Professor Pyg "cut his brain apart and took away everything human." The severity of the brain trauma turned him murderous. Scarlet, also a victim of Pyg's surgical mutations, explains that the damage "made him kill his wife, children, and everyone and everything he'd ever loved."

"Life Is Swell in a Padded Cell"

Psychological positivist theories are among the most commonly represented in comic books, with plots typically revolving around psychopathic villains who haunt heroes and wreak havoc on innocents. Sigmund Freud, the founder of psychoanalysis, suggests that behavior is not rational; rather, it is a culmination of the presence of free-floating guilt that is often self-destructive. This theory holds that within those who commit crime or other deviant acts is a sense of guilt so strong that they feel they deserve punishment. These individuals commit crime in order to bring punishment onto themselves (though this desire remains repressed and unknown to the individual). Similarly tormented individuals take shape in comic books, for example, DC supervillain Doctor Light. After murdering the physicist Jacob Finlay, Light suffers tremendous guilt over taking control of the light-manipulating suit that Finlay had originally developed. He continues to use the suit for his own selfish purposes, only to be haunted by the ghost of Finlay, which, in turn, propels him into guilt-induced acts of crime. After being defeated many times by various superheroes, the humiliated Doctor Light is revealed in *Identity Crisis* to have raped Sue Dibney and later, in *Final Crisis,* is shown in the midst of a rape orgy before being burned to death by the Spectre.

Another Freudian notion relevant to comic books is that childhood trauma is repressed in the unconscious, but can percolate up into the conscious mind and cause dysfunctional and neurotic behavior. Freud, believing dreams were a means of accessing repressed and hidden desires and trauma stored in the unconscious mind, innovated the use of dream analysis and hypnosis to understand and treat psychological problems.[26] The life of villain Victor Von Doom, depicted in *Books of Doom*, contains strong references to Freud's theories. Von Doom is overcome by nightmares in which images of his lost lover, Valeria, his father being taken away by the authorities, and his mother being possessed by a demon all weigh heavily on his psyche. The conflation of his lover and his parents is reminiscent of Freudian pan-sexualism, which links sexual desire to events involving one's parents in childhood.

Other notions of psychological disturbance are found in comic book villains, including psychopathy, which is frequently implicated as a motivating factor for their criminal behavior. Psychopathy is defined as "a deviant developmental disturbance characterized by an inordinate amount of instinctual aggression and the absence of an object relational capacity to bond."[27] In other words, psychopaths are aggressive, selfish individuals who are unable to form genuine emotional connections with others. Not all criminals are psychopaths; however, psychopaths are more likely to engage in violence and criminal behavior than their nonpsychopathic counterparts and are more likely to recidivate.[28] One of the foremost experts on psychopathy, esteemed psychologist Robert Hare, writes that psychopaths operate with a "stunning lack of conscience; their game is self-gratification" at others' expense.[29]

Such psychopathy is found, for example, in *Batman: Streets of Gotham*, in which the villain Firefly has planted incendiary chips into victims, wreaking havoc in Gotham. Citywide, citizens simultaneously burst into flames as Firefly delights in their destruction. His motivation rests not in any instrumental gain but rather in his delight in the suffering of others: "I really have no interest in money . . . my true joy comes from watching them [the victims] dance . . . and knowing how much agony it brings to Batman."

Psychopathy should not be confused with mere antisocial behavior. Psychopaths are not just "breaking the law"; rather, they are incapable of appropriately processing emotions and affect, including the recognition and appreciation of the consequences of their behavior on others. In *The Mask of Sanity*, psychiatrist Hervey Cleckley points out that behind their "normal" façades, psychopaths are at best manipulative and hurtful, and at worst murderous.[30] While many criminals exhibit antisocial personality traits, such as those outlined in the American Psychiatric Association's diagnostic manual, psychopaths seem to lack *humanity* at some level.[31] Forensic psychologist Reid Meloy suggests that it is possible that a dysfunctioning limbic system (part of the brain structure related to emotions and affect) renders the psychopath "reptilian"-like in affect. Meloy writes that the limbic structures that regulate emotions are present in mammals, but generally reduced or absent in reptiles. Therefore, the system that impacts parental drive, hoarding behavior, and social behavior is missing in reptiles, and they exhibit an "inability to socialize in a consciously affectionate and genuinely expressive manner."[32] Psychopaths are reptilian-like in their inability to sincerely connect emotionally with others. Meloy suggests that the reptilian state may be recognized, in part, as an "absence of perceived emotion in their eyes" or the "evil eye" of predation.[33] He notes that this recognizable characteristic is frequently modeled in Hollywood portrayals of psychopaths.

Scholars have not agreed upon a single specific cause of psychopathy, though there is growing consensus among researchers that it is likely to have a genetic basis. There is less support for environmental factors as causal, though such factors are not entirely discounted. According to psychologist James Blair, an expert on affective cognitive neuroscience, genetics may "determine the level of emotional dysfunction, while the environment would influence how this genetically determined emotion dysfunction was expressed."[34] Further, there is no "cure," and psychopaths show resistance to treatment.

Despite uncertainty about the exact causes of psychopathy, most experts agree on its general characteristics. Dr. Hare suggests that the symptoms of psychopathy fall into two broad categories: emotional/interpersonal and social deviance. Individuals who are psychopaths have deficiencies in the ability to create meaningful emotional attachments with others. They may be charming, but are superficially and deceptively so. They are unable to empathize with others and lack remorse for their actions. Additionally, psychopaths have a history of antisocial behavior, impulsivity, and irresponsible actions. These individuals present a profound danger to society. Dr. Hare, however, notes that popular-culture representations of psychopaths are somewhat misleading. For example, not all psychopaths are serial killers. Rather, it is more common that psychopaths walk "among us" in our daily lives, as our bosses and neighbors, engaged in legitimate occupations in such fields as medicine, law, business, and others.[35]

Psychopathy in comic books is often explicitly correlated with childhood trauma or abuse. For example, in *Punisher Max: Butterfly*, psychopathic behavior is a consequence of childhood trauma, specifically incest. A young girl (nicknamed "Butterfly") repeatedly sexually assaulted by her father grows into a psychopathic hit woman, able to emotionally dissociate herself from others and dehumanize her victims. Butterfly's first victim was murdered during a "consensual" sexual asphyxiation gone wrong—the safe word she uttered was ignored by her "boyfriend" and she struck back, surprised at how "easy" it was to kill and how "little" emotion she felt. Feeling she has little left to lose, Butterfly blossoms into a killer for hire. On a hit job targeting members of the Mafia, Butterfly expresses that she has no remorse for targeting members of the mob. She states, "[T]hese wiseguys with their families . . . besides the children, I despised all of the them . . . made no exception for the women . . . [who] looked the other way to maintain their illusion of the great American dream."

Butterfly's identity is shaped by the patriarchal authority and abuses she has endured throughout her life. In a moment of reflection, she states, "I don't think I have ever really enjoyed being a woman. But I've enjoyed

Table 5.1. Characteristics of Psychopaths

Emotional/Interpersonal	Social Deviance
Glib and superficial	Impulsive
Egocentric and grandiose	Poor behavioral controls
Lack of remorse or guilt	Need for excitement
Lack of empathy	Lack of responsibility
Deceitful and manipulative	Early behavioral problems
Shallow emotions	Adult antisocial behavior

Source: Robert Hare, *Without Conscience: The Disturbing World of Psychopaths among Us* (New York: Pocket, 1995), 34.

women. Enjoyed people, moments, the endless procession." To overcome, she exhibits power in the way that she knows how—through violence. Unfortunately for her, the consequences of her occupational choice catch up with her and ultimately she meets her fate at the hands of the Punisher.

In *Batman: Hush,* Bruce Wayne's long-time childhood friend Thomas Elliot is revealed to be a raging psychopath. As a young boy, Thomas plots to kill his parents but is thwarted. Bruce's surgeon father saves Thomas's mother from impending death after she is injured in a car wreck staged as an accident by the young boy. Thomas is greedy and wants his parents dead so he can quickly gain their inheritance. A follow-up story, *Heart of Hush,* reveals that Thomas's parents were wealthy, self-indulgent drunks. After Thomas's unsuccessful attempt to murder his mother, she remains an overprotective tyrant, forcing him to care for her. Thomas, resentful of his caretaking responsibilities, ultimately murders his mother.

Several psychopathic villains appear in *Arkham Reborn,* which details the efforts of Dr. Jeremiah Arkham (later revealed to be the villain Black Mask) to construct an asylum in Gotham City that offers rehabilitation for the criminally insane. For the villains in this book, extreme childhood abuse was most frequently implicated as the causal factor underlying their criminal behavior. Alyce Sinner, for example, was raised by parents in a religious-inspired cult that planned a mass suicide to expedite them into eternal life. Angry that her parents disapproved of her relationship with her boyfriend, Alyce murders all the cult members before they have a chance to ascend. She uses her superficial charm and somewhat sweet appearance to gain employment at the asylum. Embracing her sinful nature, Alyce colludes with the Black Mask to destroy

Arkham's plans for building a new asylum for the purpose of rehabilitation. The psychopathic nature of other villains in *Arkham Reborn,* including Killer Croc, Poison Ivy, and Scarecrow, is equally explicit. Of the seeds of pathological behavior, Dr. Arkham explains, "We are all what our childhood made us."

The Joker represents the classic psychopathic killer in comic books. His lack of humanity was boldly represented in Alan Moore's critically acclaimed *Batman: The Killing Joke* (1988). Buying a dilapidated carnival property, the Joker kidnaps Commissioner Gordon and takes him on a tortuous journey through some of the worst behavior a person can perform in a madcap, psychedelic-colored homage to deviance. The Joker cages Gordon like a beast and has cherub-like creatures prance him around on a dog leash, beat him, and sexually humiliate him. The Joker explains,

> So when you find yourself locked onto an unpleasant train of thought, heading for the places in your past where the screaming is unbearable, remember there's always madness. Madness is the emergency exit. You can just step outside, and close the door on all those dreadful things that happened. You can lock them away. Forever.

With a sing-song cadence, he rhymes, "Mister, life is swell in a padded cell, it'll chase those blues away . . . you can trade your gloom for a rubber room, and injections twice a day!"

In a more recent graphic novel, *Joker* (2008), written by Brian Azzarello, the Joker is released from Arkham Asylum. As he attempts to regain his foothold in the Gotham underground criminal network, even fellow villains are perplexed by his release from incarceration. The Penguin says to the Joker, "[W]e heard you were released. No one can figure how." The Joker replies, "Well . . . I'm not crazy anymore . . . just mad." The Joker embarks on a killing spree, the depravity of which shocks even his criminal sidekick, Jonny. As the story concludes, Jonny realizes the extent of the Joker's wickedness: "[T]here will always be a Joker. Because there's no cure for him. No cure at all. Just a Batman."

In essence, these comic books depict a type of dissociative state in which the Joker is aware, and celebrating, that he is escaping painful memories by slipping into a psychotic fantasy land of violent crime. The work of forensic psychologist Lawrence Schlesinger similarly documents the real-world sexual sadist as using violence as a means of relieving inner discomfort.[36]

Schlesinger believes that such behavior is conscious on the part of offenders, at least at the moment they allow themselves to slip away. In this sense, the behavior may represent splitting, in which a coping activity is not integrated into the sense of self as normally understood by the individual, allowing the individual to transgress. Others, like criminologist Abbie Stein in her analysis of the personal narratives of violent offenders, believe that dissociation occurs—the blurring of fantasy and reality in which there may be less conscious control over the behavior.[37] She highlights the notion that "volatile selves . . . lurk in the corners of conscious awareness" rather than exist in the full light of the conscious mind. As a "default defensive position," psychotic violence acts as a barricade against full absorption of the horrors of past trauma while also serving as a means to "master . . . a timelessly recurring trauma" and "to find the logic of one's own catabolism through the destruction of others."[38] But that "logic" can be considered a pseudo-logic in which one's powerlessness to control the original trauma is transformed into the power of controlling something or someone else.

Calculations of Crime

One of the most frequent explanations for villainous behavior is found rooted in the classical criminological concept of rational choice. If not portrayed as psychologically addled, villains are alternatively shown to be cold, calculating rational thinkers. Comic books in general rebound between the extremes of psychological turmoil in which the villains are actually the victims of events beyond their control and rational beings who are in control of their behavior and choose evil actions. This bipolar nature of the medium reflects the larger debate in criminal justice as to accountability.

While the foundations of criminal law emphasize individual accountability, defense lawyers have long brought evidence to bear in criminal cases to show shades of gray in culpability. Thus, the drive for individual accountability in criminal law is tempered by affirmative defenses such as the insanity defense. At the same time, what unites notions of psychological trauma and individual accountability is the focus on the problem of crime being contained in the individual, not society. The individualization of the crime problem is the fundamental idea that readers are likely to take away in nearly every mainstream comic book.

According to rational choice theorists, the engagement in criminal activity is the result of calculated decisions in which offenders weigh the consequences of their actions. Considerations such as the decision to become involved in criminal behavior and the evaluation of situational factors vary according to the type of crime under consideration. Rational, or conscious, purposive choices may not be the "best" choices, but they represent the offender's determination that the potential benefits of engaging in a particular crime outweigh the potential negative consequences.[39]

Rational choice theorists acknowledge that background factors such as "personality and upbringing" influence whether or not an individual is likely to become involved in criminal behavior. These factors, however, are deemphasized in favor of a focus on the process of decision making when the criminal opportunity presents itself. The underlying assumption is that human behavior is motivated by the desire to experience pleasure (increase rewards) and avoid pain (decrease the potential for punishment). In the words of utilitarian philosopher Jeremy Bentham,

> Nature has placed mankind under the governance of two sovereign masters, *pain* and *pleasure*. It is for them alone to point out what we ought to do, as well as to determine what we shall do. On the one hand the standard of right and wrong, on the other the chain of causes and effects, are fastened to their throne. They govern us in all we do, in all we say, in all we think: every effort we can make to throw off our subjection, will serve but to demonstrate and confirm it. In words a man [sic] may pretend to abjure their empire: but in reality he will remain subject to it all the while.[40]

Bentham emphasizes that the pleasure-pain principle is fundamental to human nature; therefore, most individuals have equipotentiality, or equal ability to conform or rebel against the law. Modern adherents of rational choice make a distinction between criminal involvement, or the decision to become involved in, continue, or desist from criminal behavior, and the criminal event itself.[41]

In our sample of comic books, rational choice is sometimes represented as a motive for villainous behavior, although the outcomes are not always fruitful. For example, in *Identity Crisis,* a murder mystery unfolds when Sue Dibney, the wife of reserve member of the Justice League the Elongated Man (a.k.a. Ralph Dibney), is found dead in the couple's apartment.

Members of the Justice League embark on a quest to find the killer, with Batman leading the charge, declaring, "It's the first rule of solving a crime. If you want to know who did it. You need to find out who benefits. Who benefits?" Batman suggests that the killer has made a utilitarian calculus in an effort to reap rewards from the crime. He eliminates villains from consideration on the basis of the understanding that there is no benefit to their involvement. When long-time butler and confidant Alfred suggests that the Suicide Squad may be responsible, Batman states, "It's not the squad, Alfred . . . the squad doesn't benefit. There's no gain."

In narrowing his focus on the identity of the killer, Ray Palmer (a.k.a. Atom) reflects on the words of Batman: "Who benefits? . . . So who benefits when the family member of a hero is killed?" Slowly, Palmer realizes who stands to gain: "The family members of all the other heroes." Presumably, the death would serve as a unifying bond among the remaining heroes and their loved ones. It is revealed that Palmer's ex-wife, Jean, "accidentally" killed Sue in a desperate plot to romantically reconcile with Palmer. Despite the reliance on the concept of rational choice as an explanation for Jean's behavior, she is promptly incarcerated in the Arkham Asylum for the criminally insane. This reveals a striking disconnect between her capacity for making "rational" choices and the criminal justice response to her behavior.

Similarly, the *Fantastic Four: Foes* suggests that the motivation for criminal behavior is the result of a cold, calculated plan. The villain, Mad Thinker, aided by thief and shape-shifting sorceress Threska, devises a criminal plan to allow him to "retire" to a paradise where he can "live to his heart's contentment" and have anything he desires. When his carefully laid plans are ultimately thwarted by the Fantastic Four, he states, "I had every step planned out in *great* detail. Everything up to this moment."

Choice is also singled out as a primary motivation in *Batman: Battle for the Cowl*. Here, Jason Todd, a former Batman sidekick who in an earlier story arc met his demise at the hands of the Joker, resurfaces to assume the mantle of a "vigilante Batman" determined to kill criminals to restore order to Gotham City. Todd is ultimately defeated by superhero Nightwing (a.k.a. Dick Grayson), who laments Todd's evil transformation. Nightwing recognizes that "cruel childhood events" shaped Todd's life but that ultimately Todd rejected the opportunity to make good: "[S]ome people don't want to be saved, because saving means changing." Here, Nightwing's message is that though negative social circumstances may impact development, those tragedies are not destiny.

Lex Luthor, one of the most iconic of all villains, is obsessed with the notion that we create our own destiny through the choices that we make. In *Lex Luthor: Man of Steel*, he burns with contempt because Superman is *not* a man but rather an alien that represents ideals and abilities beyond the reach of humans. For Luthor, Superman represents an obstacle for humankind since humans are incapable of reaching Superman's potential. He states that Superman is "something no man can ever be. I see the end. The end of our potential. The end of our achievements. The end of our dreams." Instead, Luthor envisions himself as the savior figure, or "hope," for the world. When speaking of destiny, he asserts that it is something that "we hold in our hands," suggesting that destiny is something that can be shaped by human agency. Destiny is not something that happens *to* us; rather, it is something we control. For Luthor, the mere existence of Superman smothers the hopes and aspirations of humankind. Characterizing himself as "an idealist," Luthor places his faith entirely in humans to achieve greater potential, not in reliance on a superman.

Realizing that he cannot defeat Superman, Luther devises a plan to shame Superman—to create an image of Superman that would evoke distrust and disappointment from the populace. Using a mentally ill child molester as a scapegoat, Luthor concocts a plan in which Superman would publicly "save" the molester from impending death. Knowing that Superman will be compelled to save him, Luthor believes that the gathering crowd will be driven to rage against Superman because they will be deprived of seeing the child molester meet his grisly death. However, Luthor's cynicism about the vengeful nature of the public is ultimately proven to be misplaced.

The theme of choice reverberates throughout the story. Though his intentions are fused with selfish pride and arrogance that he projects onto Superman, Luthor suggests that the choices he has made, in fact the very ability to make choices, are the characteristics of a great man.

Urban Renewal

Attributing the behavior of comic book villains to individual pathology or choice is a mainstay in comic books, though other explanations are also represented, if less frequently. Comic book characters are never static, but are invented and reimagined over decades to reflect the social conditions and public concerns of the day. Plots involving fighting corporate crime, social problems, political neglect, and corruption in early superhero comic books have gradually shifted to a more micro-level focus on individual responsibility. One casualty of this shift is the relative neglect of ecological factors as contributors to criminal behavior. Though the books regularly focus on social decay in settings such as Gotham City, the dystopian conditions are framed as being a result of individual or organized criminal behavior. They are not considered spaces in which social capital is compromised, thus actually contributing to higher crime rates. Here, we argue that what is missing from the narratives is as important as what is present.

Criminological theories such as that of social disorganization are rarely represented in comics. Social disorganization theory involves the ecological conditions of inner-city life as originally theorized by the Chicago School of sociology in the 1920s and 1930. Pinning crime on such variables as poverty, homelessness, low home ownership rates, absentee landlords, unemployment, low educational attainment, racial and ethnic discrimination, and neglect by politicians, the theory addresses weak social institutions that would normally curtail crime. Early Chicago School sociologists tracked delinquency information by neighborhood, revealing that although residents change, rates of delinquency remain relatively stable, indicating that institutions, not individuals, cause delinquency.[42] Social disorganization theorists posit that social institutions such as schools and churches become failed enterprises for reigning in delinquency. For example, because parents are forced to work low-income jobs to make ends meet, they are unable to afford child care. This results in youths without parental or institutional control who turn to delinquency and gang activity to fill the gap. Updating the theory for modern times, criminologist Robert Sampson and sociologist William Julius Wilson explored the intersection of race, place, and poverty. They did so to show how racial inequality has historically led to conscious political decisions that serve to contain concentrated minorities in areas of poverty and neglect.[43]

Deadshot: Urban Renewal provides one rare example of social disorganization–related content in our sample of contemporary comic books. Deadshot cleans up the Triangle neighborhood of Star City, which suffers from poverty, landlord neglect, gang activity, and discrimination (its residents are largely black, Mexican, and Russian). Deadshot's motivations are to

THAT'S THE TROUBLE WITH A BAD SEED"

save his daughter, who lives in the neighborhood, and to avenge the death of his son. Along his path to do so, the comic book provides a graphic portrayal of the injustices of inner-city life. For example, a slumlord fails to provide a secure living situation for residents; rather than fix the problem, the slumlord seeks revenge for the complaints and attempts to poison one resident's dog. The streets of Star City are depicted as overtaken by black and Mexican gangs who fight each other, leaving hard-working residents in the midst of a dangerous situation. Beyond this depiction, there are several other ways in which race is implicated. The portrayal of Deadshot, a white male, swooping in to save the inner city could also be read as potentially racist in itself, locating crime and social disorganization in racial and ethnic communities and underrepresenting white criminals in white socially disorganized areas. It also potentially plays into the antiquated notion of crime fighting as the white man's burden when, in fact, both crime and crime fighting involve all groups in society. The work of criminologist Kenneth Tunnell, for example, has sought to expand social disorganization theory to rural spaces in Appalachia, where run-down trailers, makeshift home extensions and yards filled with mechanical junk indicate a white, rural concentrated poverty often overlooked by criminologists focused on the minority inner city.[44]

Caped Crusaders Are Not Critical Theorists

Almost completely absent from comic book narratives are those for which critical, Marxist, or feminist criminological theories may apply. Although we employ cultural criminology, a critical theoretical perspective, as the basis of our exploration of comic books, none of the villains' stories in our sample imply the antecedents of criminal behavior important to critical theories, such as capitalism, racism, or patriarchy. We find that the majority of narratives run counter to the tenets held by critical criminologists, who attribute the real causes of crime to capitalist systems that encourage competition and consumption at all costs. They also concern themselves with social systems and practices that perpetuate patriarchal notions of men as more entitled to economic and social power than women and help to maintain racism, which undervalues nonwhite communities, criminalizes minorities, and leads to differential police enforcement.

Deadshot finds himself in The Triangle, a multicultural neighborhood where streets are filled with prostitutes, interpersonal disputes turn to physical fights, and graffiti abounds. (*Deadshot: Urban Renewal*, Christos Gage, Steven Cummings, Jimmy Palmiotti, DC Comics, 2005)

Critical theory questions the locations of power in our society and how that power is used in the operation of the criminal justice system. It disavows the naturalness of what is considered a crime, who is labeled as criminal, how society responds to crime, and how the media portray crime and criminal justice.[45] In *The Rich Get Richer and the Poor Get Prison*, for example, Jeffrey Reiman builds the case for the criminal justice system being largely structured around processing poor and minority offenders who cannot find meaningful work and living wages in the capitalist system. Meanwhile, the same system ignores or is lenient toward white-collar and corporate offenders.[46]

Critical criminologists do not individualize crime, but rather point to the larger social power dynamics that play themselves out in the routine, daily drama of crime and justice. In this sense, our sample reveals that comic books tend to portray criminological themes in a way that fails to question the larger foundations of society. We found that the most frequent explanations for crime revolve around psychological and rational choice perspectives, which have in common the contention that problems are embodied within individuals. As a result, the power structure in society remains uninterrogated and disembodied. In subsequent chapters, we take seriously the conspicuous absence of a critical consciousness in our sample of mainstream American comic books and expand upon how this affects the kinds of messages about criminal justice readers may consume and consider.

6

"AREN'T WE SUPPOSED TO BE THE GOOD GUYS?"

HEROES, DEATHWORTHINESS, AND PATHS TO JUSTICE

Upset that he slept through 9/11 after a pathetic self-deprecating bender, age-old superhero Savior 28 goes into a deep, reflective, and depressive spiral, emerging with an alternative to his violent approach to injustice. Haunted by a phrase from the Buddha that his wife often repeated, "What is most needed is a loving heart," he decides to work toward peace. Addressing a crowd, Savior 28 explains,

> I knew in that moment that I would never lift my hand in violence again. Never try to solve another problem with my fists. No one knows . . . better than the man who tried to live by the sword . . . how hopeless that path is. No one knows . . . better than the warrior . . . that peace is the way!

Savior 28 comes to embrace a peace-building philosophy and addresses the United Nations General Assembly calling for peace and cooperation in the fight against terrorists. As a guest on *Larry King*, he exposes the lie that weapons of mass destruction are stockpiled in Iraq and rails against an invasion. In other addresses to his followers he preaches about the brutality and arrogance of the modern world, where people handle problems by hijacking airplanes and torturing terrorist suspects, suggesting that human kindness and compassion are culturally devalued.

Savior 28's call for justice is similar to critical criminologist Richard Quinney's concept of peacemaking criminology. This theory links human suffering to the causes of crime and suggests that only through eliminating one's egocentric self can one avoid crime. The aim of peacemaking criminology is to decrease suffering through working toward social justice: "Without peace within us and in our actions, there can be no peace in our results. Peace is the way."[1] The approach has been criticized by mainstream criminologists for lacking social-scientific merit and being devoid of empirical support; nonetheless, peacemaking criminology draws on religious and spiritual wisdom to envision a new society that rejects unbridled capitalism and its inequalities and fights against racism, sexism, and classism.[2]

The response to Savior 28's change of heart is one of shock and disapproval by the Bush White House and the American public. Rumors that Savior 28 is mentally unstable abound. Ultimately, in order to save the American establishment from the complications that Savior 28 could incite with his message of peace—putting out of business the military-industrial complex, for example—the book's narrator, a former Savior 28 sidekick, kills him.

In this self-contained story, *The Life and Times of Savior 28* implies that there is little room for a superhero who works toward peace. The genre itself is embedded in dichotomous notions of good and evil. Even beyond the superhero genre we find comic book characters often acting out justice-related dramas that serve as musings on how heroes should behave in fighting for justice. Comic books are replete with stories that devalue peacemaking approaches while privileging violent responses, necessitated by the crisis at hand and the problem of a corrupt and incompetent criminal justice system. Heroes often contemplate the extent to which they can violate the rule of the law in order to ultimately preserve it, and whether they should go so far as to kill the purveyors of evil, a theme we refer to as "deathworthiness."

This chapter explores the heroes' path to justice with the acknowledgment that mainstream comic books, and in particular the superhero genre, virtually prohibit a peacemaking approach to justice and instead frequently reinforce retribution in response to threats to the social order.[3] Given that the very structure of mainstream comic book stories allows little room for deviation outside these normative responses to conflict, we turn to the various paths to justice taken by the heroes and their implications in the context of criminology and criminal justice. Our analysis finds that mainstream comic books offer a continuum of paths to justice with some heroes adhering more closely to the rule of law than others.[4]

Ultimately, we suggest that these paths to justice, including calculations of whether to kill an opponent to achieve justice, or calculations of death-worthiness, operate in a social context in which the criminal justice apparatus is deemed inadequate to serve the interests of the people. Negotiating these moral boundaries through the implementation of extralegal justice—operating on a continuum of deathworthiness—is emotionally satisfying to many readers and reflects and shapes larger notions of what it means to achieve justice in contemporary society.

In a World of Peacemaking, Comic Book Heroes Would Be Obsolete

In the *Ultimates: Super-Human*, Nick Fury assembles an elite government unit of superheroes, including Tony Stark (a.k.a. Iron Man), Bruce Banner (a.k.a. the Hulk), Wasp, Giant-Man, and the revived Captain America, which aims to take on terrorism and national security. In the story, the superheroes worry about becoming obsolete in a time of peace, lamenting that without a particular mission or violent foe to fight, their existence may be in jeopardy. As Wasp comments, "If it wasn't for this two-year merchandising campaign Stark tied us into, I bet they'd be pulling the plug right now." Luckily, Bruce Banner's role as the team's punching bag, and his failure to create a super-soldier serum that he was working on, leads him into a bout of depressive anger during which he decides to become the Hulk and threaten public safety in his wrath. Hulk's Manhattan rampage gives the Ultimates a mission and an enemy. Bruce explains, "I was only trying to help. This was all part of the plan, you see. I was only trying to come up with a menace you could all get together and fight." As a subplot in the story, Thor was asked to join the Ultimates but initially turned down the job because he was critical of the American government acting as "thugs in uniform who will smash any threat to a corrupt status quo." He is depicted as a drunk, burnt-out peacemaker who tells Nick Fury and Bruce Banner,

> Go back to your paymasters and tell them [I am] not interested in working for a military industrial complex who engineers wars and murders innocents. Your talk might be of supervillains now, but it is only a matter of time before you are sent to kill for oil or free trade.

The weakness of Thor's noninterventionist stance in the face of a crisis is quickly evident as he launches into action upon hearing about the potential destruction of Manhattan. Thor's message is that as a superhero he must engage in violence to protect the public in crisis and that any superhero who denies this duty has clearly lost his or her way. Indeed, the crises are so great that Nick Fury explains how drastically the heroes are needed: "[W]e're living in crazy times. . . . Crime is becoming super-crime. Terrorism is becoming superterrorism."

Retributive violence as a solution to the crime problem, as opposed to a peaceful or critical alternative, represents a comic book formula that insists on maintaining an us-versus-them status quo. Although there are some comic books that offer critical alternatives to the comic book formula, these stories are usually independently published and remain outside mainstream continuity.

More often, however, the situation portrayed in comic books reflects Savior 28's situation: the critically engaged hero must be killed in order to maintain the American military-industrial complex. Or, as is the case with the aforementioned *The Ultimates* plot, criminal crises and threats to public safety must come down the pike at regular intervals if the Ultimates are to enjoy continued funding by the government. Similarly, in the lead-up to the real-life war in Iraq, erroneous assertions by the Bush administration that weapons of mass destruction (WMDs) were stockpiled in the country justified an American invasion. Critical commentators have since argued that the alleged WMDs served as a deliberately false pretext to allow the military to expand and create a wartime economy.

Heroes and the Rule of Law

Crime-and-justice plots in comic books explore the Western notion of the dichotomy between good and evil as being fundamental to human existence. The great philosophers of the West, such as Augustine, Aquinas, Anselm, Descartes, and Kierkegaard, all believed in a distinction between good and evil.[5] And, the distinction is frequently made explicit in comic books through both the narrative and the art.

For example, in Arkham Asylum in a darkened cell under a red hue, Batman stands over the Joker and states, "There was good and evil. Red

Nick Fury, reimagined as an African American hero, discusses super-terrorism with the Hulk's alter ego, Bruce Banner. (*The Ultimates: Super-Human*, Mark Millar and Bryan Hitch, Marvel, 2005)

and black. Life and death. The joke and the punchline" (*DC Universe* #0). In *Justice League of America: The Tornado's Path*, Superman, Batman, and Wonder Woman convene to assemble the next generation of the Justice League and note the qualities that they seek in a hero. They consider Captain Marvel for the league, not because he is the strongest or most powerful but rather for his inherent benevolence. Superman suggests, "[H]e's *good*. Not just a good fighter. Truly good." An "inherently good" hero will be entrusted to tread a righteous path to justice.

In a retelling of the origin of Superman in *Superman: Earth One*, readers are reminded of Superman's inherent goodness as Pa Kent offers advice to a young Clark Kent, who arrived on Earth as the only survivor of his home planet, Krypton. Pa advises Clark that there will be a day when he will stand up for what's right, when he will show the world who he truly is. In suggesting a moniker for Clark, Pa reveals what makes Clark special. He states, "[Y]ou're more powerful than any other man in history. . . . [Y]ou're unique in the world. Extraordinary. Not just any man . . . and more than just a man . . . a Super-man . . . Superman." Pa makes clear that Clark *is* Superman, and that Clark Kent, the ordinary human, is merely a façade, a mask that is necessary for Superman to do good in the world.

Superheroes represent models of righteousness, or, as former comic book writer and editor Danny Fingeroth states, the superhero "does the right thing. Perhaps more importantly, *he* [sic] *knows what the right thing is.*"[6] In *Holy Superheroes!* Greg Garrett finds that the superheroes in comic books provide a model of behavior for readers, a moral compass pointing in the direction of faith and goodness rooted in Judeo-Christianity. The heroes are inspirational figures, ones who teach wisdom and life lessons. They fight against evil, operating under a moral code of self-imposed restraint, frequently coupled with a firm "no kill" policy.[7]

Apocalyptic, criminal crises that threaten public safety are rarely handled adequately by law enforcement and government in general, necessitating heroes and superheroes acting either as adjuncts to the authorities or outside the law altogether as vigilantes. Driving home the need for heroes and superheroes, comic books often portray law enforcement and government officials as utterly incompetent or corrupt.[8] Often the police are shown as either dimwitted or lacking the necessary resources to battle against the crime problem.

As one group participant stated,

> I hear a lot of frustration at, you know the sort of ineffectiveness of justice, [that] prisons don't work, evidence doesn't work. This doesn't work. That doesn't work. . . . In a democracy, the wheels of justice grind slowly, down to the lowest level, so it is natural to be frustrated. It is natural to be angry, even irrational, and that's why . . . we like heroes who shoot shit and ask questions later, you know, shoot shit justifiably.[9]

According to the participant, the vigilantism in comic books is justified because of the portrayal of a profound ineffectiveness of legitimate authorities to provide justice for people harmed by crime. As we have argued, this crisis is an overwhelming theme across mainstream comics and may be one of the most powerful and dominant take-away notions, greasing the way for the vigilante to advance a violent and individually meted out type of street justice.

For example, in *Route 666*, the police are seen reclining in their station reading the crime news in tabloid newspapers, ignorant of a dangerous plot brewing. Spider-Man encounters corruption as city workers try to prevent him from clearing an accident until their people can do it—because the longer it takes, the more overtime they earn (*The Amazing Spider-Man* #647). They are busy eating donuts during the traffic pileup, seemingly indifferent to calls from people who are suffering or injured as a result of the accident.

At times, officers are explicitly called out for their incompetence such as in *All-Star Batman and Robin the Boy Wonder*, when Batman rescues a female victim of sexual assault and warns her not to bother reporting her victimization, telling her the cops are "useless . . . worse than useless." Batman's concerns are confirmed when he violently confronts a police officer to get information on the status of a villain and is told, "It's all rigged. He walks tomorrow. Lack of evidence." Joshua Foster, father of a missing boy in *Jonah Hex: Special Edition*, hires Jonah Hex for his vigilantism after explaining, "I have employed both the sheriff and the Pinkerton's. They have repeatedly failed me. As it stands I fear that you are the last hope of my ever seeing my boy Jacob again." In *Fables* (#19), the mayor, Old King Cole, and the Wolf from Little Red Riding, who works as Fabletown's detective, argue about being unable to gain a conviction of Prince Charming for the murder of Bluebeard. Old King Cole blames it on the detective's inability to gather admissible evidence, but the detective faults Fabletown's convoluted rules of evidence and due process requirements.

In the late 1960s, law professor Herbert Packer introduced his oft-cited "two models of the criminal process" illustrating the tension in the criminal justice system between crime control (the emphasis on public safety) and due process (the emphasis on individual rights). Those who advocate for crime control would support strengthening law enforcement and reducing legal constraints on police officers, while those who advocate due process would favor rules that protect individual rights such as requiring the *Miranda* warning or implementing the exclusionary rule. This tension is never fully resolved in our society, and new threats continually reignite calls for crime control at the expense of due process. After the attacks on 9/11, our "homeland" security apparatus—law enforcement at the federal, state, and local government levels—failed spectacularly, ultimately resulting in the passage of legislation that expanded the powers of law enforcement. Because the threat to the social order was framed by the media as a "new kind of evil" and one more severe than we have ever faced, there was minimal resistance to legislation that severely curtailed our liberties.[10]

Similarly, for the most part, the mission of the superhero remains in conflict with that of due process. In their study of crime and justice in Superman and Batman comic books, criminologists Bradford Reyns and Billy Henson found that in the vast majority of their sample, the books featured narratives focusing on crime control to the exclusion of due process.[11] Similarly, our analysis found that if there is some question about due process, excessive use of force, or a potential violation of civil rights, the concerns are usually brushed aside.

The inadequacies of law enforcement extend beyond individual police officers and court officials into condemnation of the criminal justice system as a whole. It is not merely a few individual actors who are deficient and incapable of serving justice, but rather the entire apparatus is a failure. With institutions such as Arkham Asylum functioning as revolving doors, the prisons are never adequate to incapacitate the criminals for any extended period of time, and the courts are portrayed as a farce. For example, in *Identity Crisis,* "getting back to normal" is a world in which villains are freed from the courtroom en masse as a result of legal technicalities.

Corrupt law enforcement is also a regular feature of comic book plots, making justice impossible to achieve without the hero's intervention. In *Criminal: Coward,* corrupt police are in cahoots with local drug bosses to move thirty-two kilos of pure-grade heroin. Similarly, corruption is rampant in *All-Star Batman and Robin the Boy Wonder,* with numerous images of police abuse of power. The narrator states, "There's something rotten in Gotham City. It wears a badge." Batman, in an exaggerated characterization of this superhero, warns his sidekick, Robin, "Lesson number one: never talk to cops. Not in Gotham. Never let a cop near you. Not in Gotham. . . . [T]hey'll kill you just as soon as look at you." In one scene, Batman expresses his frustration with the police department as he watches murderers being "escorted to freedom by Gotham's finest." Likewise, *The Runaways* involves a cabal of villainous parents whose organization had bought off high-ranking members of the Los Angeles Police Department, complicating their teenage children's quest for truth and justice.

In the Marvel universe, corruption in law enforcement is particularly rampant. The corruption begins at the top with Norman Osborn, who has risen to power following the events of *Secret Invasion* and targets superheroic "persons of interest," turning government national security entities into his personal black operations. He forms government-sponsored teams recruiting various villains to form the Dark Avengers and, in a twist of irony, has them pose as known superheroes. Osborn promotes himself as the Iron Patriot, the man who purportedly keeps America safe. Meanwhile, he is actually a threat to safety when, for example, in *Daredevil: The List,* it is revealed that Osborn has reinstated police officers that were formally suspended for excessive use of force. In his power grab, Osborn implements a zero-tolerance policy he believes is necessary to maintain social order. He states, "[W]e must be seen to crack down hard on anyone who

The criminal justice system is frequently portrayed as woefully inadequate or corrupt. Here, a legal technicality allows criminals to go free. (*Identity Crisis*, Brad Meltzer and Rags Morales, DC, 2005)

defies the rule of law . . . because I *am* the rule of law." Lamenting the corruption, Daredevil declares, "[T]hey handed Norman Osborn the keys to the kingdom. They own the courtrooms. They own the police force . . . and now they're murdering people in their homes."

Means to an End

Incompetency and corruption provide a backdrop that signals the need for superheroes—those who are willing to move beyond the constraints of the existing criminal justice system. At the same time, not all heroes agree as to the proper path to justice, making comic books an important site for cultural and philosophical musings about the means of obtaining justice and safety for victims and society in general. Although most paths to justice reflect extralegal responses to crime, or taking the law into one's own hands, there are nuances as to how violent one can act in that vigilantism.

Most often, scholars have focused on the most iconic superheroes to demonstrate the contrasting approaches to the crime problem. Superman has been described as working within the boundaries of the law, and therefore as being a "value-neutral proponent of American justice," while Batman is "motivated by his own values and his obsession with vengeance."[12] As a result, Superman is more likely to focus on due process concerns while Batman is more likely to focus on crime control, engaging in more acts of aggression and physical force.[13]

In our research, we have found that *The Punisher* series tends to portray the most extreme abandonment of the rule of law in favor of extralegal moral crusading. Typically, the Punisher never attempts to work within the legal system and immediately jumps into his vigilante mission in any given story arc. The plot inevitably moves toward retaliatory, illegal, and individually accomplished responses to crime that must be tolerated, and even welcomed, in a time of crisis. The narrator in *The Punisher* (#33) explains, "[H]e judges [criminals], he passes sentence, then he blows them away. Justice happens in the time it takes to pull the trigger." In contrast, in the first decade of the 2000s, Wonder Woman plots have shown little tolerance for extreme violence in the pursuit of justice, though Wonder Woman has often used violence when backed into a corner by villains. This "ambassador of peace" prefers to talk through issues with her foes as a representative of her home country in a transnational governing body.

In between the Punisher and contemporary Wonder Woman are moral gray areas as to the means of justice that heroes negotiate and debate with each other. Dr. Henry Pym (Ant-Man, Giant-Man), in "Oral History of the Earth's Mightiest Heroes," a supplemental text to *The New Avengers: The Heroic Age* (#1), explains that until he scientifically created the ability to grow and shrink, he was not the "adventurous type" and was "not a man who believed in violence as a means to an end until I learned that sometimes it is the only way." Changed by the crises they encounter, comic book heroes often put aside nonviolent ideals in order to accomplish a greater good. As Daredevil states in *House of M* (#6),

So I'm saying that whatever restraint or personal boundaries you usually put on yourself in the name of good and right . . . well, I think there's no place for any of that here . . . in the fight we have in front of us. We can't lose this. We have to win.

The fight Daredevil refers to is the crisis facing the X-Men and their mutant community brought on by the Scarlet Witch, whose powers are so great they are reality altering: any emotional outburst by her sets the world out of whack and potentially into apocalyptic chaos. In order to prevent further antimutant sentiment, and to make sure the world remains intact, the X-Men must reign in the Scarlet Witch at all costs. In the process, the X-Men unofficially take on the role of government in protecting mutant-kind, as when the mutant community is ghettoized in San Francisco (before moving onto their own land, called "Utopia").

In the *Justice League: Cry for Justice* miniseries, Green Lantern laments that the Justice League has not been seeking justice vigorously enough. In a dramatic speech, he points out that Martian Manhunter's killer remains on the loose because the league has not been passionate enough in seeking justice through any means possible, including retributive violence. The league's heroes debate the issue with Green Lantern, with most of the heroes—including Superman and Wonder Woman—preferring to adopt steady, measured methods to rein in villains. After a heated argument with the other Justice Leaguers, Green Lantern and Green Arrow secede from the league in order to vengefully hunt down villains who have previously evaded their grasp. They are later joined by Supergirl, Ray Palmer (a.k.a. the Atom), and Captain Marvel.

While heroes use violence as a means to an end, explicit justifications related to crisis-proportion threats abound. Reiterated throughout our sample of comic books is a just war philosophy in relation to mass criminal events. As theologian Mike Alsford explains in his analysis of heroes in Western culture, war has been justified in Western societies as a response to violent aggression as a last resort to establish peace.[14] Christian philosophers like Augustine have put forth that such a just war should have a specific focus, be sanctioned by the highest authorities, be proportional to the offense, distinguish between combatants and noncombatants, and be winnable. In America, the rhetoric of war, and the continuous use of the war metaphor, has been invoked to sustain public policies directed toward social problems as diverse as poverty, drugs, terrorism, and obesity, among others. In particular, former president George W. Bushʼs use of the war metaphor helped create support for a preemptive war in Iraq allegedly to prevent weapons of mass destruction from falling into enemy hands. In his address to a joint session of Congress and the American people in September of 2001, President Bush stated, "Our war on terror begins with al Qaeda, but it does not end there."[15] Later in the buildup to the war in Iraq, on September 8, 2002, National Security Advisor Condoleezza Rice warned of the imminent danger posed by the enemy, stating, "The problem here is that there will always be some uncertainty about how quickly he can acquire nuclear weapons. But we donʼt want the smoking gun to be a mushroom cloud."[16] During the debates in Congress about whether to vote for Bushʼs war resolution against Iraq, Republican supporters in Congress used the language of "imminent danger" and "imminent threat" that the weapons, including allegedly nuclear ones, posed in order to invoke self-defense under a just-war philosophy. Use of this rhetoric ultimately justifies, if not requires, immediate action.

Similar rhetoric is reflected as comic book heroes are obliged to fight the latest apocalyptic war against evil. Oftentimes one hero has to convince the rest of a team to unite forces in putting down a particularly dire threat. The debate in most comic books is not whether there is *ever* a just war, but whether the current crisis is such a situation—and it often is. For example, in *X-Force & Cable: The Legend Returns*, the future, known to superhero Cable due to a confluence of events, involves the villain Skornn dominating the world and annihilating all mutants. Cable explains to his potential allies,

> X-Force—and members of the Mutant Liberation Front—the only hope for our people—for all civilization—rests with . . . working together towards a common goal—our mutual survival. Some will live to fight another day, some may not. But if we donʼt fight together weʼll all die alone!

The sense of urgency in crisis is summed up by Havok in *X-Men/Black Panther: Wild Kingdom*. After listening to Black Panther detail the human experimentation the villain Dr. Paine had been perpetuating on the people of Niganda, Havok quips, "Why are we standing around talking when this psycho is still on the loose?"

Role Reversals

In their willingness to operate outside the law as a means to an end, many heroes have a lot in common with the villains they are fighting. We found many plots that relied on hero and villain role reversals. The Thunderbolts series explores the roles of heroes and villains. The Thunderbolts are a group of villains who pose as heroes, and for many story arcs do indeed help people. However, their ultimate goal remains betraying society later on, when people least expect them to hatch a nefarious plot.

The flip-flopping of good and evil, hero and villain, has long characterized comic book universes. Fans consider it one of the reasons why Image comics, publisher of Spawn, gained ground in the 1990s—fans wanted explorations of darkness more than staid good or evil characters.[17] Plots that involve an antihero, a hero who is fighting an ultimately good fight despite either a flawed character or questionable methods, are at times viewed as an example of blurring of the boundaries of good and evil. However, we suggest another way of looking at the antihero: rather than being an alternative to the formula, it is merely a twist on it, with characters alternating in and out of transgressive behavior. Cal MacDonald, for example, is a monster-hunting private detective in *Criminal: Macabre*. He comes to his vigilantism as a former cop who was relieved of his duties after being found passed out on drugs in his squad car. Far from a reformed addict, MacDonald pops pills and takes along his "friend" Jim Beam to find vampires, ghouls, zombies, and other horrific residents of a dystopian Los Angeles. Despite this sordid background, like many other heroes in comic books, he maintains an us-versus-them status quo by augmenting law enforcement in their fight against various creatures of the night. Likewise, the Eisner Award–winning series *Criminal* features the antihero Leo Patterson, a professional thief who brings down a gang of drug traffickers and corrupt cops. As one comics blogger wrote about Leo and other antihero characters in the series, "[T]hey all have valid reasons for doing what they're doing. They're not doing it simply because they're evil. They're doing it for what they truly feel is their own personal greater good. They're often wrong, but they're reasoned about it."[18] In *Irredeemable,* published by BOOM! Studios, the superhero Plutonian breaks under the pressure of constant expectations to save the world, switching sides, mystifying his friends and foes alike. Although in the past Plutonian received accolades from the majority of his commentators, the taunts of the few who remarked that he is not doing enough cannot escape him. After his superhero status is publicly revealed by his ex-girlfriend and disseminated to the rest of the population, Plutonian lashes out against everyone. Unlike traditional superhero tales, *Irredeemable* presents a hero-gone-bad—one who breaks the sacred trust between the hero and citizens. As writer Mark Waid writes in *Comic Book Resources,* the series interrogates the nature of heroism, asking such questions as, "How did the Plutonian come to this? What became of the hope and promise once inside him? What happens to the world when its savior betrays it? What makes a hero *irredeemable?*"[19] The companion series *Incorruptible* flips this concept by portraying the supervillain Max Damage having a change of heart after witnessing Plutonian's rampage and renouncing his former life of crime. The series follows Max as he faces the challenges of "making good."

With the *Heroic Age,* Marvel has made a concerted effort to decrease the role reversals and reconstruct heroes with a "brighter tone." Writer Brian Michael Bendis has stated that "instead of deconstructing superheroes because it's fun to do, we're actually holding them up and saying don't we wish we had heroes like this and wouldn't that be great?"[20] The focus on a more stable hero has led to such storylines as the *New Avengers* (#5), in which the sky opens up in an invasion of creatures from another dimension, starkly externalizing evil and necessitating several exorcisms by Doctor VooDoo and the Avengers.

Is This Torture?

While historically Captain America exemplifies American values and national pride, more recently, at times, he has served as a counterhegemonic response to a government that infringes on personal liberties in the age of the war on terror. In the aftermath of the *Civil War* storyline, Captain America (#22) discusses with Sharon Carter the importance of standing up against the government when it is oppressive. The proposed superhero registration act would require all costumed superheroes to unmask, reveal their identities, and register with the government. Carter argues that when superheroes intervene, even with the best of intentions, others' lives are put at risk; therefore they should oblige and register with the government. She states that to refuse is "against the law. And the rule of law is what this country is founded on." Captain America counters, "[N]o . . . it was founded on *breaking* the law. Because the law was wrong" (*Captain America* #22). Ultimately, however, he finds that breaking the rules is hollow because it leads to death and destruction, and he returns to a commitment to the rule of law.

More frequent, though, is the presence of a zealous nationalism in comic books that typically runs counter to democratic principles. Ultimately, in the cosmic battle between good and evil, there is no room for due process, as violence is justified as righteous, and each side of the apocalyptic movement offers "roads to heaven that are paved with the corpses of those they detest."[21]

Though the heroes are almost never official agents of the government, they may, at times work as government adjuncts. Nonetheless, they are expected to abide by an ethical code that protects human rights rather than abuses them. While there is some contention among comic book characters (and readers) over the appropriate use of deadly force on the part of heroes, there is little controversy surrounding the use of violence. Excessive force is on continuous display and is widely regarded as an acceptable, if not desirable, mode of conflict resolution. Usually, the superheroes make explicit that the threat is too great, the crisis too severe to abide by the rule of law or consider due process concerns. In *New Avengers: Power*, heroes Luke Cage and his wife Jessica Jones have realized that their baby has been kidnapped. They state, "We don't have time to be subtle. We don't have time to play by the rules of engagement. . . . [W]e have to think differently. We have to think like a Skrull on the run." (Skrulls are an alien race, often enemies, in the Marvel universe.) Similarly, adhering to constitutional procedures is seen as an impediment to justice in *Batman: Battle for the Cowl*. Commissioner Gordon talks with the new district attorney about department protocol. The DA states, "I'm the new district attorney, Gordon. There are protocols that need to be adhered to. I just can't go around wiretapping and arresting people on a hunch." Gordon presses, "[T]hen you'll just wait until some innocents get killed. That's what you're saying, right?" Seconds later, an explosion occurs and the new district attorney dies. Following constitutional procedures is not only unwise, but potentially deadly.

Part of playing by the rules involves protecting the constitutional rights of those innocent until proven guilty. The interrogation of suspects provides a rich context for exploring the parameters of justice and the circumstances in which heroes may flaunt rules that state and federal agents must not. For real-life law enforcement officials, interrogators are bound by constitutional guidelines outlined in the U.S. Supreme Court's decision in *Miranda v. Arizona*.[22] The *Miranda* decision was made to curtail coerced confessions, both psychological and physical, because historically, it was not uncommon for the police to engage in the "third degree."[23] Although the *Miranda* warnings are ubiquitous in popular culture, particularly in crime-related television shows, comic book heroes are often lauded when they break free from such constraints. Since they are not (usually) government officials, superheroes are not bound by procedural safeguards, but rather are bound only by self-imposed constraints.

Superheroes routinely, either alone or in concert with law enforcement officials, subject suspects to violent interrogations. When the superheroes in *Identity Crisis* are determined to find the murderer of the wife of one of their own, they resort to brutal interrogations of all villains who may have information leading to the suspect, querying, in a series of panels featuring different superheroes, "What" "do" "you" "know!?" The panels on this single page illustrate that all the heroes tread the same path—use of force as a means of extracting the truth.

Similarly, in *Secret War*, a S.H.I.E.L.D.[24] agent is interrogating a suspect, brutally beating him to gain information about the persons responsible for underwriting a criminal underground network of bank robbers. The physical tactics are successful, and after a few blows, the criminal is willing to give up the information, stating, "[O]kay . . . I'll tell you anything you want—jush—jush—I wantsha a deal. I wansha deal to shttay outta Rykker'sh." Batman also frequently flouts the law while attempting to gain information from a suspect. In *Batman and Robin: Reborn*, Batman "interrogates" a suspect by dragging him face down on the pavement alongside the high-speed Batcycle.

The heroes are often unashamed of resorting to violence. In *Batman: Hush*, Batman interrogates the Riddler, incarcerated at Arkham Asylum. The interrogation becomes violent when the Riddler taunts Batman about the loss of his former incarnation of Robin, Jason Todd, at the hands of the Joker. After hearing the scuffle, a guard enters the room and asks, "What happened?" Batman stands over the bloodied Riddler and replies, "He fell." This deliberate torture is also apparent in *Justice League: Cry for Justice*, as a grimacing Prometheus (actually Clayface, who has been forced to shape-shift into Prometheus's form), in the custody of Green Arrow and Green Lantern, cries out, "I'll talk! I'll talk! I'll talk! For God's sake!"

GREEN ARROW: Is this torture?

GREEN LANTERN: Prometheus is a villain, Ollie. He's a murderer.

GREEN ARROW: Yeah, but aren't we supposed to be the good guys?

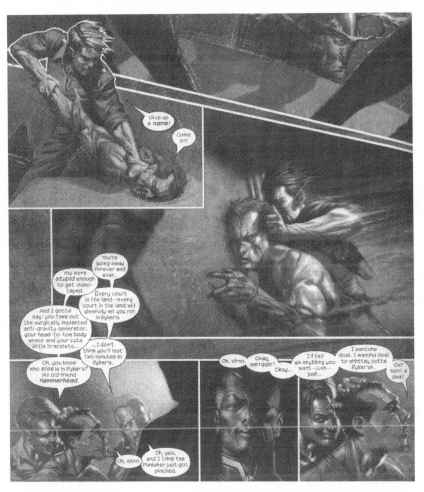

Interrogations in comic books are frequently violent in nature and considered justifiable in response to criminal threats to the social order. Here, a S.H.I.E.L.D. agent interrogates a criminal suspect. (*Secret War*, Brian Michael Bendis and Gabrielle Dell'otto, Marvel Comics, 2005)

Though cognizant of the potential irony of the good guys using dirty tactics, many focus group participants felt that such behavior was necessitated by the criminal crisis at hand. Like Green Lantern, many indicated that the gravity of the crisis and even the sense of urgency that crisis often sets up justified extreme measures. One stated, "[S]ometimes you don't have time to be diplomatic. There's no more talking, no more words, there's no one there to stop it and those times, I think that you just have to [use violence]. And I'm not saying there are not repercussions for that, because there are."[25] Others framed the violence in terms of being "strengthened through adversity" to act definitively.[26] Even if the long-term consequences leave the hero living with his or her own moral depravity, the short-term need to urgently stop the criminal crisis trumps all, suggesting that for some, a real hero is one who does the dirty work in order that others can be free from it.

Taken as a whole, the implication is that, although unsavory, violence is a necessary tactic that ultimately serves the greater good. Rather than view this justification of violence as a cheap plot point, we view it as important in two ways: (1) as a reflection of historical moments in United States history when the government asserted unbridled power and trod over individual rights in the face of threats such as those from the Japanese during World War II or communism during the Cold War, and more recently during the war on terror, and (2) as contributing to the larger culture's vocabulary of motives, that is, as part of a larger cultural discourse that privileges expressions of violence in certain contexts even if its use remains ineffective or, worse, counterproductive.

First, we may view the heroes' reliance on violence as reflecting our real-world concerns over threats that seem overwhelming, if not apocalyptic, in nature. Drastic times call for drastic measures. When faced with terror threats on domestic soil, patriotism surged and Americans rallied behind the government. This created an opening for government officials, particularly law enforcement, to operate unchecked, using such tactics as "enhanced interrogation techniques," waterboarding, and other torture, as authorized by the Bush administration.[27]

The controversy surrounding enhanced interrogation techniques flared in the aftermath of 9/11. Though techniques such as simulating drowning, forcefully grabbing, slapping to cause pain but avoid internal injury, forcing the subject to stand naked in a cold cell, and dousing with cold water have not been proven to elicit useful actionable intelligence, supporters of the Bush administration continue to argue for their implementation.[28] In fact, former vice president Dick Cheney suggests that the very act of engaging in public debate about the use of such techniques is dangerous and should be avoided. He has stated, "The terrorists see just what they were hoping for—our unity gone, our resolve shaken, our leaders distracted."[29]

Despite the fact that it has not been proven effective, enhanced interrogation remains appealing as a concept because it taps into our powerful desire for self-preservation—to protect our "way of life" at all costs. The presence of torture in these comic book story arcs is not just a plot point, but rather engages our sense of (in)security in the world and reverberates throughout popular culture.[30] It is the struggle with this conflict—the balancing of public safety against the necessity of protecting individual rights in a democracy—that is played out among superheroes and villains in comic books time and again. For the readers, this is an attractive, transgressive pleasure. The path to justice is a tumultuous one, and negotiating these moral boundaries, if only in a fictional universe, serves as one means of wrestling with real-life moral anxieties.

With Power Comes Great Responsibility

Comics scholar and philosopher A. J. Skoble muses that superheroes are playing in philosophically murky water as they place themselves above others in knowing and accomplishing the ultimate good; a usurpation of the Lockean social contract in which civil society gives up private vengeance in order to allow the government to provide objective judgment and responses to violence.[31] Such a situation brews in the *Secret Avengers* (#1), when Captain America takes over where villain Norman Osborn left off, but on the side of "good." Captain America has been asked by the U.S. government to form a secret team to avert national security dangers before they happen, thus making an end run around normal criminal procedure and transparency with "stealth tactics and preemptive intervention."

If the social contract is void, as comic book heroes often make it, then the famous question posed by Alan Moore in *Watchmen*—"Who watches the Watchmen?"—is a poignant one. And, in an ironic notion of societal checks and balances, the villains fill this role. In many comic books, the villains are the ones who question the moral goodness of the heroic quest for justice. For example, in *Justice*, Lex Luthor explicitly challenges the status quo of superheroes who swoop in and save victims from danger, but never work toward a world of social justice in which such dangers are prevented altogether. Although Luthor's social justice agenda is merely a ploy to gain citizen support for his evil plot to rid the world of ne'er-do-wells, nonetheless, he asks an important question and acts as the balance to the superhero agenda.

Similarly, in *Villains United*, six rogue villains are assembled by Lex Luthor to battle the Secret Society of Supervillains. Though the six ultimately serve as mercenaries for hire, they also serve as a check on the heroes' questionable ethical behavior. After it has become known that members of the Justice League of America "mindwiped" Dr. Light (the villain who brutally raped Sue Dibney), Catman cries foul. He tells Green Arrow, "[G]ood guys don't lobotomize people who are already in handcuffs. . . . [P]eople are going to die, because you took the shortcut."

Another example can be found in *Sleeper: All False Moves* when the villain Tao pontificates about the role of heroes as upholders of the status quo. As he is describing to the protagonist, Holden Carver, how he came to be the mastermind of an international organized crime and terrorist group, he explains, referring to himself in the third person, "[H]e was not sure what he wanted to do in the world. But he soon realized it was not being a costumed hero. That was a life of empty gestures. Always fighting the symptom and not the cause. Sweating blood for the status quo." Tao indicates that he is much more interested in manipulating heroes in order to shatter their illusions about good and evil and to ultimately create such chaos around the world that the heroes would destroy themselves, and with them the "tedious" world as we know it. His words are accompanied by a picture of him with a big-toothed grin in front of his computer and video command center, plotting world manipulation. Here, the villain is portrayed as one who believes fundamentally in his brand of evil, reminiscent of former president George W. Bush's construction of terrorists as "evildoers" in a biblical sense, wholly saturated in the intent of harming good society as the result of a moral or philosophical perspective. In this sense, the evil is not easily suppressed while it is also broadly defined as evil-writ-large, necessitating a machine of response in countless theaters of war in a long saga.

The serial nature of the medium tends to rely on plots featuring a determined and never-ending evil that routinely threatens the status quo. As comics scholar Douglas Wolk remarks, a true ending to the evil "would cause the kind of permanent change that's fatal to ongoing narratives."[32] Instead, in most comic books in our sample, the cat-and-mouse game of hero and villain continues, with both living to confront another day with many of the same villains.

Deathworthiness: To Kill or Not to Kill

Our sample of comic books, in eschewing plots that would radically alter the status quo, instead often played with whether heroes would kill villains as part of their path to justice and what it means to kill or not to kill. In *Midnighter: Anthem*, Midnighter consults a computer genius and known child molester named Chester in order to crack a computer code. In a rush to punishment, once Midnighter retrieves the code he proceeds to snap Chester's neck, effectively giving him the death penalty for his crimes against children. Upon returning to his hideout, Midnighter tells his accomplice Mindy that Chester was expendable. She replies, "Took him out then? Good riddance t' bad rubbish." In this particular storyline, Chester was viewed by Midnighter and Mindy as deathworthy, deserving of an extralegal death penalty without ever being given due process. Unlike the methodical procedures of the formal criminal justice system, in the world of comic book punishments, the death penalty is often administered only on the basis of the vigilante's discretion.

In real-life criminal cases, determinations of eligibility for the death penalty are made by prosecutors as they decide on the charges to be filed, a part of the criminal justice system that offers little transparency. If a case is a capital one and it proceeds to trial, the determination of the defendant's guilt and the determination of punishment (whether to sentence the defendant to death) are two separate phases. The first stage involves culpability; in it the jury determines whether the defendant is guilty of a capital charge. If so, the juries then judge the defendants' deathworthiness as a separate deliberation from that of their culpability. Notably, if death is not a possible sentencing option based on the charges of conviction, then judges can constitutionally decide sentences from the bench without the jury. Thus, determinations of a defendant's deathworthiness is a distinct jury deliberation, designed to put this important decision in the hands of many people rather than one judge. As legal scholar Phyllis L. Crocker explains,

> [T]he question of what punishment should be imposed on the defendant for committing a murder is more than a statement about his culpability for the crime; it is a judgment about his character, his record, his background, the circumstances and character of the murder, and the harm caused, not only to the victim, but to the victim's family.[33]

Thus the capital sentencing phase seeks to uphold the constitutional requirement of fostering individualized and careful sentencing in death penalty cases. Mandatory death sentences based solely on a determination of guilt would make the penalty more arbitrary and would not necessarily take into consideration prevailing values in society.[34] As Justice Potter Stewart's opinion in the Supreme Court case *Gregg v. Georgia* explains, "[T]he decision that capital punishment may be the appropriate sanction in extreme cases is an expression of the community's belief that certain crimes are themselves so grievous an affront to humanity that the only adequate response may be the penalty of death."[35] Because of the serious and extreme nature of the penalty, case law allows for a nearly unlimited amount of testimony from the defendant as to potential mitigating factors that would show that the defendant is not deathworthy, despite being found guilty of murder.

Because empirical studies have shown that the death penalty is unlikely to be a deterrent to crime, and by definition, putting someone to death cannot be rehabilitative or restorative, the public policy rationales for the death penalty can only be for purposes of incapacitation and retribution.[36] Retribution as a community value is usually cited as the primary reason why the death penalty is constitutional and on the books in many states, with the understanding that juries should reserve it for cases in which the circumstances and the character of the offender are particularly extreme. For example, a review of New Jersey death penalty cases revealed that "a greater percentage of sexual assault [murder] cases advanced to penalty trial and received the death sentence than did all death-eligible defendants. This demonstrates that offenders who commit sexual assault murders are considered more deathworthy than those who commit other death-eligible homicides."[37] One dominant theme in our sample of comic books is the deathworthiness of particular villains, based on considerations of the heinousness of the villain's crime, the impact the villain has had on victims, and the inherent nature of the hero. The deliberations are often quick and ad hoc in nature and based only on the musings of the self-appointed vigilante heroes.

Despite the lack of due process, however, we find that heroes in our comic book sample often have their own personal rules as to when it is appropriate to kill a villain. For instance, Batman has a code or self-imposed rule that limits his license to kill in pursuit of justice regardless of the nature of the crime being avenged. A comic book podcast host puts it this way,

> [A] big question in the comic is, "why is the Joker still alive? Why doesn't Batman finally kill him and end it?" . . . and that's what sets Batman apart from most other non-superpowered crimefighters is that Batman has the ability to takedown crime, but he's still got a code, and he does it within the code . . . [I]f Batman takes out the Joker, then the Joker has won.[38]

Therefore, a determination of a villain's guilt in murder does not necessarily mean that the villain will be murdered as a resolution to the plot. Comic books also bifurcate culpability and the question of deathworthiness, but do so without formal due process.

In our research we found that although not all characters are deathworthy, many enemies, and even peripheral characters, may be killed along the path to justice. Despite the systematic nature of the vigilante justice in comic books and the bifurcation of issues of guilt and deathworthiness, protagonists differ in their approaches. Responses range from avoiding death as punishment in all cases to more bloodthirsty policies of killing anyone morally depraved or criminally guilty along the path to justice. We found four broad levels of deathworthiness: (1) the avoidance of killing with the possible exception of the purpose of self-defense, (2) the killing of those responsible for harms done to others, (3) the killing of those morally depraved, for any reason, whom they encounter along the path to justice, and (4) the killing of innocents as collateral damage in the battle between good and evil.

Generally, heroes explicitly and repeatedly assert their mission as one of avoiding the death of adversaries. In the *Batgirl: Year One* motion comic, Batman and Robin subject Barbara Gordon (a.k.a. Batgirl-in-training) to numerous tests to determine whether she is worthy to wear the cape. After completing a training exercise, Robin informs her, "I don't think you passed . . . [Y]ou used lethal force against your last opponents . . . [W]e don't do that . . . [W]e don't kill, even to defend ourselves."

Moreover, at times there are explicit references to show that the heroes are not fatally wounding their opponents. For example, in *Daredevil: Return of the King*, Daredevil exacts a preemptive strike against the Owl, but carefully avoids fatal injuries by severing the nerves in Owl's arms and legs. Daredevil says,

> I have heard every word this monster said . . . I know what he was planning to do to Dakota. So I take away his arms and legs. I know just which

nerves to sever . . . [H]e'll survive . . . [I]t won't even look like much . . . but the Owl is done hurting people I care about.

For other heroes, killing is often necessary, requiring little mental deliberation. In *Astonishing X-Men: Ghostbox*, during a mission with Armor, Wolverine offers training and words of advice. He states, "[L]ike we practiced . . . you watch our backs." Armor replies, "[A]nd not kill anyone, right?" Wolverine instructs her, "[I]f it comes down to it with some bastard out there, you kill him without even thinking about it." Similarly, the modern X-Force unit, a black operation, including Armor and Wolverine along with Warpath, Domino, and others, is willing to kill its enemies in order to prevent the genocide of mutantkind.

Others, such as protagonist Christopher Chace, a martial artist and professional impersonator in *Human Target*, express difficulty with showing restraint. In the story arc "For I Have Sinned," he wrestles with whether to seek revenge on Father Mike, a pedophile priest, who abused Nat Clarke, now an adult and a problematic criminal. Chace muses,

I watch Nat Clarke. As he beats hookers, sells dope and porn. Lives out his sordid life. Is he like this because of what Father Mike did to him? Or was he just born an evil bastard? Some are. I could kill him. I could kill Father Mike. I possess a godlike power over their destinies.

Upon catching up with the priest and dangling his body out a high-rise window, Chace desires to kill him, but Father Mike explains that it would accomplish nothing and that in more recent years since the abuse of Clarke, he has been working on redemption through good works. At the end of the comic book, Father Mike is seen abusing another boy, and ultimately Nat Clarke kills him. This storyline, therefore, represents a notion of deathworthiness in which it is not ethical for the crime fighter to kill the criminal in pursuit of justice, but those he has directly wronged have that right. Before shooting Father Mike, Clarke says, "Remember me, Father Mike?"

Some protagonists' approaches to deathworthiness extend to anyone who has caused harm to others, as is the case with the hero Knockout. In *Secret Six*, after defeating Vandal Savage and Dr. Psycho, Knockout asks her compadres, "The guards have surrendered. Shall I kill them?" This implies that the group of six had not subjected the deathworthiness of their opponents to a policy determination in the past, and indeed, the Secret Six at this time were a relatively new group of villain avengers. Catman replies, "Without Vandal they're no threat to anyone. We won. That's enough," indicating that he has a utilitarian notion of whether offenders should be put to death, a clear rule emerging from Knockout's off-the-cuff contemplation of the question. Knockout herself seems to prefer a more permissive policy in which all those guilty of carrying out a murderous plot should be put to death. She responds, "Your mercy tastes like vomit on my tongue."

Wolverine represents a superhero who must actively curb his desire to kill in every adversarial situation. In *X-Men Origins: Wolverine* the plot involves a retelling of Wolverine's roots as Weapon X, subjected to a military laboratory experiment in which his human characteristics were replaced by those of an animal in order to enhance his preexisting mutant abilities, bolstering his "animalistic" urges. Professor Xavier of the X-Men discovers his powers as a fighting machine and invites him to join his X-Men Academy, where superhero mutants learn to control their powers and use them for good. When Wolverine accepts the opportunity, an army unit comes after him and he kills the entire unit, leaving a pile of dozens of bodies in a large pool of blood. The professor describes it as "death, indiscriminate and uncaring." The professor subsequently has to talk Wolverine down from killing him as well, explaining, "[I]f you kill me, the animal wins. I believe the man inside you is stronger. Now prove it." Wolverine is able to control himself at this point and ultimately joins the X-Men, but continually must rely on other X-Men to rein him in when he is in the red zone of blood-lust. In addition to struggling with his beastly instinct, Wolverine also expresses fewer moral barriers to violent behavior than other X-Men.

Similarly, anyone morally depraved is eligible to die in *The Punisher*. In one storyline a street junkie is thrust off a building to his death after confessing to the Punisher that he will do whatever it takes to get more drugs (*The Punisher* #33). In *Birds of Prey: Platinum Flats*, the heroes are willing to sacrifice a second-rate villain, Calculator, in order to get to the Joker. Infinity, an operative working with superhero Oracle, states to Calculator, "We need to draw them out, Calculator, and we know they're after you. So you're the bait. You'll have to trust us to keep you alive." In the melee that follows, Calculator is obliterated by the villain Gizmo.

At times, a determination is made that the killing of one (or several) innocents is in the interest of good ultimately prevailing over evil. In *Secret*

War, after destroying all of Latveria, while overlooking the carnage, Nick Fury (or rather, his model life decoy) explains to the heroes, "They hate us. I didn't start this war, but damn it to hell, I'm not going to lose it. This fight was absolutely worth sacrificing you for. It was worth losing my job for. And it was worth killing for." For Daredevil, the decision to use lethal force even against innocents is a wrenching one, but ultimately comes down to the numbers. In *Daredevil: Dark Reign; The List* #1, the villain Bullseye taunts Daredevil by claiming that his "no kill" policy has cost innocent lives. Bullseye states, "Just think of all the innocent lives you could have saved if you killed me when you had the chance!" Later, Daredevil laments, "One hundred and seven. That's how many innocent people died here tonight . . . because of me." Daredevil contemplates his actions and wonders, "[B]ut what if one sacrifice could make it right? One life to save many?" In this instance, Daredevil is not referring to his own life as sacrifice, but rather another's life, in order that Daredevil may lead a clandestine group of ninjas and use them as a force for good rather than evil.

`Heroes often debate among themselves their policies on deathworthiness. In the *House of M*, the X-Men and Avengers convene in a conference room to determine the fate of Scarlet Witch (a.k.a. Wanda Maximoff). Scarlet has lost control of her mutant powers, endangering the world. Colossus presents the dilemma:"[I]f word got out that the Witch was responsible for what happened to the Avengers . . . that a mutant killed the beloved heroes of this city . . . it would set the mutant/human relations back to the Stone Age." Emma Frost declares, "What is there to say? Put her down." Others respond, "No!!" "What is she, a dog?" After much wrangling, Frost demands a vote on whether the heroes will kill the Scarlet Witch. One hero states, "I'll never agree to killing her." Wolverine responds with a utilitarian calculus: "Someone do the math for me . . . [H]ow many more of you does she have to kill before you snap out of it?"

Black Widow also kills innocents along the pathway to justice. In *Black Widow: The Things They Say about Her*, she fires a machine gun, killing numerous "criminals" only tenuously identified as such by the fact that they were found in a notoriously crime-ridden alley. Likewise, in her rescue of women being experimented on by a nefarious pharmaceutical company, Black Widow enters the company's factory, slits a middle manager's throat, and later exits as an explosion decimates the workplace. Indeed, collateral damage to innocents often results when they are unfortunate enough to

Using a utilitarian calculus, Daredevil contemplates the morality of human sacrifice on the path to justice. (*Daredevil: Dark Reign; The List* #1, Andy Diggle and Robert de la Torre, Marvel, 2009)

be in the way on the path to justice. In *Scarecrow: Year One,* Batman and Robin tear through a town looking for Scarecrow, leaving numerous people injured in their wake.

> BATMAN: We did it by the numbers.
> ROBIN: Yeah, well it's a big city . . .
> BATMAN: Meaning?
> ROBIN (jokingly): If we're gonna beat up the whole town . . . I'd like to bring my lunch.

Despite personal codes as to whether and when to kill, heroes are often found deliberating about whether a particular situation is so extreme as to be an exception to the rule. Green Arrow embraces lethal force as a response to harms done directly to his family in *Justice League: Cry for Justice.* In this miniseries, he is put on trial for the vigilante killing of Prometheus, who had attempted a genocidal plot to destroy Star City. Green Arrow falls out of favor in the superhuman community; even his secessionist team members determined that he went too far in killing, rather than capturing, Prometheus. The members of the Justice League confront Green Arrow, asking, "Is this what we've become? Executioners?" Green Arrow responds, "That bastard deserved to die." Flash retorts, "It's not your call to make. It's not even our call. We're the Justice League not the Vengeance

League!" However, Green Arrow believes the killing a just response to genocide—particularly a genocidal event that resulted in the mutilation of his son, Red Arrow, and the murder of his granddaughter, Lian.

Cry for Justice prompted an extensive discussion among fans on the ethics of killing. Some fans suggested that Green Arrow is no longer a "hero" because he allowed his emotions to dictate his path to justice—killing Prometheus in response to the death of his granddaughter. For example, a commenter on the DC Message Boards states, "[S]hooting Prometheus in the head by you, Green Arrow, is not justice. It's vengeance. There's a difference. . . . So, Ollie. You are now a vigilante killer. You are a criminal." Others argue that Green Arrow's behavior was justified, and even laudable. One commenter stated, "In my opinion, it was both vengeance and justice. . . . Prometheus deserved to die, and I completely understand the emotional pain Ollie suffered from him." And still another appreciated the moral questions raised by Green Arrow's actions:

> One of the things I enjoy about comics is the explorations of good and evil, justice and heroism and corruption and vengeance. I know what I believe in, but I'm not bothered by reading stories about characters who cross lines I wouldn't or who live in those ethically murky areas.

Contextualized Justice

In *Daredevil: The Devil's Hand*, Daredevil (a.k.a. Matt Murdock) expresses his regret at the lawlessness and corruption that is rampant in New York City. He states, "The forces of law in this city have become the forces of injustice. . . . [W]ithout justice, this city will tear itself apart." Daredevil has taken control of the underground group of former assassins known as "the Hand" and is prepared to use them for good against the forces of evil. They gather in a shadowy cavern, with red hues outlining the devil-horned costumes. In his clarion call to the group, he shouts, "They think they can kill with impunity. They think they have nothing to be afraid of. They are wrong! We shall be the thing to fear! And fear us they shall. We shall be the voice of their conscience. We shall be the pain of retribution." As superheroes Iron Fist and Luke Cage look on with horror, Daredevil kills long-time foe Bullseye by impaling him with a *sai*. The *sai* is Elektra's weapon of choice—and, a detail not to be lost on long-time fans, the same weapon that Bullseye used to kill her years earlier (*Daredevil* #181).

The members of the Avengers debate whether Daredevil's behavior is of concern. Luke Cage states that Daredevil is "setting himself up as judge, jury and executioner" while Iron Fist muses that that is what superheroes do every day. Though Daredevil's position is a rather explicit example of vengeance—one that fans would presumably clamor for—the reception to the story has been lukewarm. The problem appears to be that Daredevil is "normally" a more nuanced crime fighter, not prone to use fatal methods to protect the people of his New York neighborhood, Hell's Kitchen.[39]

Here, readers are expressing what we consider "contextualized justice." This is the tendency of readers to make judgments regarding "justice" according to whether or not the behavior fits the mythology of the hero(es). In this way, justice is relative—some behaviors, such as killing, are acceptable for some characters but not others. For example, readers generally accept that the Punisher routinely seeks death against his enemies but are horrified by the prospect of Superman, Spider-Man, or Daredevil doing the same, regardless of the crime committed.

One blog post expresses dissatisfaction with the Daredevil storyline as follows,

> *Shadowland*, after eight months of main-title build-up and one issue of its own, is stupid and ham-fisted garbage.... Matt Murdock loses it and agrees to become the new ruler of The Hand and acts somewhat more "hardcore" than he's generally known for, while his friends wring their hands on the sidelines and endlessly discuss "what to do about Matt because he's lost it this time for sure!"[40]

The inherent goodness of the hero is of paramount importance in judging his or her behavior, with the understanding that no superhero is perfectly good all the time. In this light, the punishment of the offender should fit the hero and his/her mythology rather than the crime or the criminal. In fact, some of the most vitriolic responses from fans arise when a hero is found to be acting "out of character."

For example, on a website discussing the *Civil War* storyline involving Tony Stark's (a.k.a. Iron Man) transformation from a "major hero that advocated freedom" to a "fascist" advocating detention of superheroes that refuse to reveal themselves and work alongside the government, a reader remarks, "The problem for me is that they have characters acting totally opposite to their established selves."[41]

Another killing by a superhero startled the DC Universe and comic fans alike. In *Superman: Sacrifice,* Wonder Woman (a.k.a. Diana Prince) murdered villain Maxwell Lord. Wonder Woman is an Amazonian princess from the island of Themyscira and a reluctant warrior most known for her aversion to violence and reliance on diplomacy. As an ambassador of peace, and blessed by the gods, Wonder Woman uses her powers to fight for justice—only using force as a last resort.[42] In a preemptive strike, Wonder Woman, resident diplomat of the Justice League of America, resorted to lethal force to eliminate the threat posed by villain Maxwell Lord. Wonder Woman snapped Lord's neck after learning that Lord utilized "Brother MK I" (a powerful surveillance device originally created by Batman) to take control of Superman's mind. Lord taunted Wonder Woman by stating that he would not relinquish control of Superman's mind and the only way he could be stopped would be if he were killed. Lord points out that if he can control Superman, and all other heroes as well, then anyone can.

The story provoked much debate among fans over the proper use of deadly force among heroes. What is clear is that readers take these actions seriously—even though they are perpetrated in a fictional universe. In 2005, IGN website posted its "Defending Wonder Woman" article offering justification for Wonder Woman's actions, basically suggesting that her Amazonian culture (the "warrior way") mandates that she destroy an enemy that could otherwise not be stopped. Though most readers agreed that Wonder Woman made the right decision to end Maxwell Lord's life, hundreds of letters to the site prompted a follow-up post eight days later titled "Defending Maxwell Lord."[43]

Still, other readers were disappointed in Wonder Woman's actions and felt that the killing was contrary to her nature. For example, one focus group participant expresses the transgressive pleasure in violence, but also acknowledges that if the violence is inconsistent with the character traits of the hero, then it is ultimately unsatisfying: "I don't deny there's a bit of a monster in each of us, and it's fun to see the monster, and sometimes meeting the monster means watching Wonder Woman rotating Max Lord's head around. And in that particular case, I thought it was hackneyed

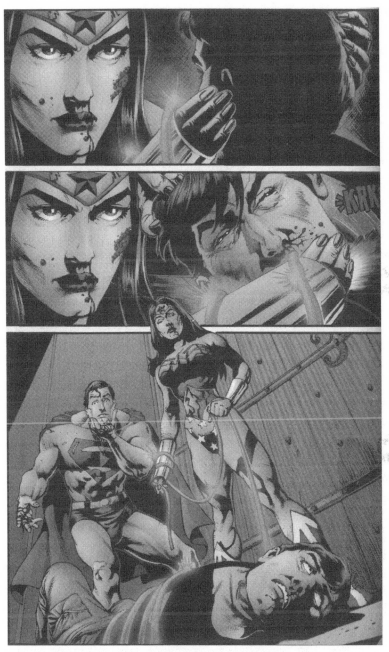

In a rare implementation of deadly force, Wonder Woman kills Maxwell Lord, ultimately neutralizing his threat to humankind. (*Wonder Woman* #219, Greg Rucka, Rags Morales, David Lopez, Tom Derenick, Georges Jeanty, and Karl Kerschl, DC, 2005)

storytelling."[44] Another commenter offered alternatives that would have incapacitated Lord, rather than killed him. On the online Comic Vine discussion board, the commenter offered suggestions for incapacitation, then stated,

> Is my ranting about this going to change anything? No. Am I *that* upset about it? To a degree. Did I lose a certain amount of respect for Wonder Woman? A small amount, yes. . . . Now of course, I can here [sic] fans saying, "DC's no-kill policy is outdated." I disagree, but if others think so (and I know some do), that is fine.[45]

What may have raised the ire of some readers was the way in which Wonder Woman was unapologetic about her actions. For example, in a story arc titled "Affirmative Defense," Wonder Woman states, "I made my decision. I stand by it as the proper one." An entry on the Comixology website explains the controversy of the killing, placing the discussion in the larger context of American notions of crime and justice,

> When Wonder Woman killed the villain Maxwell Lord during the Infinite Crisis storyline, battle lines were drawn by fans as to whether or not this was a consistent action for the character. One group claimed she was a warrior and did what she needed to do for the greater good. Another pointed to her lovingness or some other abstract part of her character to say that this action was abominable. . . . The closest we can get to guessing how she should of [sic] reacted are two competing lines of American thought: the concept of martial order for the greater good as afforded to the police, even though this is arguably a case of more direct murder since he was restrained, or the traditional superheroic ideal that killing is never justified.[46]

Again, the mythology of the character factors into the way fans receive characters' decisions about how to achieve justice. One of our focus group participants suggested that Wolverine's particular approach to violence made him relatable as a character. He states,

> [Wolverine] kills people, but he's not a killer. To separate that out, I mean that he only kills people when he has to and if he doesn't have to, he

won't. . . . I can't relate to [other characters like Superman and Shazam] who I both like, because I grew up in the streets, saw a lot of gang violence, stuff like that. For me, Wolverine was more a guy I knew. You know, you've got to fight your way out of a situation.[47]

Similarly, with regard to heroes' vigilantism, one focus group member states,

You know, we all want these characters, these merciless characters, to be our heroes, but then you really stop to think about it and it doesn't work because everyone has a little Joker in them, we all have Joker in us, and everyone has a little Punisher in us, but do you really think people want to go into that place, to be that person?[48]

Interestingly, we found that most readers in our focus groups emphasize that comic books are "merely" fiction, existing apart from the reader's morality. Sensational responses to crime are more tolerated in the fictional world than in the real world, yet a certain grounding, relatability, believability, and internal consistency also reign. Fans want exciting plots that toy with the potential for violence, and sometimes deliver on that violence, but in ways that fit the established character formulas they have come to know and love. Taken further, comic book justice is individualized and even idiosyncratic justice, a kind of fantasy in which one vigilante's worldview trumps all and is not negotiated by various parties in a bulky criminal justice system. And because justice belongs to one hero—one character— the reader can explore it as *this* or *that hero's* justice, experiencing it without having to necessarily condone it in any real-world sense.

Focus group participants, online comics bloggers, and discussants routinely exhibit an emotional thrill in following their long-loved heroes along their paths to justice, for better or worse. It is often the emotional and dramatic brinkmanship of whether a hero will kill or not kill a foe, given his or her character development, that acts as a visceral experience for readers.

"TAKE DOWN THE BAD GUYS, SAVE THE GIRL"

GENDER, SEXUAL ORIENTATION, AND COMIC BOOK JUSTICE

In 2005, DC Comics' *Villains United* introduced Scandal Savage, the daughter of supervillain Vandal Savage. Scandal is among a rogue band of six villains available for hire as a mercenary team. In *Villains United*, Scandal rebuffs the advances of her teammate, Deadshot, and proclaims that she is a lesbian. In the final issue of the series, Scandal's girlfriend is revealed to be Knockout, a mole in the rival villain "society." In the subsequent *Secret Six: Six Degrees of Devastation*, Scandal feuds with her supervillain father, Vandal, who is insisting she father a child by a man of his choosing.

The Scandal Savage plot can be read as commentary about superheroes, supervillains, and power. Scandal is consistently thwarted by the men in her life, and at least one of them, her father, views her primarily as a means of procreation. In one scene, Deadshot sleeps with her girlfriend, Knockout, and she kicks him in the face, screaming, "Betrayer! How could you? How could you?" She also assaults housemate Catman as he attempts to mediate the situation. From there, she moves on to her father's house, where he is determined that she produce an heir with the unattractive Dr. Psycho. When her father and Dr. Psycho are defeated, at least in the short term, Scandal jokes, "A tubal ligation is in order, I think." Despite Scandal's attempts to live on her own terms as a lesbian and leader of her own villain squadron, her behavior skirts the patriarchal order and, as a result the male villains turn her body, and the body of her girlfriend, into contested sites.

Contemporary comic books open up possibilities in terms of the gender and sexual orientation of their characters. In recent years depictions of superheroes and crimefighters have gone beyond the white, male historical standard, with minority, lesbian, gay, bisexual, and female characters becoming more prevalent in best-selling comic books. At the same time, despite a technical inclusion of diverse characters, as is evident in the just-described comic book plot involving Scandal, underlying messages about crime and justice emerge in a world dominated by heterosexual, white males.

In this chapter, we are concerned with comic books as cultural artifacts illustrating the intersection among sexual orientation, gender, victimization, and crime fighting. This becomes particularly important given that mediums such as comic books can be considered a reflection of broader social contexts—gendered and hierarchical patterns that are particularly pronounced due to the graphic nature of the medium. Put simply, along the path to justice these characters operate in the context of the male, white, heterosexual realm, with women primarily portrayed as young, sexual objects in need of protection.[1]

We begin our analysis with a focus on victimization and the paternalistic undercurrent running through many contemporary comic books. In order to understand this dynamic, we situate our analysis in the perspectives that gender is a fluid concept and that crime and victimization are enacted in gender-specific ways. We discuss the hypermasculine nature of male heroes and the way females must negotiate their crime fighting in ways that express femininity in culturally approved ways. We suggest that messages about heroism in the context of a patriarchal, or male-dominated, society contribute to larger notions of crime and justice, and we examine how readers receive these messages and interpret the relatively narrow range of "who" and "what kind" of person may be a hero and who are the anticipated victims.

We acknowledge that the lack of diversity in comic books does not lie solely with individual creators, writers, and artists but rather is influenced by a number of factors, including editorial decisions and industry standards. For example, mainstream comic book content remained dictated by the Comics Code until the 1980s. Specifically, the Code required adherence to the heterosexual norm and forbade deviation from the norm in terms of marriage and sexual relationships. It wasn't until 1989 that gay people were positively portrayed. The modifications to the Code included the following with regard to the depiction of adult sexuality: "Scenes and dialogue involving adult relationships will be presented with good taste, sensitivity, and in a manner which will be considered acceptable by a mass audience. Primary human sexual characteristics will never be shown. Graphic sexual activity will never be depicted."[2] Through the Code, and the dominance of heterosexual perspectives in American cultural discourse in the twentieth century in general, comic books would remain the domain of an explicit and uncontested heterosexuality until the relaxing of the Code in the late 1980s.

The persistence of sexist and heteronormative depictions in comics, therefore, may stem from a variety of factors, including the cultural history of comic books, the fact that the industry is still largely dominated by men, and expectations of certain types of content by fans themselves. At the same time, the loosening of the Code has resulted in some shifts in the possibility for alternative imaginings related to sexual orientation and gender, suggesting that content is slowly diversifying.

Protecting the Victims

Although most criminological theories focus on motivations for criminal behavior, one branch of criminology, "victimology," is devoted to the study of victims and patterns of victimization. Victimology gained traction in criminology during the 1970s. It was during this time that various social movements such as the women's rights movement, the civil rights movement, and the gay rights movement began to bring attention to issues of inequality and discrimination that often manifest as violence directed toward minorities. Studies in victimology have consistently demonstrated that victimization is not a random process.[3] For example, victimologists have discerned patterns of victimization by type of person: younger people, minorities, and males are more likely to be victimized than their counterparts, while women are more likely to be victims of sexual assault and victimized by nonstrangers than their male counterparts. Further, property crimes occur more frequently than violent crimes, and victimization is more likely to occur in urban areas than in rural or suburban areas.

Despite the relatively consistent patterns of victimization, media accounts are frequently replete with misrepresentations. Researchers have shown that the news media overemphasize violent crimes and focus on sensational cases that resonate emotionally with viewers and readers.[4] Likewise, studies have found that fictional media often contain similar misrepresentations.[5] Despite the reality that violent victimization is more likely to be the fate of young urban minority males, studies have shown that media news stories as well as entertainment disproportionately feature white women as victims.[6]

In our sample of comic books, males are frequently portrayed as victims; however females are subject to particularly brutal, and at times sadistic, forms of victimization. Subsequently, the message conveyed is that women require particular protection from the forces of evil. For example, young women are imprisoned and experimented on in *Black Widow: The Things They Say about Her*. The Gyncorp Corporation patents biotechnology and is a relic of the Cold War Russian organization that created super-soldiers, from which Black Widow originates. In *Wolverine: The Brotherhood*, a sex slavery cult imprisons young women and abuses them in the backwoods of Oregon. In another example, a wife and child are taken hostage by Razor-Fist, a villain operating on behalf of villain Norman Osborn, as they flee the destruction of the floating city of Asgard in *Siege: Captain America*. Young girls and children are also shown being kidnapped in *Sam & Twitch*, *New Mutants: Return of Legion*, and *Batman: Streets of Gotham*. And, in *X-Men: Messiah Complex*, the Scarlet Witch obliterates the X-gene, thus making mutantkind (which forms the X-Men) an extinct group. Predator X, a villain seeking to maintain this extinct status, kills all infants in Cooperstown, Alaska, to prevent the rumored birth of the last mutant baby. These events reach a pinnacle in the subsequent saga of Cable, who protects one of the last-born mutant children, Hope, after the mutant genocide. Cable is depicted as a hypermasculine defender that protects Hope through stealth violence and time travel. His outfit includes a special harness that allows the baby girl to attach to his chest.

The notion that women are in need of male protection is reinforced through many mainstream comic books, such as in the marital relationship of Luke Cage and Jessica Jones. Though Jessica is a former superheroine and private detective, she becomes Luke's protected wife, sent to Canada with their baby for safe-keeping during the events of *Civil War*.

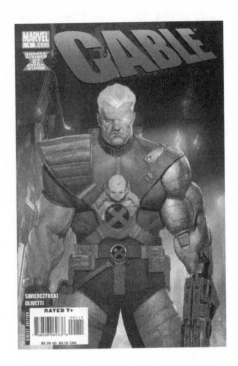

Hypermasculine superhero Cable
protects baby Hope, the messiah of the
mutant race. (*Cable* #1, volume 2, Duane
Swiercynski and Ariel Olivetti, Marvel,
2008)

She is later concerned when Luke joins the New Avengers for fear that this
will take him away from the family too often. Sharon Carter, ex-field agent
of S.H.I.E.L.D. and on-and-off girlfriend of Captain America, stays behind
ostensibly to hold down the fort at headquarters as Captain America and
the rest of his team run a rescue mission in Mars. Unfortunately, while
doing so, she is attacked by members of the Shadow Council (*Secret Avengers* #1), indicating that she is not only incapable of being effective in the
field but also incapable of securing headquarters.

In *Red Robin*, the criminal organization known as the League of Assassins is at war with a rival criminal organization, the Spider Council. Red
Robin (a.k.a. Tim Drake) is traveling the world, working to take down
both. While he is overseas, Lucius Fox sends his daughter Tam to bring Red
Robin back to Gotham City. While Red Robin is battling the assassins, Tam
finds herself in danger from the Spider Council. As Red Robin swoops in
to save Tam, he thinks, "It feels good. No compromises. Take down the bad
guys. Save the girl." He's rewarded with a kiss by Tam, who blushes with
embarrassment. In *Identity Crisis*, Green Arrow attempts to shield his wife,

Black Canary, from the aftermath of Sue Dibny's murder, even though she is also a superhero in her own right. The story features numerous glosses on Sue's death as symbolic of men's failure to protect their wives and girlfriends from violence and injustice.[7]

Female superheroes are often given conflicted and emotional character flaws in order to create plot situations in which they need to be protected. In *Runaways*, Nico is one of the only Japanese American leaders of a superhero team, yet she is regularly shown experiencing emotional insecurity and the inability to identify what she is feeling in certain situations. She is depicted clinging to men in her life for emotional protection. Similarly, Daredevil describes Elektra as "an amazing woman. She feels things very deeply. But sometimes—if I can put it like this—that can make her reckless" (*Ultimate Elektra: Devil's Due*). Accordingly, Daredevil must keep an eye out for Elektra, standing ready to come to her aid.

In addition to protecting women and children, male superheroes must also ward off potential threats to their masculinity that may result in devastating consequences. In one instance, a defeat at the hands of the Hulk propelled superhero Hank Pym to domestic violence. In *The Ultimates: Super-Human*, an argument ensues between Hank (a.k.a Giant-Man, Ant-Man) and Janet Pym (a.k.a. Wasp). As they prepare to celebrate with Tony Stark after a series of media interviews about the defeat of the Hulk by Thor and Captain America (a.k.a. Steve Rogers), Hank reveals his jealousy of Janet. Feeling "small," Giant-Man derides Janet about her outfit: "You don't want me to tell you what you look like. Are the push-up bra and high heels for Rogers' benefit or for Tony Stark's by the way? . . . You've turned me into a laughingstock."

After exchanging insults, Hank hits Janet across the face, drawing blood. As he apologizes, Janet strikes back. The panels highlight each blow, giving the reader a closer sense of proximity to the violence. In the final panel, he expresses regret, but a wider perspective showing the physical disarray surrounding Hank indicates that it is far too late.

In one of our (all-male) focus groups, participants discussed their reactions to the domestic violence incident between Hank and Janet. Reactions to the story were overwhelmingly positive, with readers saying that portraying domestic violence in such a "realistic" fashion made the story more interesting. Many felt that the story was realistic because they had witnessed domestic violence in their own lives.

Hank Pym strikes his wife, Janet, the first blow in a domestic battle. (*The Ultimates: Super-Human*, Mark Millar and Bryan Hitch, Marvel, 2005)

PARTICIPANT: My first reaction . . . was shock . . . this was done more real-
istcic . . . and uh, it was done really, the way I had seen scenes like that
personally.

ss: In real life?

PARTICIPANT: Yeah, growing up. It seemed very real to me . . . the words that
were said, the way he reacted, the jealousy, the insecurity on his part, the
flirting on her part.[8]

Much of the discussion focused on Hank and his reaction to feeling "small"
and powerless as a man. Mentioning that the comic book played on the
concept of "Giant-Man," many participants found that Hank's reaction to
the threat to his masculinity was one of the strongest components of the
story. The participants recounted the ways in which Hank suffered blows
to his masculinity. For example, Hank was easily "taken out" by the Hulk
and then subjected to media scrutiny that was ultimately embarrassing for
the hero. The male readers in this focus group were most engaged with
Hank, the threat to his masculinity, and the way he should be treated by
the superhero community; the participants were less focused on discussing
Janet and her victimization. This ability to relate to the male characters is a
recurring theme in our research and may be contrasted against the "relatability" of many of the female characters for male readers, a point we discuss in more detail later in this chapter.

One storyline featuring antigay victimization received a flurry of attention from readers and the press (*Green Lantern: Hate Crime*).[9] In this story
arc, Green Lantern (a.k.a. Kyle Rayner) receives a call indicating that his

gay assistant, Terry Berg, has been attacked by perpetrators who saw him involved in a public display of affection with his boyfriend, David. While David escapes, Terry suffers a skull fracture, two broken legs, a collapsed lung, and a number of broken ribs. In the aftermath, several things happen that expose societal attitudes toward gay men and these types of attacks. In one scene, Terry's father refuses David access to Terry in the hospital, saying that David was the cause of the crime and had made Terry gay. In another scene, an investigating police officer suggests a gay panic defense to Terry, implying that Terry's flirtations provoked the attack. The officer also asked Terry if he was using drugs at the time. Meanwhile, Green Lantern is angry about the police response and proceeds to physically assault one of the offenders in jail until he confesses and names his accomplices. Green Lantern finds the accomplices and beats them, but stops short of killing them.[10]

In an analysis of reader response to the issue, Valerie Palmer-Mehta and Kellie Hay found that five of thirty-one published responses were dissatisfied with the *Green Lantern* hate crime plot because of its focus on gay issues, with one reader expressing concern as to the effect the story might have on children. Six of the letters objected to the vigilante violence Green Lantern engaged in and felt that he should not be reduced to using such brutal tactics. Over half of the letters were appreciative of the story and labeled DC Comics as "progressive" for taking on the issue of violence against gays, and one letter writer even shared his own account of antigay victimization.[11] Understanding these gendered dynamics and the various reactions to them requires a consideration of the ways in which gender and sexual orientation are accomplished with regard to crime and justice in a patriarchal society.

Holy Masculinity, Batman!

In her groundbreaking book *Gender Trouble: Feminism and the Subversion of Identity*, Judith Butler contends that gender is not made up of essential identities but rather is *performative*, and only exists in the process of doing.[12] Butler is rejecting the notion that gender should be viewed as a simple binary connected to one's biological sex. Similarly, criminological theorist James Mersserschmidt explains that gender, race, and sexual orientation are not merely static labels but identities that are actively accomplished within a particular social context.[13] Our physical appearance, style, relationships, and behaviors are enacted in specific social contexts that at times reinforce the dominant social order or may challenge it. In essence, these ways of "doing gender" reflect or challenge the power structure from which they emerge. Crime and crime fighting are enacted in a patriarchal, or male-dominated, context that entails specific gendered performances.

It is in this context in which "hegemonic masculinities" are performed. Sociologist R. W. Connell describes hegemonic masculinity as involving forms of masculinity and femininity that are hierarchical, emphasizing the dominance of men over women. Connell states, "'[H]egemonic masculinity' is always constructed in relation to various subordinated masculinities as well as in relation to women."[14] Hegemonic masculinities are cultural ideals that represent what it means to be a "real man" or a "real woman" in society. For example, hegemonic masculinity is heterosexual, while subordinated masculinity is homosexual. Femininity that challenges traditional gender expectations, for example women who are independent, strong, and assertive, is subordinated to femininity that reinforces "the interests and desires of men."[15]

We suggest that comic books are cultural artifacts that contribute to the cultural construction of hegemonic masculinities. Specifically, we suggest that comic books contribute to and reflect ideological notions of "who" and "what type" of person may be considered heroic. In fact, Connell writes, "Indeed the winning hegemony often involves the creation of models of masculinity which are quite specifically fantasy figures, such as the film characters played by Humphrey Bogart, John Wayne and Sylvester Stallone."[16] These characters exemplify contemporary masculinity through their sex appeal, toughness, and muscular stature. Further, Connell points out that "maleness" is more than just the presence of male chromosomes. She states, "[T]he physical sense of maleness . . . involves size and shape, habits of posture and movement, particular skills and the lack of others, the image of one's own body, the way it is presented to other people and the ways they respond to it."[17] Thus, the physical sense of maleness (and femaleness) is consistently negotiated through social action. This process of "doing gender" is enacted in a patriarchal world.

The patriarchal world of comic books is exemplified through an examination of one of the most tragic dramas in comic book history, according to many readers, the death of Peter Parker's girlfriend, Gwen Stacy, in 1973 in the pages of *The Amazing Spider-Man* #121. Among die-hard comic book fans, the death sent shock waves through networks of young male readers. They had been vicariously delighted that the gawky Peter Parker had a girlfriend, but were emotionally distraught by her death during one of Spider-Man's rows with his arch-nemesis, Green Goblin. As comics scholar Arnold Blumberg writes,

> The death of Gwen Stacy cannot be overestimated in terms of its historical importance to the comic book medium and the superhero genre in particular. As vast and cosmic in scope as some superhero adventures can be, one of the genre's greatest and most tragic moments was a tale told of one young girl—an intimate, heart-rending story about the death of a superhero's one true love.[18]

This notion of "a superhero's one true love" is construed from the explicitly male point of view of the comic book, written for the reader to identify with Peter Parker as Spider-Man. The tragedy squarely reinforces the "norm" in comic books as a construct of male loss of a female companion—who had been characterized in traditionally feminine ways as sweet, kind, accommodating, and Peter's spiritual center. Such a loss fits into adolescent notions of awakening and self-becoming, not just for Peter Parker but for comics as a whole. Blumberg explains,

> The death of Gwen Stacy was the end of innocence . . . when a defeated hero could not save the girl, when fantasy merged uncomfortably with reality, and mortality was finally visited on the world of comics.[19]

The death of Gwen Stacy is a prime example of what scholars have called a gendered gaze—the story is told from the vantage point of a male and reinforces the notion that men act and women merely appear. Journalist and critic Douglas Wolk explains that the "maleness" of contemporary comic books is "self-perpetuated," partially a result of an industry that has been dominated by white, male creators.[20] This created a fan culture with expectations of male insularity in terms of how characters interacted and how plots played out. He recalls that in the early 1990s, Marvel produced a voluminous document outlining how the company could better connect with female readers, ultimately revealing that they had only two titles that were created for female readers: *Barbie* and *Barbie Fashion*. More recently, DC attempted to market Wonder Woman to female readers by having writer George Perez shift the character to make her more identifiable to women by incorporating Greek goddesses into Wonder Woman's genealogy and making reference to "environmental and social sustainability."[21] Although there was a slight uptick in female readership, it did not last after Perez's tenure.[22] Other attempts at targeting a young, female readership have also failed, such as DC's short-lived Minx imprint that released titles such as "The Plain Janes" and "Re-Gifters" in a digest format.

The above is perhaps not surprising as historically, it was virtually unheard of (with the exception of Wonder Woman) for women as crime fighters to carry their own title for any length of time. Women were more frequently portrayed, according to journalist and writer Charlie Anders, as "tagalongs, also-rans, and girlfriends" who try to marry superheroes.[23] Classic Spider-Man's underlying romantic plot centers on whether his ideal mate is the soft-spoken and patient Gwen Stacy or the more outspoken and independent Mary Jane. Successful journalist Lois Lane melts into submission when it comes to her love for Superman. In *Daredevil* history, girlfriend Karen Page represents the emotionally taxing situation of loving a heroin addict, giving Daredevil plenty of opportunity to wrestle with saving her as she succumbs to drugs. And the superheroine Storm was "retconned" (her origin story was expanded) to include her as a girlfriend and mere "distraction" to Black Panther's quest to find his father's killer as a young man. Although they ultimately marry after he becomes King of Wakanda, Black Panther makes it clear that his marriage proposal stems from his loneliness at the throne and is not about Storm's feelings for him and whether the relationship fits into her life (*Black Panther* #14).

We found that mainstream comic books are so frequently male associated, in terms of both content and readership, that many comic book readers consistently expressed a need to justify their consumption of any female-centered titles. For example, one comic book podcast featured hosts that seemed bemused by the simultaneous publication of more than one female-led title. They opened their episode with the following query for the listeners: "This is one of those things, do they need a *Power Girl* series and a *Supergirl* series going on concurrently? [a short pause] . . . and I'm going to say most definitely."[24] The male hosts seemed proud that they accepted the simultaneous publication of two female-led comic book series. The absurdity of their query becomes crystal clear when one recognizes that it would never occur to the hosts to ask whether the audience "needed" a Batman *and* a Superman *and* a Spider-Man *and* a Captain America (and so on) series at the same time.

Another comic book fan podcast gave an overall positive review of the ongoing *Batgirl* title, only after clarifying that the (male) hosts did not read female-centered titles as youths. Further, they explained that while they may have trouble relating to a young woman superhero, they would not have the same trouble relating to a young male superhero (e.g., Blue Beetle) because they had "been there." The hosts spent several minutes expressing their pleasant surprise that the writers made Batgirl "relatable" to the (male) readers, somehow making the character "accessible." However, the hosts did not apply that same level of scrutiny to other titles that feature rather outlandish protagonists such as aliens, zombies, cyborgs, or any number of otherworldly entities that do not resemble twenty-first-century reality on Earth. The hosts explain that they find Batgirl interesting because her vulnerabilities and insecurities are on prominent display. They state, "[I]t's not a male or female thing. . . . [W]e have all been there. . . . [S]he has those moments all the time."[25]

Further, we found the majority of our focus group participants quite willing to admit that there remains significant stigma attached to reading female-centered titles. One focus group participant noted, "I think that is because of the demographics of the readership. I think most males don't want to read a female-centered title. . . . I think there is something, there is a stigma attached to being a male reader of a female comic. . . . [P]eople will joke about it."[26] While acknowledging the stigma, they are also quick to note the irrationality of it. For example, another participant stated, "There is definitely a resistance . . . a very loud . . . I wouldn't say the whole fanboy movement, but there's definitely an element there, that like you said, oh you can't read female books, that's like gay or something . . . oh but seeing two guys in tights beating up each other, like that's not homoerotic?"[27] There tended to be a consensus among the focus group participants that men are more loyal readers than women because the depiction of women in comics tends to be "sexualized" and therefore alienating to women.

Fighting Crime like a Man

Male crime fighters in comic books sport a hyped-up version of masculinity, or hypermasculinity, with such characteristics as a brawny stature and a macho orientation.[28] For these characters, hegemonic masculinity is often represented through body image; hypermasculine heroes that represent confidence, strength, and power. The necessity of brawn to the crime fighter is illustrated in Captain America's origin story, retold in *Steve Rogers: Super Soldier*. Steve Rogers, an emaciated 98-pound weakling rejected from the army, is transformed into a muscular superpower after ingesting the super-soldier serum provided by a secret military project codenamed Project: Rebirth. Without the serum, Rogers was not only unsuitable as a superhero; he was also unfit to serve his country.

At times, the muscular features take on astonishing proportions. In *Punisher vs. Bullseye*, Bullseye is hired by the mob to take out the Punisher. The cover illustration shows Punisher's brawny physique with larger-than-life weaponry to match. Similarly, Cable's bulging muscles and the postapocalyptic weaponry strapped onto his large frame in *X-Men: Second Coming* (#1) serve to emphasize his role as a protector figure to one of the last mutants of a dying breed. In the character guide at the back of the comic, Cable's exceedingly muscular arms are drawn to be twice the width of his head. In Marvel's *The Call of Duty: The Brotherhood*, a tribute to the first responders of 9/11, the firefighter protagonist has been described by one critic as "a heartthrob with Ken doll good looks, who battles increasingly outlandish and even paranormal threats."

Frequently, superhero masculinity is characterized by scarred bodies indicating that heroes are battle tested. For example, Batman is often shown shirtless with fresh wounds and scars from previous altercations. Alfred, Bruce Wayne's long-time butler, is frequently charged with mending his wounds. Similarly, in *Nightwing: The Great Leap*, a series of images show the scars on Nightwing's body as he dresses in preparation for confronting Two-Face.

To fight crime, male heroes are expected to *look* heroic, to maintain a hypermasculine physique, and to "do crime fighting" in a gendered way that privileges heterosexuality. This is demonstrated by the ways in which sexual orientation remains the source of jokes as gays tend to be marginalized within the world of the comic books. In some mainstream comic books, antigay asides are common. For example, in an issue of *Dark Wolverine*, Dark Hawkeye (a.k.a Lester; the former Bullseye) approaches Dark Wolverine (a.k.a. Dakin) before a combat operation saying, "Well, look at you," and Dark Wolverine quips, "Yes, do. Don't worry, I won't tell anyone you want to tap my . . . assets." In *Batman and Robin* (#6), when villain Flamingo enters the scene Robin quips, "I was expecting scary, not gay." And, in *Human Target*, the protagonist's sidekick is driving with a client, in a bearded disguise. Chance, as the narrator, says as an aside, "Probably not the first time Bruno's been out with a beard."

However, the past decade has shown a willingness to integrate gay and lesbian crime fighters into the mainstream. For example, the first decade of the 2000s has seen the rise of the gay superhero in characters such as Midnighter, Apollo, and Batwoman. These contemporary characters negotiate sexual orientation in an environment characterized by hypermasculinity and hyperfemininity dominated by hegemonic masculinity, yet remain for the most part confident in their crime-fighting abilities and secure in their sexual orientation.[29] For example, in *Midnighter: Fait Accompli/Anthem*, the ongoing gay relationship between superhero members of the crime-fighting team the Authority, Midnighter and the Apollo, continues. Introduced in 1998 and wed in 2002 in the pages of *The Authority: Transfer of Power*, the couple represents one of the most stable and enduring gay relationships in comics. The two dote on each other in the opening pages of *Anthem*. In a plot to thwart terrorists from controlling the oil market in the Middle East, references to Midnighter's sexual orientation abound.

> OLIVIA (villain): Please, if . . . if you let me live, you . . . can do anything you want to me.
> MIDNIGHTER: Sorry sister. I'm pretty adaptable, but I don't swing that way.

And, when the Midnighter encounters Shock and Awe, two-headed Siamese twins in one body, one twin makes a quip that the Midnighter look great in leather, and he responds, "Save it sister—this one zigs when he ought to zag." Interestingly, the "ought" in this statement seems to refer to heterosexual normativity and to Midnighter's sense of his own difference as potential liability or weakness in the context of crime-fighting masculinity. It could be interpreted as a break in character in the sense that the Midnighter tends to be proud and upfront about his sexual orientation, not apologetic.

Similarly, Rictor and Shatterstar, two male mutant superheroes, embraced and kissed each other after Scattershot emerged from being controlled by a mysterious villain named Cortex, in the August 2009 issue of *X-Factor*. Witnessing the display of affection, Guido, also known as the Strong Guy, quips, "Uh-kay. Didn't see that comin." The subplot about Rictor and Shatterstar is not picked up again until a few issues later (#49) when Guido and Rictor are driving as Scattershot sleeps off exhaustion. Guido, Rictor's friend, wonders why he didn't know about the relationship and accuses Rictor of merely reacting to the recent break-up by his former girlfriend. Rictor reveals that he had been involved with Shatterstar before the relationship with his ex-girlfriend, effectively disclosing his bisexuality. Rictor explains, "Look . . . what a guy does . . . who he is . . . it's his business." Although Guido is slightly uncomfortable, as pointed out by Shatterstar, who wakes up during the conversation, this seems to be a suitable resolution to the situation and implies that Guido accepts his friend Rictor for who he is.

The introduction of gay characters, though, is not met without resistance. In the introduction to *Green Lantern: Brother's Keeper*, writer Judd Winick explains his rationale for a story that featured a hate crime committed against Green Lantern's gay assistant. Winick acknowledges that there was some backlash to the mere presentation of a gay character in the story arc. He states that "reaction to the story ran the gamut" from responses suggesting that sexuality (or rather homosexuality) is an inappropriate topic for comics to the accusation that the author was "pushing an agenda."[30] As for his motivation for the story, Winick states, "Almost all the heroes . . . were white, male, heterosexual, Americans. That isn't the world we live in . . . [T]he world we write about is an enormously diverse one; it should at least compete with our reality."[31]

Though the presence of these characters arguably represents a certain degree of acceptance of diversity, there remains a tension around the portrayal of gay characters as crime fighters. This is exemplified by the 2002 release of the western comic *Rawhide Kid: Slap Leather*, published by Marvel. Characterized by some as a step backwards in the portrayal of gays and lesbians, the Rawhide Kid is obsessed with fashion and home décor, dispels advice about moisturizers, wears fashionable sunglasses from Paris, and shows off his body by doing calisthenics in his underwear and target-shooting in his chaps, sans pants. Rawhide Kid was described by one blog commentator as "a [l]imp-wristed caricature, [who] embodies every homosexual stereotype, [and acts as a] [s]tunt re-creation of an old Marvel Western star whose homosexuality is the joke-premise of . . . [the] mini-series."[32] Sharpshooter Rawhide Kid shows up to save the day in a town in which the sheriff is consistently emasculated and incompetent at defending the town against the deadly Cisco Pike gang. Rawhide Kid is welcomed to the town by the sheriff and deputized.

Although Rawhide Kid is effective in fighting the outlaw Cisco Pike gang on behalf of the innocent townspeople, he is clearly depicted as a man outside the norms and values of that town. Once he has saved the town from the gang, he moves on despite invitations from the sheriff and his paramour to remain and settle down. His reasons consist of vague references to being a tumbleweed at heart, a common trope in the larger western genre, but an alternative interpretation suggests that there is no role for a gay cowboy in the fabric of a nineteenth-century western town, where the church is the central institution and the definition of manhood is courage under fire and a lady waiting at home. Considering that the town mayor is named Bush (with an overt resemblance to the former president), who responds to the Cisco Pike gang by saying, "Terrorism will not be tolerated and the evil ones will be punished," it is safe to assume the nineteenth-century frontier town is being likened to Bush-era conservatism, a status quo that merits preservation by those who would fight against outlaws.

While some have commented that *Slap Leather* reinforces gay stereotypes, others find in *Slap Leather* a challenge to hegemonic masculinity in the portrayal of a hero that "defends queer masculinity, and punishes those who commit anti-sissy crime."[33] Certainly, Rawhide Kid is comfortable in his own skin and it is others who are confronted and challenged to question their own assumptions and stereotypes surrounding heroic gunslingers. Arguably in camp style, *Slap Leather's* Rawhide Kid fully embraces the gunfighter culture by being the most skilled and accomplished gunslinger around, while also challenging traditional notions of masculinity and embodying numerous gay stereotypes.[34]

The debates over whether or not gay characters are legitimate heroes reflect our larger cultural values surrounding the general acceptance of gays and lesbians. That there would be dissent among some readers about the inclusion of gay heroic crime fighters is not surprising given the history of prejudice and discrimination against gays and lesbians. Specifically, the relationship between gays and lesbians and law enforcement historically has been tumultuous. The criminalization of homosexuality and the erroneous, yet mainstream, perception of homosexuality as a mental illness—spurred in part by the inclusion of homosexuality in early editions of the American Psychiatric Association's Diagnostic and Statistical Manual of Mental Disorders—contributed to the harsh treatment of gays and lesbians. In addition, the police have a sordid history of abuse and harassment toward gays and lesbians.[35] Historically, police raided gay bars and enforced liquor licensing laws in an effort to shut them down.[36] Incidents such as the 1969 police raid on New York City's Stonewall Inn that resulted in days of riots brought awareness to police brutality against gays and sparked the gay rights movement.

Our concept of who is capable of being a hero is tied to the hierarchical notions of hegemonic masculinity and is negotiated over time. Gays and lesbians challenge hegemonic masculinity and pose a threat to the status quo. In addition to the criminalization of gays and lesbians, part of the inability to envision these individuals as legitimate crime fighters stems from institutional forms of discrimination. For example, in the United States, law enforcement agencies historically avoided hiring gays and lesbians as police officers. Since many states do not have laws prohibiting employment discrimination based on sexual orientation, there was no concerted effort to eliminate institutional bias from hiring policies. Even when hired, police officers frequently feel the need to remain closeted to avoid prejudice and discrimination from fellow officers and the community at large. However, over the past several years, some law enforcement agencies have begun to actively recruit gay and lesbian officers and fully integrate them into the force. As a result, there is a cultural opening in which gays and lesbians may be perceived as being as heroic as their crime-fighting heterosexual counterparts. That gay comic book heroes are emerging, and at times remain contested, reflects our cultural ambivalence toward sexual orientation.

Female Crime Fighters

The notion of crime fighting as a historically masculine endeavor is reflected in the challenges that women faced as they entered police work.

Criminologists Susan Martin and Nancy Jurik explain, "Women are perceived as a threat to the men's physical safety, group solidarity, and occupational identity as macho crime fighters. In addition, women's presence undermines the close association of their work with masculinity and men's control over social order."[37] Women have long had a difficult time being accepted into the male-dominated positions of law enforcement. During the 1800s, in their earliest foray into law enforcement, women's work was relegated to female-oriented positions such as serving as jail matrons and caring for women and children. Women in law enforcement were marginalized and faced near-insurmountable employment barriers. Once hired, they were restricted in their duties and underpaid. It would take decades, lawsuits demanding changes in hiring practices, and the momentum of the women's movement for women to become fully integrated into the police force. In fact, it was not until the 1970s that women were allowed to serve as patrol officers.[38]

Female crime fighters must negotiate their crime fighting in a way that embraces "emphasized femininity" while simultaneously demonstrating competence in a role traditionally thought of as the domain of male protectors. In comic books, female crime fighters frequently represent what Connell terms "emphasized femininity," a construction focused on female "sexual receptivity in relation to younger women and motherhood in relation to older women."[39] Here, females comply with more traditional gender expectations such as a focus on domesticity, child care, nurturance, and empathy even while they fight for justice. For example, in *Fantastic Four: Foes,* Sue Reed (a.k.a. Invisible Woman), Reed Richards's (a.k.a. Mr. Fantastic) wife, fulfills traditional gender roles as she takes care of their two children. Additionally, she frequently expresses discontent when she perceives that Reed is paying too much attention to his work and not enough to her. In *Planet Hulk*, the Hulk fights against a despotic ruler who enslaves his people with the help of the ruler's warrior underling Caiera. Though Caiera originally acts as Hulk's ally and bodyguard, the two marry after Hulk becomes king of the planet. She then no longer is shown practicing warriorship and instead takes a submissive, female back seat to the Hulk's imperial duties.

The treatment of women who deviate from traditional gender roles in comic books is a reflection of larger cultural notions regarding the appropriate behavior of women in contemporary society. In their study of media images of marginalized girls and women, criminologists Meda Chesney-Lind and Michele Eliason note, "A review of the media fascination with 'bad girls' and crime provides clear evidence of the assumption that if women begin to question traditional femininity, they run the risk of becoming like men, that is more violent and sexually 'loose' (often conflated with interest and involvement in lesbian activities . . .)."[40] Here, women who deviate, for example, those who are romantically linked with other women, tend to be portrayed as man-like and violent, if not mentally ill. Frequently, the media tend to equate lesbians with masculinity and thus implicate a propensity toward violence. The "lesbian as psychopath" motif was apparent in the portrayal of New York Police Department lieutenant Molly von Richthofen in *Punisher War Zone: The Resurrection of Ma Gnucci*. Molly's personality has somewhat hardened after her initial appearance in the earlier *The Punisher: Welcome Back, Frank*. In both stories, Molly's sexual orientation is central to the plot. In *Welcome Back, Frank*, she rejects the advances of the male police commissioner and is given undesirable assignments. She expresses her disdain to her partner,

> You're the unluckiest cop on the force and I won't sleep my way to the top, which is why they give us lousy jobs like this one. We are expected to fail. The creeps who run this department want us to fail. We can rely on no back-up, no support, nothing—except what we do ourselves.

Molly rails against the misogyny she has faced after years of service with the police department. She states that promotions are rewarded under certain circumstances, "if you're a good little girl and let the chief shove his hand up your skirt" (*Ma Gnucci*). Molly has long been disgusted with her treatment at the department and by the time she reappears in *The Resurrection of Ma Gnucci*, she is exhibiting psychopathic tendencies.

Molly is charged with investigating an Italian Mafia family once believed wiped out by the Punisher. In her personal life, she is consumed with jealousy of her girlfriend, who is bisexual and openly dating men. She violently terrorizes a potential (male) love interest of her girlfriend, bloodies the face of the (female) bartender who dares to speak a kind word to her girlfriend, and, to further cement her psychopathic tendencies, is shown coolly executing a miniature poodle as he urinates on the street.

Molly's violence may be interpreted as rage against the patriarchal constraints under which she operates both at work and at home, and is always infused, at least implicitly, with her sexuality. While Molly is certainly a competent law enforcement officer, her honor and integrity are belied by her abuse of power. Violence is used as one means of negotiating her sexual orientation, which is never far removed from her objectification as a female. In her confrontation with the Mafia, she partners with the Punisher and in the process undergoes numerous humiliations culminating in a "bra and panty" showdown captured by the media. There is a space for the lesbian crime fighter, but only firmly in its place within masculine hegemony. As the *New York Globe* headlines reported the showdown, *"Lethal Weapons! Sexy Lesbian Lieutenant in Punisher Team-Up Carnage!"*

Another depiction of "lesbian as psychopath" appeared in *Rawhide Kid: Slap Leather* with Catastrophe Jen, a buxom, African American, man-hating, "butch" outlaw and critical part of the killing machine that is the Cisco Pike gang. Unable to control her desire to kill men, she is seen assassinating fellow outlaws who joke about her gender or attempt to seduce her. Even among the outlaws, Jen's propensity for killing is sadistically out of control. Cisco Pike scolds her, "Damn girl, get a hobby 'sides killin' our own men, would ya?" However, unlike the Rawhide Kid, who was destined to roam the Wild West, she has a place in the frontier town of Wells Junction. In the final scene of the story arc, the sheriff is shown marrying his paramour and Catastrophe Jen has been outfitted as the new deputy in town, perhaps suggesting that gay men, such as Rawhide Kid, must wander alone, but lesbian manhaters can be subsumed, their rage redirected and controlled.

Despite the presence of lesbians as psychopaths, there are other characters that fare better. One of the most high-profile gay superheroes to appear in comics is Kate Kane (a.k.a. Batwoman). The original Batwoman ("Kathy" Kane) initially appeared in *Detective Comics* (#233) as a love interest to Batman. She was introduced, in part, to blunt the criticism from Frederic Wertham that Batman and Robin were gay.[41] Abiding by the Comic Code at the time, Batwoman adhered to traditional gender norms, carrying a purse, "a perfume bottle of tear gas, charm bracelet handcuffs, and makeup powder."[42] In 2006, Batwoman was reintroduced in DC Comics' year-long series 52. In this appearance, Kate Kane appears along with her ex-girlfriend, former Gotham City Police Department (GCPD) detective Renee Montoya. In this reintroduction of the characters, both are tough, successful, independent women.

Batwoman later appears in *Batwoman in Detective Comics* (#854)—as DC Comics' first openly gay superhero.[43] Here, Kate's sexual orientation is

After her clothes are burnt off, Detective Molly von Richtofen continues to fight for justice alongside the Punisher. (*Punisher War Zone: The Resurrection of Ma Gnucci*, Garth Ennis and Steve Dillon, Marvel, 2008)

treated rather nonchalantly. However, the intersection among sexual orientation, patriarchy, and crime fighting is consistently confronted, including a discussion between Kate and Maggie Sawyer, captain of the major crimes unit of Gotham City Police Department (#856). The two women discuss the prevalence of gay women on the police force as well as the GCPD's antidiscrimination policy. The comic book received rave reviews from fans and won a Gay & Lesbian Alliance Against Defamation (GLAAD) Award for its portrayal of Kate and her expulsion from the military as a result of the misguided "don't ask don't tell" policy.[44]

In the first few pages of the issue, Batwoman demonstrates her physical agility and competence as a crime fighter as she violently "interrogates" a witness that has needed information. Further, she demonstrates that she is not merely some bumbling, incompetent "costume" as she corrects Batman on his inaccuracies about the criminal gang activity and smirks at his crime-fighting advice:

BATMAN: Do something about your hair. One pull, the fight's over for you.
BATWOMAN: I'll take it under advisement.

The next panel demonstrates that Batwoman is several steps ahead of Batman's advice when she reveals that she wears a wig during crime fighting—she will remain unharmed during hair-pulling fights.

The Eisner Award–winning series penned by the same writer, *Gotham Central: Half a Life*, follows Renee Montoya, as she is forcefully outed at the precinct after a picture of her kissing another woman is posted on the station bulletin board. Batwoman and Renee later reappear together in *The Crime Bible* miniseries, where the sexual tension between Renee and Kate is expressed through physical altercations—a *bat*fight rather than a catfight.

Together, *Detective Comics* and *Gotham Central* indicate a shift in the portrayal of sexual orientation and female crime fighters in comic books—a move from a Batwoman that serves as a distraction from Batman's perceived homosexuality to a Batwoman that is, in her own right, an independent, competent crime fighter. Renee Montoya's experience in *Gotham Central* reflects realistic concerns among lesbian law enforcement officers that misogyny and homophobia still persist, and that the negotiation of sexual orientation is a process that operates within the hierarchy of masculine hegemony.

Hypersexualization

If female crime fighters manage to keep up the crime fight, they still must be eye candy for male readers via the gendered constructions of the comic. Given the visual splash of publishing technology, contemporary visual culture, including comic books, may be best understood as a haptic event—one that aims for emotional resonance to communicate and entertain. The sexualized imagery adds to the thrill of the book for adult readers and aids in conjuring up a virtual experience rather than merely being a good story. As Laura Mulvey pointed out in her article on "Visual Pleasure and Narrative Cinema," cinematic images are constructed from the perspective of the male gaze. She writes, "In their traditional exhibitionist role, women are simultaneously looked at and displayed, with their appearance coded for strong visual and erotic impact so that they can be said to connote *to-be-looked-at-ness*."[45] While she confines her analysis of the three modes of voyeurism (the camera, the audience, and the characters) to cinema, the acknowledgment

This two-page spread introduces the reader to DC Comics' first openly gay crimefighter, Batwoman. (*Batwoman: Elegy*, Greg Rucka and J. H. Williams III, DC Comics, 2010)

of the pleasures in looking and the representation of the woman as an erotic object of the characters in the story as well as an erotic object for the audience are certainly relevant to other mediums as well.

The cover of *Marvel Divas* #1, for example, shows Firestar, Black Cat, Hellcat, and Photon in skin-tight, breast-accentuating bodysuits, reminiscent of the silhouette graphic for the television show *Charlie's Angels*. *Green Lantern* #18 shows villain Star Sapphire straddled over Hal Jordan in a suggestive dominatrix stance. In another example, Shazam appears distracted by Supergirl and her exposed midriff during the events of *Justice League: Cry for Justice*, and the Atom jokes that Shazam's hormones are interfering with his judgment.

In his analysis of female superheroes, author Mike Madrid finds that by the 1960s, female superheroes were drawn in a sexually suggestive manner, but it was not until the late 1980s and 1990s that female characters were portrayed as ultra-violent and hypersexual. Larger cultural phenomena occurring at the time, such as the emergence of supermodels flouting physiques attainable only by the genetically gifted, or surgically modified, and the cultural mainstreaming of pornography, were perhaps influential. As Madrid describes them, females in mainstream comic books serve as "a cross between a stripper and a homicidal killer . . . the Bad Girls."[46] Popular culture commentators have noted the "pornification" of female heroes as they are being drawn with more accentuated curves than in past comic book eras. These characters' proportions are wildly exaggerated, with large, exposed breasts and skimpy costumes that would most certainly serve as a hindrance to crime fighting. The anatomical anomalies of women in comics may relate to a culture of reshaping women's bodies (plastic surgery, etc.), connected to Michel Foucault's notion that contemporary men and women reproduce cultural hegemony by disciplining their own bodies.[47] In essence, women's bodies have become "cultural plastic."[48]

Nearly all of our focus group participants acknowledged the hypersexualization of the female characters and most suggested that at times it was embarrassing to read the books in public (e.g., on the subway) due to the graphic nature of the illustrations. One participant stated, "I think most of the female superheroes are just guys with breasts basically, written by guys to just make guys get off."[49] Another participant commented on the landmark six-hundredth issue of *Wonder Woman*, which, with much fanfare, ushered in a new costume change for the superhero with Wonder Woman out of her one-piece bathing suit–style costume and into pants and a jacket. Despite the outfit change, to arguably more modest attire, one participant still found the images sexually suggestive. He pointed out that the provocative illustrations of her body positions made Wonder Woman "more suggestive than she's ever been," "With *Wonder Woman* issue #601, the artwork is like basically he took something out of porn, and just drew it, with her bending over all the time, her breasts are like spilling out."[50]

X-Men member Emma Frost in recent years has taken on an off-the-shoulder, low-cut outfit that highlights her bust. Exceedingly skinny waists that accentuate bust sizes are also routinely drawn. She-Hulk, in her self-titled *Jaded*, is portrayed in a midriff-baring, form-hugging top that emphasizes her skinny waist and large breasts. Similarly, in *Ultimate Elektra: Devil's Due*, Elektra sports a skimpy red costume in which the top button of her pants is consistently undone to emphasize her waist and to draw the eye toward her pelvic region.

The focus group participants were quick to point out that the males are also sexualized, but while the men serve as role models for boys and young men, the women serve as objects: "When teenage boys look at superheroes, they're like, I want to *look* like that . . . but when they look at a female superhero they are thinking I want to *be with* her, not I want to look like her."[51]

Creators, however, often take a rather lighthearted approach to the blatant hypersexuality. Power Girl's famous tight white keyhole top, which reveals her cascading cleavage, serves as one of the most glaring examples of hyperfemininity among female protagonists and was prominently featured on the cover of the 2009 first issue of the eponymous comic book. When asked about the attention surrounding Power Girl's appearance, artist Amanda Conner declared that she has embraced the "cheesecake factor" of Power Girl, indicating that it is "part of [Power Girl's] personality." Conner states, "I like how she seems to have a sense of humor about the whole cheesecake thing, and doesn't take it too seriously."[52] Power Girl, with Conner as artist and Jimmy Palmiotti as writer, received acclaim from fans, with one blogger stating that the book was simultaneously "horribly offensive *and* totally spot on in its feminist/pop-culture critique. . . . [I]t's just *fun*."[53]

One weekly comic book podcast included a discussion of how a change in Batgirl's body shape as drawn by a new artist on the *Batgirl* team created distractions for the reader. For example, the artist transformed Stephanie Brown from a "real girl" with an "athletic frame" to a character who "grew in cup sizes" and now has "lip injections." The podcast host suggested that the modifications were a disappointment.[54] Similarly, fans have documented instances of "porn face," described as at least one artist's tendency to keep drawing women with the same orgasmic expression, one example being the repetitive female images in *Uncanny X-Men: Sisterhood*.

In other cases, long-lived and well-developed characters are reduced to sexual objects through quips by male characters. For example, in *Teen Titans: Cold Case*, Deathstroke's daughter, Rose Wilson (a.k.a. Ravager) is asked by Robin, "Do you still think you can sleep your way onto this team?" Likewise, when Forge shows up in the plot in *Astonishing X-Men: Ghostbox*, he says to Emma Frost, "I didn't recognize you with your legs together." And in another disturbingly sexualized depiction of a female

Power Girl sports her signature keyhole top, an example of hyperfemininity in comic books. (*Powergirl* #1, Justin Gray, Jimmy Palmiotti, and Amanda Conner, DC, 2009)

superhero in contemporary comics, Cinder (a.k.a. Carla Morelli) uses her literally boiling hot female anatomy to burn and kill a male antagonist during sex. The comic featuring Cinder, *Brightest Day: Teen Titans/Villains for Hire*, earned the distinction of being one of the five worst comics of 2010, according to the Comics Alliance blog.

On the flip side, portrayals of females in comic books may be read as hypersexualized *and* empowering at the same time.[55] This point of view is often linked to postfeminism, which, as with Carrie Bradshaw in *Sex and the City*, celebrates the woman who can have her Manolos and her fiery independence at the same time. In this vein, Marvel's *Divas* attempts to show superheroines as both avid shoppers and crime fighters, taking time out from the latest mission to date eligible bachelors. In *Mighty Avengers* #6, the Wasp (a.k.a. Janet Pym) laments, during an invasion of mole-like monsters, that the "finest shopping district in America" is being destroyed. Later in the series, disheveled from another battle, she exclaims, "First my shops, now my hair!" Here we see that emphasized femininity is not merely how the female superhero looks but also her consumption habits and how she spends her free time when not fighting crime.

Hypersexualization and Violence

In regard to criminal justice themes, the crime fighters have shifted to include more gay and female characters, but still they are a numerical minority within comics, and often they are minor characters in the overall history of a comic books series. Further, gay and female characters have a shorter life span than their heterosexual counterparts; they are easily discarded, and often victimized in brutal and sadistic ways.

Gail Simone, a prominent writer at DC Comics, was so turned off by the treatment of female superheroes in comic books that she published on her now-oft-referenced *Women in Refrigerators* website that lists those who have met "untimely ends." Simone was originally inspired by a 1994 *Green Lantern* storyline involving Kyle Rayner's girlfriend, Alex DeWitt, a short-lived character. After devoting herself to helping Kyle transition to being the new Green Lantern, Alex is killed and stuffed into a refrigerator, having little part to play in the massive DC saga. Simone writes, "Not every woman in comics has been killed, raped, depowered, crippled, turned evil, maimed, tortured, contracted a disease or had other life-derailing tragedies befall her, but given the following list . . . it's hard to think up exceptions."[56] Indeed, even the most iconic female superhero, Wonder Woman, has been critiqued as "an excuse for stories about sexual domination and submission" given the number of times characters, including Wonder Woman herself, are bound in her "magic lasso" in the early, Golden Age stores.[57]

In the 2007 cover for *Heroes for Hire* #13, the female heroes are shown tied up, their breasts exposed, with phallus-like tentacles caressing them as they face the prospect of being raped. Blogger Steven Padnick expressed his criticism: "These are supposedly superheroes, people who protect others from rape. To show them as potential victims, to make their (potential) rape a sales feature, denies them of their capability as heroes and their existence as developed characters, and makes them into sex toys, to be leered at."[58] Gay comic book characters do not fare much better. The late author and screenwriter Perry Moore compiled a comprehensive list of over seventy, mostly minor, gay characters and notes that a majority of them are killed soon after their introduction.[59]

Whether as a consequence of the way the violence is portrayed or because of the nature of the victim and/or offender, some scenes of violence produce significantly more controversy among fans than others. One such scene occurred in DC's *Identity Crisis*, originally released in 2004. In what is essentially a classic murder mystery, the superheroes set out to solve the murder of Sue Dibny, the wife of Ralph Dibny (a.k.a. Elongated Man). During their investigations, Ralph recounts the story of the rape of Sue years ago by villain Dr. Light. The flashback is chilling and graphic in its portrayal of Dr. Light pulling Sue's hair from behind, holding her wrists at her back, amid her screams of protest. As a result of the rape, the superheroes mind-wiped the villain to ensure protection against future attacks.

The comic received rave reviews as well as stinging criticism. Some fans decried the use of rape as a cheap plot point. For example, a commenter on the science fiction website io9 states, "Black Cat, Catwoman, Sue Dibny. What links these [female] characters? They had rape retconned into their background as a way of making them edgier. It's lazy writing, offensive, and a cheap ploy to pad out the background of the characters."[60] Another fan writes of the rape scene,

> We never see how it affected her—all that matters is the effect it had on the male superheroes plus Zatanna. It's very much the old-fashioned view of rape: women are property, so rape is where one man damages another man's property. The rapist is actually committing a crime against the "owner" of the woman, not the woman herself. That's sort of what *Identity Crisis* seemed to be saying.[61]

Similarly, in 2004, the death of Stephanie Brown (a.k.a. Robin, Batman's female sidekick) raised the ire of fans. Anders writes that shortly after Stephanie rose to the ranks of Batman's sidekick Robin, she was brutally murdered. He explains, "[I]n a series of unfortunate events, Batman canned her, she accidentally set off a Gotham City gang war, and finally fell into the hands of a skull-faced villain called Black Mask, who tortured her to death with a power drill."[62] Many fans were upset at her horrific demise, particularly the sexualized nature of her murder. Girl-Wonder.org, a website created by fans in response to the Stephanie Brown murder, writes, "Her breasts and hips are emphasized and her body is twisted into unlikely but sexually suggestive poses. This is how a teenage girl; a superhero; a Robin is depicted as she is being fatally brutalized." Further, Girl-Wonder notes that the power drill–clutching Black Mask was immortalized in plastic form as a DC Direct action figure, part of the popular toy line for collectors. But the horrific murder was not the only reason fans were upset. They felt further insulted when subsequent DC storylines failed to properly acknowledge the existence of Stephanie. Whereas Batman crafted a memorial to remember the earlier fallen Robin (Jason Todd), there was no memorial for Stephanie. Contributors to Girl-Wonder explain their outrage: "It damages the integrity of Batman as a text and as a character to ignore the contribution Stephanie Brown made to the mythology. We believe that our intelligence has been insulted by those in control of these characters and this mythology."[63] More recently, Stephanie Brown's murder has been "retconned," revealing her death to have been faked. Batman's reluctance to put up a memorial to Stephanie is attributed to his skepticism about her death. Whether this turn of events was the result of fan outrage or an independent editorial decision remains contested. Regardless, the "retcon" falls squarely in the critique of the aforementioned *Women in Refrigerators*, indicating that crime-fighting females, like the crime-fighting racial minorities described in the next chapter, often suffer from a shorter life span than their white male counterparts. However, the fan ire indicates a new space for the possibility of enduring female characters.

The simultaneous moves forward and steps backward characterize the overall decade or so of comics we sampled. There is an opening up of issues of sexual identity, potentially ushering in a wider variety of gay, bisexual, and transgendered heroic characters in the future. Although there are more female characters in crime-fighting mode than ever before, their sexualization, insecurity, and relatively short life spans temper the progressive nature of mainstream comics. Overall, a mixed message is at work here, with the white male heteronormativity of the comic book landscape still acting as an important mainstay in the medium.

8

"AREN'T THERE ANY BROWN PEOPLE IN THIS WORLD?"

RACE, ETHNICITY, AND CRIME FIGHTING

In the medium of comics, in which graphic representations communicate ideas, the identity marker of race has often been stereotypical and problematic. Although racial identities intersect with other identities such as gender and sexual orientation, a separate treatment of race as it plays out in criminal justice themes yields important information about messages of racial identity that contemporary comic books impart. Racial identity is not static in its depiction in comic books; rather, there is a plethora of constructions that sometimes privilege certain racial identities over others. As scholar Marc Singer explains, "Race in contemporary comic books is anything but simplistic. If some titles reveal deceptively soothing stereotypes lurking behind their veneers of diversity, then others show complex considerations of identity."[1] Though latter-day writers speak of their work as multiracial and diverse, contemporary comics are not immune to stereotyping. Some feature token minority characters, or minority characters with bit supporting roles that, in effect, play into racial clichés. Still, it is important to note that a select few comics, most independently published, have been able to portray minorities in American society and to do so more thoughtfully.[2]

Our focus in this chapter centers on the intersection between race/ethnicity and crime fighting, acknowledging that crime fighting is performed within a heteronormative context that privileges the white, male, patriarchal perspective. We interrogate how comic books, as one facet of popular culture, further reinforce the notion of heroism as embodied by white males. In particular, we consider notable heroic black, Asian, Latino, and Native American characters. The current racial and ethnic diversity found in comic books may indicate that the medium is transitioning from the white world of ages past into one with a globalized cast of characters, but we find that this transition is far from complete. Viewing the books with a critical eye toward race reveals much about how they reflect and shape larger cultural notions of what kind of person is considered heroic in American society.

Racial Identity and Criminal Justice: The *Criminalblackman*

Critical criminologists have long emphasized the role of racial and ethnic identity in struggles for power and authority in criminal justice.[3] Some have called for redressing historical power imbalances between white Americans and minorities through more diverse imaginings of people in popular culture.

Criminologists have examined both the quantity and the quality of minorities represented in both fictional and nonfictional media. Studies have consistently shown that the news media tend to reinforce the perception of minorities, particularly blacks, as criminal, while underrepresenting them as upstanding citizens.[4] There are few representations of heroic minorities, leaving the impression that when minorities are represented in media, they are to be feared. As criminologist Delores Jones-Brown has argued, the history of representations of blacks as criminals in the media has led to individual blacks being treated as "symbolic assailants" in the real world, regardless of their actual behavior.[5]

Similarly, critical race theorist Katheryn Russell-Brown notes that although positive portrayals of persons of color exist in the media, these are often coupled with subtle images of black deviance.[6] Fictional black characters that have made positive achievements, for example, are often "reformed," ex-cons, or "rehabilitated stick up" kids.[7] In related research, Dana Mastro and Amanda Robinson found that the presence of blacks on prime time television shows has increased, though this did not necessarily correspond to an increase in the quality of the portrayal. Minorities were underrepresented as criminals and overrepresented as police officers; yet when portrayed as criminals, minorities were more "problematic" than their white counterparts.[8]

The stereotypical black male has been problematized in popular culture as a symbol of being "*too* male, *too* physical, *too* bodily."[9] bell hooks describes the development of black hypermasculine identities as a cultural adaptation to social conditions in the U.S. South, where white supremacist rhetoric feminized and dehumanized black men.[10] Coupled with structural inequalities, the legitimate avenues of economic and social success for black men being in the realms of sports and music caused black men to seek control over their lives through physical strength and sex appeal— forced to use their bodies to achieve success rather than their minds. This, in turn, led to American notions that black men had "bodies not minds" and were even bodies out of control.[11] The cumulative effect of these images of deviance produces what Russell calls the "criminalblackman," the mythical notion that being a black male is intrinsically connected to criminal behavior. This racist cultural construction has served to thwart the perception of blacks and other racial minorities as heroic figures. In popular cultural images, we find little room for heroic representations; rather, these images more frequently reinforce and perpetuate racial stereotypes.[12]

A Conspicuous Absence

One of the most striking observations about race and ethnicity in contemporary American comic books is the virtual invisibility of racial and ethnic minorities as characters. For example, media scholar Phillip Lamarr Cunningham writes that as of 2010, there were only three Marvel comic book titles featuring lead black superheroes.[13] Other heroes of color are also conspicuously absent. The lack of diverse superheroes is a reflection of the larger history of neglect of persons of color in heroic roles in mainstream popular culture. It has been over forty years since the appearance of the first black superhero (Black Panther in *Fantastic Four* #52), yet the dearth of titles featuring minority superheroes persists. Cunningham points out that minority supervillains have also received short shrift. Cultural theorist Stuart Hall notes that in society, the process of fully integrating those who are marginalized occurs in fits and starts, and that "what replaces invisibility is a kind of carefully regulated, segregated visibility."[14] In essence, while comic book readers may ultimately see an increase in the number of minority characters, those characters may still be sidelined in supporting roles.

The minority characters who do appear in comic books seem to lack the staying power of their white counterparts. For instance, throughout his superhero career Paul Johnstone, as the black superhero Shadowhawk, fought for justice while HIV positive, having been injected with infected blood by vengeful gangsters. However, he succumbed to the virus and died in 1995. Ryan Kendall as Black Condor was killed in *Infinite Crisis* (#1) by the villain Sinestro in 2005. Impala, a Zulu warrior, died in 2001 (*Justice Society of America* #28). Black Mask slit superhero Orpheus's throat during the events of *Batman: War Games* and Bishop, member of the X-Men, died in the Ultimate Marvel universe in 2005.

Sometimes black superheroes are resurrected from the past only to be killed off, as was the case with Black Goliath in Marvel's *Civil War*. As one comic book blog discussant wrote,

> [Black Goliath] wasn't around much but showed up during Civil War to join back with the Avengers just in time to get killed by (fake) Thor. I'm like . . . really? They had to pull the black hero no one knew much about back into the fold just to kill him off? Hadn't seen anything like that since G.I. Joe created a one time black character called Cool Breeze only to kill him off in one issue.[15]

Ironically Black Goliath's last words in comic books were, "Get ready for the shortest comeback in history, Thor!"

Another comic book discussion board participant blasted the death of Freedom Beast, a South African superhero who was arrested for photographing the beating of a black individual by white Afrikaner policemen. After Freedom Beast's release from jail, his superhero mentor Maxwell provides him with an elixir and special helmet that confer upon him the power of mind control, super strength, healing ability, and the capacity to unite any two animals into a powerful hybrid. However, Freedom Beast is soon killed off by allies of the villain Prometheus in *Justice League: Cry for Justice*. One commenter expressed displeasure at the storyline on Dwayne McDuffie's website forum. The late comic writer McDuffie was the cofounder of Milestone Media, a publishing company under the umbrella of DC Comics that was specifically formed to address the lack of racial and ethnic minorities in comic books. The commenter stated,

> I've been polite about James [Robinson's] all-white JLA spinoff, as I know that he did not have full control over the roster, but this just pisses me off. It's bad enough that Connor Hawke is no longer a superhero, but now they went and killed off one of the few non-stereotypical black heroes [Freedom Beast] just to act as fodder.[16]

"Connor Hawke" in this comment refers to the second Green Lantern, son of the first, and a character of mixed white, black, and Asian identity—a rarity among comic book characters. In the contemporaneous *Green Arrow/Black Canary* (#12-14) storyline, Connor Hawke lapses into a coma after being shot by members of the League of Assassins, losing his archery abilities as well as his mental faculties.

We asked focus group participants their thoughts on the lack of racial and ethnic representation in comic books. One participant stated, "The reason I became a Marvel fan faster than a DC fan was because, just as a Latino, when I was growing up reading comics, every DC hero was white. I couldn't relate to that. I was like, aren't there any brown people in this world?"[17] Though there are more "brown people" in comics today, the source of this participant's frustration largely persists. Unlike other mediums, such as television and the movies, which have seen an increase in minority characters in the past decades, comic books remain a largely white world. Focus group participants echoed this problem of invisibility, maintaining that it was vital for comic book writers to include characters from diverse backgrounds. Although the quality of those representations is important, many participants expressed the desire to simply see an increase in the number of minority characters. When asked about this, participants stated,

> PARTICIPANT 1: I think [we need] mere representation. I think the first time you see a black face in the comic book, as a black reader, you're like, this is awesome. I read Spider-Man from the beginning pretty recently and when Joe Robinson showed up, it was like my world changed. . . .
> PARTICIPANT 2: But he was good character. If he was a "Stepin Fetchit" character, it would be a different story.

PARTICIPANT 1: . . . But I also read Luke Cage, and those [characters] were not always strong or diverse . . . or what I agreed with. . . . [I]t was more stereotypical. I didn't always feel great about reading it, but when I wore a costume for the first time at a con[vention] it was Luke Cage.

Early minority superheroes did indeed reflect the aforementioned stereotypical portrayals. As a result, they may not have contributed to larger notions of minority inclusion. According to comics scholars, minority superheroes were historically absorbed into the superhero formula as exotic outsiders who helped the mainstream white superheroes preserve the American way of life. For example, in the late 1950s, in the *Legion of Super-Heroes*, each team of superteens originating from a different planet was a literal rainbow of colors: green, blue, yellow, and white. Only the white color corresponded with an actual race in the real world. By 1976 members of the legion, intended as symbols of multiracial cooperation, met up with an African American character and insisted they were color blind and inclusive because of their rainbow hues. Undermining this is the subtext that Superboy, who is white, is not marked as belonging to any race at all (though he also hails from another planet). Communications scholar Naomi R. Rockler explains, "Whiteness functions as a normative category that 'Others' are measured against. Many European Americans see race as something people of color have, but that they themselves do not."[18] As English scholar Marc Singer describes it, "[S]uperhero comics represented every fantastic race possible, as a means of ignoring real ones."[19]

Comic books, like other forms of media, are a product of their social environment. Universes where superheroes swoop in to save the day are undoubtedly inspired by the particular social milieu of the creators and artists. Some of the earliest contributors to superhero comic books were artists of Jewish descent, many of whom obscured their Jewish identity in order to be taken seriously in the comic book industry in New York. Jewish creators are responsible for some of the most popular American superheroes, including Superman, X-Men, Spider-Man, the Spirit, and Batman.[20] In his account of how Jewish history has made an impact on comic books, Simcha Weinstein cites characters that were created to "protect the innocent" and "conquer evil." Such heroes take on a whole new light when one considers that they were conceived, in part, in response to the persecution of European Jews.[21] The Jewish experience is reflected in many popular American superhero comics.

For example, author Arie Kaplan describes Superman as a metaphor for the Jewish experience in the American diaspora.[22] He likens Superman's Kryptonian name Ka-El to the Hebrew for "all that God is." Interestingly, others have taken a Christian slant on Superman, suggesting that he is a messianic figure who is more powerful than humans yet intercedes on their behalf as a savior figure. Similarly, certain traits, perceived by some as culturally Jewish, i.e., sarcastic humor and kvetching—are noted in Marvel's Spider-Man and the Thing.[23] In this sense, the apocalyptic nature of the criminal justice themes in mainstream comic books can be said to be truly Judeo-Christian.

In particular, the premise of the long-standing *X-Men* saga has been analyzed as a Jewish-inspired reverie on the tensions of ethnicity and assimilation in the United States. Created in 1963 by Jack Kirby and Stan Lee, both of Jewish descent, *X-Men* involved human mutants who discover they have superhuman telepathic or physical powers either by way of genetic mutation or exposure to radioactivity. In the early plots, when nonmutant humans become aware of the X-Men's abilities, fear leads to political opposition and attempts are made to restrict the X-Men's freedoms. The arch-villain in the series, Magneto, is a Jewish mutant who suffers through the Holocaust and loses his entire family. He advocates for a preemptive strike by mutants to eliminate all humans before humans can eliminate all mutants. The X-Men, led by telepathic mutant professor Charles Xavier, attempt to defend humans from Magneto's extreme ideology while also defending mutants again human discrimination.[24] This premise has been analyzed as a manifestation of Jewish anxiety about assimilation and anti-Semitism in America. Creators channeled this to envision a universe in which powerful protectors were available to fight the forces of discrimination and to protect the vulnerable.[25]

The X-Men, however, have become a more general symbol of racial or ethnic inequality. In many passages, various X-Men must contend with being different because of their unique powers, and in more recent years, their dwindling numbers due to the events of the *House of M.* In *X-Factor: Second Coming*, when Darwin, a half-African and half-Latino mutant, and member of the X-Factor investigative team, confronts an army of antimutant human warriors, he has this exchange with one of them,

DARWIN: We're not people to you! You see us as less than human! You think a guy with my skin color can't wrap himself around that?

WARRIOR: This isn't about race. . . .

DARWIN: You're trying to exterminate my people! How the hell is this not about race?

Here, Darwin faces the double marginality of being both mutant and a racial minority, and deliberately links antimutantism to the intolerance found in racism. Further, he takes it to apocalyptic levels by focusing on the genocidal nature of antimutant campaigns. There are echoes here of both the Holocaust and civil rights–era struggles. When Jews joined forces with African Americans in the sixties, the two much-maligned groups came together in their collective experiences with adversity for the greater good of society. Lee and Kirby had these struggles at the front of their minds when they first conceived X-Men, and their messages about tolerance and diversity endure through to today.

Superheroic While Black

The earliest black superheroes, such as Luke Cage, Black Panther, Black Lightning, Blade, and Black Goliath, were inspired by blaxploitation films, and characterized by macho street language and anti-establishment attitudes.[26] Media scholar Phillip Lamarr Cunningham writes that black superheroes have been used to "address social issues that its primarily white [and] invulnerable . . . superheroes could not."[27] DC's first black superhero, John Stewart, who was part of the elite Green Lantern Corps, emerged in 1971, during a time in which the *Green Lantern/Green Arrow* comic was focused on issues of social justice such as racism and poverty. Introduced as a replacement in the event that the previous Green Lantern was incapacitated, Stewart was described as "a proud defender of the black community."[28]

Early black superheroes were framed in terms of being heroes for *their* people, and were often placed in supporting roles in white-centric story arcs, a legacy that can still be felt today.[29] Conversely, white superheroes have historically been construed as universal heroes, ready to save all innocent people. The Falcon, for example, appearing in *Captain America* #117 (1969), was a reformed ex-con "dedicated to protecting the people of Harlem."[30] More recently, after Captain America's death in the *Civil War* crossover event, the Falcon registered as a superhero and is charged with protecting the same territory. Mr. Terrific, in the Justice Society of America

Evidence of the diversity of the X-Men, New Mutant Dani Moonstar (*right*), a Native American superheroine, rescues Karma (*center*), a superhero of Vietnamese origin, and a young child in *Return of Legion*. (*New Mutants: Return of Legion*, Zeb Wells, Diogenes Neves, and Zachary Baldus, Marvel, 2009)

(*JSA: Black Adam and Isis*), is a superhero dedicated to "ensuring fair play among the street youth" using his invented T-Sphere device, which can emit electrical charges, enable him to fly, and create holographic images. Meanwhile, Thunderbolt (William Carver), a Daredevil supporting character, is an African American military veteran. While he was avenging his brother's murder at the hands of a violent street gang in Harlem, the murderer was killed by a lightning bolt that also affected Carver. Requiring an experimental cobalt radiation treatment, Carver emerged as the costumed hero Thunderbolt, able to move at superhuman speeds.

Similarly, Luke Cage, who debuted in 1972 in *Hero for Hire*, is a petty criminal from Harlem, framed for heroin possession and sent to prison. While there, he agrees to be a test subject in a chemical experiment, during which an irate guard attempts to kill him by administering an overdose. While not killing him, the overdose gives him a unique body chemistry that provides him with superhuman strength, a power he uses to help the people of Harlem. In Marvel's *Secret War* miniseries, the opening pages show Cage encouraging black youths in Harlem to get positively involved in their community by revealing to him the identity of a neighborhood drug pusher. Cage hunts down the culprit screaming, "What's my name!" and tells the offender, "Get outta my face and get outta Harlem!"

Black Panther, the ruler of an African kingdom known as Wakanda, first appeared in 1966 amid the Black Power movement in America. However, according to the *Marvel Chronicle*, Black Panther's name was briefly changed to Black Leopard in a presumed effort to avoid linkage to the Black Panther revolutionary movement in the 1960s.[31] He is considered the first black superhero in a mainstream comic book and was created by Jewish comics icons Lee and Kirby, who also created the aforementioned social justice–inspired X-Men books. Black Panther is portrayed as culturally African, his superhero identity considered "the sacred totem of his people," a status earned only after he underwent many tribal tests and trials.[32] He was then given a special herb native only to Wakanda that enhanced his sensory perception and physical abilities. He helps out the Avengers and the Fantastic Four from time to time, but his people are his highest priority; he is placed within the framework of being primarily a hero for his kingdom.

Comic books featuring black superheroes explore race relations and social justice in ways not possible in books that render race "invisible" through the exclusion of superheroes of color. In *Super Black*, African American studies scholar Adilifu Nama points out that the reimaginings of characters such as Black Panther allow racially aware writers such as Reginald Hudlin to "emphasize the 'black' in Black Panther."[33] Nama points out that Hudlin's characters in *Black Panther: Bad Mutha* engage in racial banter designed to evoke themes of "European colonialism, racial eugenics, biological racism, and white supremacy," and Hudlin consciously uses backdrops such as New Orleans to illustrate the failures of the government response to Hurricane Katrina.[34]

Black Panther's mission to protect the African country of Wakanda remains central in the 2005 retelling of Black Panther's origin story in Hudlin's *Black Panther: Who Is the Black Panther?* Here, T'Challa has risen to the rank of Black Panther through various tests of skill and strategy. Wakanda is an African country described as historically "way ahead of the rest of the world" and has, for the entirety of its existence, resisted being conquered. Wakanda is "unfettered by the yoke of colonization . . . a high tech, resource-rich, ecologically-sound paradise that makes the rest of the world seem primitive by comparison." The American officials describe

Wakandans as having a "warrior spirit" and "technological superiority that defies explanation." This contrasts the more frequent popular cultural portrayals of Africans as backward and not fully civilized.

Although Wakanda has no history of aggressive action against any nation, American "Dondi Reese" (who bears a striking resemblance to Condi Rice and is a relatively rare example of a powerful black female character in comic books) suggests that a regime change is in order. Incidentally, while doing her job, Reese endures various racial insults hurled by U.S. military leaders against the Africans (i.e., referring to them as "jungle bunnies"). Simultaneously, Black Panther's arch-nemesis, the Klaw, is seeking revenge for the death of his great-great-great-grandfather, who was killed by an earlier Black Panther.

As the United States learns that Wakanda is in danger from the Klaw and his mercenaries, officials opt to assist by sending in an army of cyborgs that are later rejected by T'Challa. Ultimately, Black Panther, with help from his sister Shuri, drives out the Klaw and defeats the villains, proving once again that Wakanda is untouchable from outside conquerors. The racialized nature of the Black Panther saga is explicit in another story arc from 2007, *Black Panther: Civil War*. Here, Black Panther leads the faction of superheroes opposed to the Super-Human Registration Act, which when passed into law would enforce the mandatory registration of superpowered individuals with the government. A rally in support of the movement is held outside the White House with supporters of Black Panther portrayed as almost entirely people of color, while the president's aides and analysts are all white. The one exception is War Machine, who, as part of the S.H.I.E.L.D. arm of the government, is tasked with reigning in Black Panther. When one aide asks War Machine what his "take" is on Black Panther, War Machine replies, "Oh man, is Black Panther the new litmus test question? The question whites ask blacks to see if they are anti-white or too 'pro-black' or whatever?" In the ensuing civil war battle, Black Panther saves War Machine's life. Later, War Machine chastises Iron Man for continuing to treat Black Panther as the enemy despite his heroic actions on the battlefield.

Racial tensions also rise to the fore in the *Civil War* saga when superhero Bill Foster (Black Goliath) is killed by a clone of Thor in a scuffle to arrest him for not registering with the government. The black community is portrayed as outraged by his death while the white government operatives attempt to back-pedal against the media onslaught by downplaying their continued conflict with the Black Panther. One political analyst says to the president,

POLITICAL ANALYST: [Black Panther's] friend [War Machine] just called for a truce, and considering the recent death of Goliath, it was probably a good idea not to engage with a probably fatal showdown with a popular African king.

THE PRESIDENT: Point taken. In this PC-world, we'd end up looking like [the] Klan, not Patriots.

The implication here is that the death of Goliath only has the appearance of involving racism. A similar preoccupation with appearing racist emerged in *She-Hulk: Jaded*, in which She-Hulk, a bail bondswoman, returns a bail jumper to custody. The officer processing the suspect begins to chat about She-Hulk's no-holds-barred fight in the Mall of America to apprehend the suspect. She-Hulk explains that such force was reasonable in the situation and the officer replies, "Try being afraid to use reasonable force on a minority perp because you'll be crucified as racist in next day's papers."

Real-life cases in New York City, such as the controversial shootings of unarmed black men Amadou Diallo and Sean Bell, bring to light the unfortunate popular notion that the charge of racism in those events is actually a form of reverse racism on the part of the black community. This type of criticism is routinely lobbed at members of the black community who rally against police brutality and other forms of racial discrimination and corruption, obscuring the root cause—white hegemony in American society and the criminal justice system.

Race and Patriotic Heroism: An Uneasy Coupling

The American Dream has been traditionally achieved by whites, with racial others relegated to supporting roles in helping them achieve that ideal. Such is also the case in superhero comics, among them *Truth: Red, White, and Black*, which features an alternative history of the emergence of a black Captain America, Isaiah Bradley. In this story, the government uses black men as experimental subjects, injecting them with a super-soldier serum. Although

Spin doctors weigh in on race and politics when Black Panther, the King of Wakanda, joins forces with the Americans. (*Black Panther: Civil War*, Koi Turnbull, Marcus To, Don Ho, Sal Regla, Jeff De Los Santos, and Nick Nix, Marvel, 2007)

African American soldier Isaiah Bradley survives the experiment and dutifully and loyally conducts missions for the U.S. government, he is eventually betrayed by the government and imprisoned. Ultimately, the effects of the serum lead to extensive mental deterioration and Isaiah is reduced to a "shadow of the man he had been."[35] This plot contains echoes of the tragic Tuskegee experiment conducted in the United States, which used poor rural black men to study untreated syphilis.

Truth: Red, White, and Black explores the possibilities of patriotism in a sociohistorical context in which the American Dream is reserved for whites. Though the series features a black Captain America, the mainstream white Captain America, Steve Rogers, also appears. As scholar Rebecca Wanzo writes, the idea of a black superhero conflicts with "historical realities that burden the narrative with the impossibility of any of these men being embraced as ideal patriots wearing the Captain America uniform."[36] She continues, "[B]lack Captain America Isaiah Bradley epitomizes not only the failure of US democracy to work equally for all citizens but also the ways in which the fantasies of US democracy can be built on the backs of those it uses and then discards."[37]

Race was also confronted in the immensely popular *Spawn* series that began in 1992. Dead African American military hero Al Simmons chooses to return to the world of the living, but he can only return as Hellspawn, a super-powered warrior charged with leading the forces of hell against those of heaven. The series involves him trying to understand his personal history, why he was given the option to resurrect, and what he should accomplish as Spawn. In the early issues, Hellspawn uses his powers to take human form in order to find his still-living wife. Surprisingly, in *Spawn #2*, he comes back as a white man, seemingly because that's all his powers can do. Spawn soliloquizes,

> Time to change into human flesh again. Wish I could look like myself. But these powers seem to have a mind of their own sometime. I can't even change my appearance. Keep turning into this white guy. Worse yet. . . I look like some kind of California beach bum.

Many readers have debated online the significance of Spawn's shape-shifting into a white man, with some arguing that he remains black, but just appears white, as if being white were another costume. Others argue that race is a social construct and nonessential and that therefore, he is truly of no race, whether he appears one way or the other; or he is fundamentally the race that he is when he appears as such.[38] The ability to convincingly shape-shift, the transition of bodily forms, is itself a hallmark of the medium of comic books. Characters may transition from one race to another, or from one gender to another (see Brian K. Vaughn's depiction of Xavin in *Runaways*), or from young to old. Characters may shift in appearance from panel to panel or issue to issue; no other medium more easily allows such successful transformations. Over the years, creators have utilized the medium to reintroduce characters, changing their race, sexual orientation, and other characteristics.

In the early 2000s, long-time Marvel character Nick Fury, a white general and veteran of a variety of special ops over the years, suddenly appears as an African American man in the pages of *The Ultimates*. Because the world of *The Ultimates* is situated outside the Marvel continuous saga, and in a parallel universe of sorts, such a change could be executed without explanation. Off-camera, the rationale from Marvel was that it was part of the reinvention of characters in fresh new ways that characterize the "Ultimate" storylines. According to entertainment websites, making Nick Fury black was a deliberate attempt to open up the role for Samuel L. Jackson, who played him in the *Iron Man* movies.[39]

Journalists noted backlash that appeared in response to the casting of Jackson, commenting on social media, including Twitter posts and Facebook group pages, with titles such as "Nick Fury is white not black."[40] In a manner similar to the way movie roles generally call for the casting of "white" characters unless otherwise specified, superheroes that deviate from whiteness are likely to receive scrutiny. One commenter on a Comic Book Resources forum stated, "I didn't like how they got rid of normal Fury in 616 just to replace him with movie Fury, but that's just me."[41] The implication is clear: the "normal" is the white Fury traditionally appearing in the comic books. Or, as this comment from Facebook more succinctly stated, "[C]ool but nick fury was WHITE."[42] Though its origins remain unclear, one particular comment circulated among various websites and created a flurry of responses from readers:

> I don't like [the Ultimate Nick Fury] at all. Yes, it's because he is a black man. I have never liked black superheroes and I don't really think that they are believable. I didn't mind the Kingpin being black in the [Daredevil] movie because he's a villain. I don't want to relate to or care about the villains, only the heroes. I know that this may sound like a racist statement but look at the society that we live in. If you look at the majority of crimes and lawlessness in this country most of it is caused by African-Americans. The kind of movies, television and music they endorse [sic] is full of violence, drug use, abusing women, att[r]acting law enforcement officers, rape and murder. That's really all that needs to be said.[43]

This commentator's understanding of crime in the United States is not correct—most crimes are not committed by African Americans, and purporting that African Americans as a whole endorse violence is a gross and untrue generalization. However, the comment is a present-day representation of the historic stereotype of the criminalblackman and evidence of the kind of resistance some readers may have to blacks as crime fighters and heroes. What is most notable about this reader response is the notion that a black superhero is simply not "believable." It shows that for some readers, black characters can only exist within a historically white frame of reference; they simply don't ring true when cast in crime-fighting roles. This lingering white frame of reference in comics favors depicting black superheroes as heroes only for blacks while saving universal heroic status for white men. Nick Fury's treatment as a decorated general who safeguards *everyone* from homeland security threats challenges some consumers of the medium who are not comfortable with racial minorities in positions of power and authority.

On the other hand, according to our focus groups and perusal of numerous comics discussion boards and podcasts, most comic book readers embraced a black Nick Fury. One comic blog received this comment from a reader,

> I like the [black Nick Fury], simply because most African Americans are depicted as slang-speaking street hustlers. Fury is depicted as a Machiavellian soldier who covers every angle and realizes that you can't protect the world and be everyone's friend. I think . . . despite the change in pigment, the spirit of the character remains unchanged. Only in the past decade or so has the entertainment industry begun to get past the street image of the Black male. I've encountered a few people who had a fit when there was a Black captain on Star Trek, a Black man in the Iron Man armor and another wearing a Green Lantern ring.[44]

Notably, Samuel L. Jackson's performance in the role has been very popular in the *Iron Man* movies. The first *Iron Man* movie grossed $318 million in 2008. It ranked twenty-nine in all-time box office grosses in the United States.[45] However, some consumers find a black Nick Fury a nonevent. As one comment on an entertainment fan site revealed, "I doubt anyone is really gonna care that [Nick Fury]'s black. Its [sic] 2010 not 1910."[46]

Today the few black heroic characters in best-selling comics are often put in supporting roles with little play, such as Agent Deems in the *Astonishing X-Men* series or War Machine in *Secret Avengers* (#1). In the case of War Machine, though he is an Avenger, his character does not participate as often in the drama and action as the other team members. In this first issue, he is seen in a supporting role, monitoring activities from a computer and answering to Captain America and Beast, who act as the strategists. Entertainment writer David Walker notes,

> For an industry with a tremendous level of influence over pop culture and the world of entertainment, comic books are pathetically behind the times. At a time when Barack Obama is president of the United States, Will Smith is the top box office star worldwide, and the music charts are dominated by hip-hop and R&B, there is only one monthly comic book currently being published starring a black superhero (*Black Panther*).[47]

Overall, the portrayal of black characters in comic books is both progressive and stereotypical. The depiction of Luke Cage, for example, encompasses the dichotomy. He has been promoted to leader of the Thunderbolts by Captain America, the government's superhero liaison and homeland security czar. In this sense, Cage is a leader and essential to the plot development. However, his character falls back on stereotypical behavior in *Thunderbolts* (#144), in which he amasses his team of villains from those in prison. His intent is to use them for the greater good, and in return, for them to receive reductions in their prison terms. Though being shown as a leader of a major superhero team is a step in the right direction for black male heroes, Cage also exhibits the black male stereotypical origin story, which he brings up in order to convince the villains on his team that he relates to their plight. He refers to his history as a petty criminal in Harlem several times during the events of *Thunderbolts* (#144) as the reason why he understands their criminal pasts. As Captain America put it upon giving Cage the job, "You had every bad break life could have dealt. You not only turned all that around, you became an Avenger. That's the kind of leader this program needs to see." Cage's transformation from the downtrodden and exploited victim of a wrongful conviction to superhero may be read as a symbolic victory over social injustice. Or, as Nama points out, "Luke Cage is bound to issues of unjust black incarceration, black political disenfranchisement, and institutional racism in America."[48]

Independent comics have been the most notable exceptions to the poor showing of racial diversity. These lesser-known books have attempted over the years to offer more nuanced and culturally sensitive portrayals. In the 1990s, Milestone comics, co-created by a group of African American comic creators and artists, showcased black protagonists who use brains, not just brawns, to fight for justice.[49] For example, the character Static was depicted as a scrawny black teenager who could control electricity. In *Static #3* he fights a shape-shifting monster called Tarmack (who is made of tarmac) by using a variety of hardware items that chemically solidify and destroy him, including dry ice and light bulbs.[50] This was later spoofed in the *Irredeemable* series when the Volt exclaims, "I'm a black superhero with electric powers. I know I know" (#5). And later in the comic he says, "I am solidly aware that an electro-magnetic African-American super [sic] is a total cliché. I didn't order this power off the menu I swear" (#5).

In 2010, DC Comics absorbed the Milestone characters in *Milestone Forever #1* and *#2*, bringing them into DC continuity. However, despite the series hypothetically being integrated into the DC Universe, the plots take place in a community apart, with one main character counseling a reformed crack addict and another using the phrase "a little sumpin' sumpin." Many of the original objectives for the use of these diverse characters, however, remain, including the focus on intellect as well as brawn. *Brotherman,* another independent comic with notably diverse characters, was published by creators Dawud Anyabwile and Guy Sims in the 1990s. By drawing on hip-hop style, this comic, though short-lived, developed a cult following. Similarly, although only a few books were created, *Chocolate Thunder,* a combination of superhero antics, blaxploitation, and kung-fu fighting created by brothers Jeremy, Robert, and Maurice Love, also celebrated black culture and had a loyal cult following.[51]

The Intersection of Race and Gender in Crime Fighting

In turning a critical eye toward black female protagonists in comics, it is obvious that nuanced and progressive depictions are also conspicuously absent. One of the first regularly appearing black female characters in comic books was Gloria Grant, introduced to readers in 1975. A career model and friend to Peter Parker, she became the secretary of J. Jonah Jameson, the publisher of the *Daily Bugle.* Ultimately she is revealed to be the weak link at the newspaper when she becomes involved romantically with a criminal mastermind whose true objective is to get information from her bosses.[52]

One of the most popular black female comic book characters of all time is Storm, created in 1975 and recently played by Halle Berry in the *X-Men* movies. Storm arrived in comic books as an Egyptian mutant descended from an African witch-priestess. Her main power is the ability to control weather. Married to Black Panther, she has been portrayed as vacillating between accepting a more subservient role as queen of an African kingdom and remaining an assertive and accomplished part of the X-Men team. In the Uncanny X-Men saga *The New Age: First Foursaken*, she travels to Kenya for a spiritual "walkabout," during which she takes down fighting warlords and has a vision of her former lover, the Native American hero Forge. In an amalgamation of an African location, an Australian aboriginal spiritual journey, and a Native American dream vision, the comic book manages to compact a variety of cultural otherness themes into her story. Underscoring her character as an explicit construction of exotic difference, during a New York Comic Con conference presentation, in 2010, of the beta version of the online Marvel-character massively multiplayer role-playing game (MMPRG), Marvel representatives revealed that users can maneuver Storm to dance in the "walk like an Egyptian" style, based on a popular 1980s song and video by all-female group the Bangles.

Black females appear to get short shrift in the popular horror comic *The Walking Dead*. As part of the horror genre, the series suffers from the stereotypical plight of minority characters in classic horror films: they are typically early victims of the gruesome killer on the loose. Several female black characters appear in *The Walking Dead*, the first of which dies in a joint suicide with her boyfriend. In volume 5, more disturbingly, Michonne, an independent black female character who had been fighting zombies singlehandedly since the apocalypse began, is imprisoned shortly after being introduced and tortured mercilessly in a drawn-out rape scene. Although she survives the prolonged ordeal and vengefully tortures her attacker, the event is particularly startling even for a horror comic, representing the taming of an independent black character through the violent subjugation of her body. The violation of her body and her psychology as a victim eventually overshadows her self-reliant characteristics. One focus group participant mentioned Michonne as a "problematic" representation of black females, in particular because after the rape, she does not seem to have a role in the comic book "other than sleeping around a lot."[53]

Asian Crime Fighters as Supreme Martial Artists and Geeks

Heroes of Asian descent also suffer relative invisibility and stereotypical depictions. In the opening panel of *Secret Identities: The Asian-American Superhero Anthology*, authors Jeff Yang, Parry Shen, Keith Chow, and Jerry Ma present six Asian stereotypes that they believe are historically present in comic books. The authors parody these stereotypes, creating such characters as the coolie, a hard-working rice paddy laborer, and Riceman, a superhero in the shape of a pork dumpling.

Of these particular typologies, however, one that is often seen is the geeky scientist, represented in the anthology by the "unfunny" man, an eyeglass-wearing superhero who can use his eyes to release myopic blasts. Radioactive Man, for example, an enduring character since he was created in the 1960s, fulfills the Asian male geek stereotype in contemporary comics. He is a nuclear physicist whose powers include using radioactivity to incinerate whole city blocks.[54] During Norman Osborn's reign as leader of the government's homeland security team, he considers the public relations implications of deploying Radioactive Man, who is Chinese, against the villain Jack Flag and his ilk,

> OSBORN: You appear to Americans to be a radioactive foreigner running around the country sterilizing everything you look at. The uniform is purely for show. It blurs your racial features a little, and appears to contain any radioactivity people believe you are leaking.
>
> RADIOACTIVE MAN: Would it not be more effective to educate your people as to my condition?
>
> OSBORN: Educate them? See that's foreigner's talk. Joke.

Here, we see that Osborn has little faith in people's ability to understand the nuances of the situation.

The most common stereotypical construct, however, is possessing martial arts talents. One historical example that Gene Yang and Michael Kang single out in their Asian anthology is from the series *The Green Hornet*: "You have this handsome wealthy crime fighter, and the Asian martial arts expert is his chauffeur? I mean, it's demeaning."[55]

Likewise, Shang-Chi, one of the first Asian male superheroes in comic books, appeared in the 1970s as the "greatest living master of kung fu."[56]

This depiction mirrored mainstream American stereotypes that regard Asian men as either master martial artists or geeky scientists. Shang-Chi appeared more recently in *Secret Avengers* #6, when his villainous father was resurrected by the Shadow Council and threatened American interests. After Secret Avengers Captain America and Ant-Man debrief Shang-Chi on his father's return, Shang Chi looks out at the skyline of Hong Kong and reflects on how peaceful it is. Ant-Man quips, "Uh . . . is he going to start meditating?" In *X-Men: Manifest Destiny*, Wolverine trains under Master Po, "master of 82 different Chinese martial arts." Meeting in Master Po's secret lair in Chinatown, San Francisco, the two prepare for their confrontation with the Black Dragon Deathsquad, which is terrorizing the neighborhood.

Asian female stereotypes in comic books similarly involve constructions of martial arts mastery. In 1999, Asian American Cassandra Cain was introduced as Batgirl (*Batman* #567). Though not the first Batgirl, Cassandra was the first to be featured in her own title series, *Batgirl*. Cassandra was trained as a martial arts expert and assassin at an early age by her father. After her first murder at age eight, Cassandra retreated from her life as an assassin and sought to use her skills for good. Ultimately, Cassandra proves her worth to Batman and is integrated into the Bat family. Later, Cassandra relinquishes her Batgirl title to the new Batgirl, Stephanie Brown, a blond-haired heroine. During her time as Batgirl, Cassandra fluctuated from hero to villain, leaving fans uneasy about her characterization. In one blog post a fan comments on the transition from Cassandra as Batgirl to Stephanie Brown,

> A capable, powerful, intriguing, complex and Asian character [Cassandra] suddenly out of nowhere gets a character alteration that everyone hates so DC quickly changes it. Then, after a criminally short time with her being back in action, they replace her with a considerably less interesting PRETTY BLONDE WHITE GIRL![57]

Here we see that an Asian female Batgirl is short-lived and her construction as a white hero is reinstated.

Martial artistry is also the expertise of the X-Men character Psylocke, a heroine who was called "nimbo" in the 1990s for being a cross between a ninja and a bimbo. In the graphic novel *X-Men: Psylocke*, she is drawn in a skin-tight leotard with large breasts and several suggestive images of the contours of her butt and crotch. Psylocke, who has the power of telekinesis, was born white and British, but has spent many years in an Asian body. The circumstances of the body switch, according to one commentator, are "tediously complicated," involving the villain Matsu'o Tsurayaba's attempt to resurrect his dead lover in Psylocke's body. The commentator suggests that the result, Psylocke residing in an Asian body, underscores that her Asianness is merely an "affectation."[58] Another commentator on the comic book blog "Bleeding Cool" went so far as to say that Psylocke is "like a white person wearing black face."[59] Psylocke, herself, seems confused as to the meaning of her identity. In the events of *Psylocke*, she travels to Japan to seek revenge on Matsu'o Tsurayaba and to perhaps recover her original form. Unsuccessful in the latter, she attempts to come to terms with her identity. She narrates, "For so long, my life has been out of control. Chaos and serendipity wrapped in insanity. I have suffered. I have lost. Not just my life, but my very soul, my self." The end of the story shows her in a fuzzy pink bathrobe drinking tea out of a delicate Japanese teacup, reflecting about being at peace with her hybrid and conflicted identity.

Super Gang-Bangers

In popular culture, stereotypical depictions of Latinos include that they are gang members, criminals, and pregnant teens.[60] In comic books these stereotypes are both reinforced and challenged by writers, though overall Latinos are some of the least-represented minorities in mainstream books. For example, the contemporary El Diablo is a drug dealer, but he uses the profits of his trade to benefit the poor, reinforcing the criminal stereotype with a Robin Hood twist. Jose Delgado (a.k.a. Gangbuster), a Superman sidekick introduced in 1987, is a vigilante hero whose expertise is targeting street gangs. And Maya Lopez (a.k.a. Echo) is the daughter of an associate of the crime boss Kingpin, who raises her when her father dies.

Jaime Reyes is the third incarnation of DC's Blue Beetle, first appearing in *Infinite Crisis* #3. A high school student in El Paso, Texas, Jaime accidentally stumbles upon a blue scarab that has magical powers derived from alien technology. Jaime finds that the scarab can be infused into to his spine, providing him with a tracking system, wireless connection, and superhuman strength, among other benefits. In *Blue Beetle: Shellshocked*, Jaime does not fully accept his powers and becomes increasingly dependent on his peers for emotional support. The specter of Hispanic gang culture looms large in *Shellshocked*, with the adults worrying about their children taking on gang membership. Jaime's friend, Traci's aunt, asks Traci about his friend Paco. "Paco, some of his clothes—is he flying gang colors?" Traci replies, "Huh? No! He's not running with that gang. He just knows a bunch of them from the neighborhood." The gang, called the Posse, is a meta-human Hispanic gang with a worse rap than deserved. At the end of the story arc, they become accomplices in Blue Beetle's fight for justice.

Rictor is a Mexican earth-shatterer who was introduced to the Marvel universe in the late 1980s in a push to have younger and more diverse characters. Unlike most Latino characters, Rictor's ethnic identity is not stereotypical—he has no connection to gang-banging nor is he a former criminal (although it was revealed in his origin story that his father and cousins were arms dealers). Rictor receives more attention in the comics community for being in a same-sex relationship with X-Factor teammate Shatterstar, thus bucking the kind of masculinity constructions many male Latino characters feature.

Outside the superhero genre, Gilbert and Jaime Hernandez's *Love & Rockets* saga, which began in the early 1980s, features prominent Latino characters. Writing from their experience in California's Latino community, the Hernandezes center the series around Maggie, a Mexican American bisexual mechanic, and her girlfriend, Hopey. The creators populate Maggie and Hopey's world with a number of racially and ethnically diverse characters. Although their stories run the gamut from science fiction to more realistic portrayals of Mexican Americans living in a Southern California barrio, the breadth and scope of the world the Hernandez brothers created makes the depictions of street violence in some of their stories thoughtful and nuanced. As Jaime Hernandez explained about their work in a 2001 interview, "I like to think we speak a universal language in the comic. So even though these people are Mexican, you can still relate to them as people, which was our main objective. I want people in China to like our stuff."[61]

As fan Ross E. Lochkart wrote on his blog, the series consisted of "realistic black-and-white representations of normal people living normal lives. These were stories of people who looked and felt familiar, people who joked, laughed, fought, made love, and dreamed of making something of their lives."[62] One of the most revered issues of the *Love & Rockets* saga is Jaime Hernandez's "The Death of Speedy," collected in *The Girl from H.O.P.P.E.R.S.* Speedy Ortiz is a supporting character, part of the crew who occasionally clashes with another gang from a nearby town. Although Maggie is romantically interested in Speedy, her sister Esther has already claimed him—even though she has another boyfriend from the competing gang. The story is acclaimed by comics fans for dealing with the passion and ambiguity of romantic love and male violence. Speedy and his gang antagonists ultimately do not attain any benefit from the violence in *la vida loca*, and instead his loss evokes deep pain.

Although *Love & Rockets* presented Latino characters that went beyond stereotypes, many other Latino characters suffer from stereotypical portrayals. One of the first female Latino superheroes, Marvel's Araña, uses stereotypical street slang. On the other hand, she bucks conventional depictions by being an excellent student with a father who pushes her to excel academically. Though involved in a vigilante organization that uses violence, unlike a street gang, the organization seeks to restrain enemies until law enforcement can take them away, rather than seeking to kill them. Through Araña's character development, comics scholar Karen McGrath has argued that "small steps toward more varied representations of minority groups are present in this comic book series, [but] the characters are still depicted in . . . race stereotypical ways."[63] The continued depiction of Latino crime-fighting characters as reformed gang-bangers casts a shadow over the few representations of Latinos that contemporary comic books offer. Rather than Latino crime fighters being imagined as on the side of justice and the law from the beginning, they are given back stories that uphold the stereotype of the Latino gang-banger. This ultimately suggests that the typical state of people with Latino identity is to have gang identification, which then must be overcome, in order for them to be considered heroes.

Shamanistic Crime Fighting

Native American crime fighters also receive short shrift in comic books. In *Batman: The Black Glove*, the Sioux character Man-Of-Bats is shown pouring himself a glass of wine while his son Little Raven proclaims, "Dad! Come on.

Chicano gang members banter about a street encounter in a classic *Love & Rockets* storyline. ("Vida Loca: The Death of Speedy Ortiz" in *The Girl from H.O.P.P.E.R.S.*, Jaime Hernandez, Fantagraphics Books, 2007)

You know how you get when you drink." Though published in 2007, the story manages to evoke the stereotypical construct of the alcoholic Native American and superficially references the epic problem of alcoholism on Native American reservations. However, most Native American superheroes in the DC and Marvel pantheons are not portrayed in this way. Instead, they are construed as particularly spiritual superheroes who regularly draw on allegedly Native American spirituality for their power to fight for justice.

Red Wolf appeared in the Marvel universe in the 1970s as part of the company's diversification push.[64] While he was growing up on a Montana reservation, his parents were killed by corrupt businessmen. He later appeals to the Cheyenne tribal deities to allow him to avenge their deaths. The Wolf Spirit Owayodata responds by granting him superhuman senses and expert archery and tracking skills.[65] Another Marvel character, Forge, is portrayed as a skilled shaman of the Cheyenne tribe, trained in the magical arts by the sage Naze, the great trickster. Strangely enough, Forge's spiritual powers manifest in the ability to invent advanced technological devices. He has undergone such adventures as subduing the villain Adversary with his mystical spells and powers. Adversary is believed to be a demonic god who regularly gambles with the fate of the universe without concern for the damage he causes. Meanwhile, Marvel character and Native American John Proudstar invokes his ancestors as a warrior for the X-Men and is ultimately killed fighting crime.

Like black superheroes, Native Americans often are relegated to protecting other Native Americans, rather than being framed as more universal heroes. This construct, when applied to Native Americans, might be more justifiable than when used to define other minority characters. Unlike other ethnic groups, Native Americans, in the context of reservations, have the most separate criminal justice system among American systems, and their lands are technically sovereign. Nonetheless, their tribal police and courts remain a part of the American system of justice and are answerable to the federal government. Treating Native American crime fighters as merely heroes of their own people obscures the interconnectedness of American criminal justice systems and does not provide an avenue for nuanced depictions in the contexts of Native American residing in nonreservation jurisdictions. In essence, the separateness of Native American justice obscures the variety of criminal justice contexts that people of Native American descent might encounter.

In *Thunderbolts: Faith in Monsters*, Jason Strongbow, hero of the Navajo tribe, is shown debating whether to register himself as superhero American Eagle, per the guidelines of the government's Super-Human Registration Act. Originally, he was mutagenically enhanced in a mine blast while protesting the stripping of a mountain sacred to the Navajo. As a result, he developed super strength, speed, and endurance and expert archery abilities. Although American Eagle sometime helps out the Fantastic Four, he primarily stays on his reservation to fight for local justice.[66] In the Thunderbolts storyline, he confides in his friend Steve that the Super-Human Registration Act bothers him, despite the fact that if he registers he can make money being deployed on government missions. In response, Steve gives a long speech about racism and the federal government,

> Your skin's the wrong color to sign up, man. . . . You want to go to Washington and say, I'm the Injun who can kick the cheese out of Iron Man without breaking a sweat, and I'm here for some of that sweet federal money? Tell you what: I'll come with you and see if they'll do me my forty acres and my damn mule while they're at it.

At the end of *Faith in Monsters*, American Eagle is deemed exempt from registration as a resident of a Native American reservation, once again framing a minority superhero as being most relevant to his own people, treated differently than other superheroes.

A more nuanced and contextualized treatment of Native Americans is found in *Scalped*, a DC Vertigo title focusing on organized crime, drugs, and poverty on a reservation. Though there are no superheroes in the story, *Scalped* is one of the more critically acclaimed DC titles. In an interview with Newsarama, writer Jason Aaron reveals that influences for the story included the American Indian movement, the Red Power movement of the '70s, and the Leonard Peltier story.[67] In the comic, an undercover FBI agent returns to his roots at the "rez" and is determined to seek justice for two Native American activists who decades earlier had presumably murdered two federal agents, but were innocent of the crime. *Scalped* deals with a plethora of crime problems, including corruption, prostitution, illegal arms, and drug use in the context of the reservation. Aware of the potential criticisms of a white man writing about life on a South Dakota Indian reservation, Aaron responds,

> And yeah, I'm a white guy writing about life on an Indian rez. I faced the same sort of challenge when, as a guy born in 1973, I set out to write a story about life on the ground in the Vietnam War. I don't mind that sort of challenge. . . . It's noir with a rich setting, one based on a real place, and with a rich history, part of which is based on real events, but at the end of the day it's still noir.[68]

The writer of *Scalped* shows a laudable sensitivity to the racial and ethnic irony of being a white person writing about Native Americans. Recognizing this fact helps to inform the writer's sense of his work as primarily a noir piece and not necessarily a deep cultural commentary. And, if mere representations are welcomed by minority consumers, the series does fill a major gap in the lack of depictions of life on Native American reservations. On the other hand, this very popular, long-running series highlights the need for Native American comics creators, since none of its major artists, writers, or editors hails from the background it depicts.

There Aren't So Many Brown People in This World

Although contemporary comic books can rightly boast having more ethnic and racial diversity than in the past, a more careful look reveals the prevalence of stereotypes long since criticized in other media such as film and television. Comic books rarely changed as a result of analyses that uncovered the medium's white hegemonic tendencies. It does not help that creators and editors are mostly white men. This situation leads to racial and ethnic privilege being reproduced in comic books despite multicultural settings. This is why portrayals abound of black and Native American superheroes as segregated protectors of their own kind. They are made exotic as the vehicles for magic, spirituality, ancient warriorship, and ancestor worship in the fight against crime. It is also why white creators run the risk of representing their own world and experience with racial and ethnic others as mere colorful stand-ins.

When minorities are portrayed as heroes, they have often overcome dark pasts, as Latino gang-bangers or black male criminals or drunken Native Americans. The implication here remains that the minority hero has overcome something that plagues most of the other members of their community and is a unique exception to a stereotypical rule the comic books reinforce. Only Asian crime fighters seem to avoid the criminal stereotype—as master martial artists.

In the intersection between race/ethnicity and crime fighting, a heteronormative context that upholds a white, male, patriarchal perspective is prevalent even today. Through a conspicuous absence of the minority superhero, who is frequently portrayed as a token good guy or girl in a community of bad, comic books maintain a stereotype of heroic crime fighting as quintessentially white male behavior. Although some recent racial and ethnic diversity may suggest that comic books are evolving away from these problematic stereotypes, nonetheless, the overall impression is one of a dominance of portrayals of the white male as the natural crime fighter in American society.

9

APOCALYPTIC INCAPACITATION

THE "MAXIMUM-MAXIMUM" RESPONSE TO CRIME

In his article *Feeding Wolves: Punitiveness and Culture,* David Green writes that our understanding of criminal justice policy is influenced by the cultural resources we encounter on a daily basis, that the stories "we tell and retell ourselves, are crucial to the ways we understand the world and how to engage with it."[1] The solutions that we embrace to address our social problems, crime included, are informed by the cultural narratives circulating in our everyday experiences. Green suggests that those narratives that are "fed," regurgitated, and circulated in a mass-mediated landscape are the ones that thrive. These narratives may be punitive, promoting harsh, get-tough sentencing policies and the death penalty, or they may promote principles of restorative justice and peacemaking.

Criminologists tend to identify five main types of punishment rationales: retribution, incapacitation, deterrence, rehabilitation, and restorative justice. In this chapter we evaluate our sample of comic books with respect to these five basic types. Comic books are one cultural resource among many that inform American collective sentiments about punishment. Arguably, comic books, like other forms of media, hold a "preferred reading."[2] That is, while frequently capable of nuance, mainstream American comic books provide crime and justice frames for readers that privilege incapacitation solutions, but do so through an emotional and violent performance that allows for the near-experience of retribution even when the plots fall short of an "eye for an eye." The possibility of retribution as punishment acts as a perpetual tease. Plots in our sample were most often moving toward incapacitation, creating tension that provides pleasure for the reader and a means for vicariously experiencing transgression. Meanwhile, alternative solutions, such as rehabilitation, restorative justice, and deterrence, are less prevalent in comics and in some cases even actively devalued as suitable responses to crime.

Devaluing Rehabilitation

In mainstream American comic books, there is a conspicuous disconnect between crime causation and the preferred punishment. As shown in chapter 5, crime is often depicted as a consequence of childhood trauma and maltreatment leading to psychological deficits and personality disorders. In typical criminological discourse, this etiology most easily lends itself to the punishment goal of rehabilitation. Samuel Walker describes rehabilitation as reducing crime "by treating criminals and transforming them into law-abiding citizens."[3] Rehabilitation calls for the implementation of a variety of programs that may include psychotherapy, education, anger management counseling, and vocational training, among others.

However, in comic books the solution to the crime problem rarely includes any consideration of treatment and rehabilitation. For example, villains in the DC universe are frequently sent to the infamous Arkham Asylum, where patients/prisoners are considered beyond repair. The idea of rehabilitation is merely an illusion. In *Justice* Batman says of Arkham, "[N]o one wants to even admit the possibility of ills for which there are no cures." Similarly, at the end of the graphic novel *Joker*, Joker's sidekick Jonny declares the folly of rehabilitation—at least for the Joker. He states, "[T]here will always be a Joker. Because there's no cure for him. No cure at all. Just a Batman."

Similarly, Blade calls hunting and killing vampires the "cure" for their condition in *Ultimate Avengers 3* (#1). He explains that vampires are suffering from porphyria, a virus that affects hemoglobin in the blood, framing his prey as regular people who happen to have an illness. Whereas most medical conditions logically imply a rehabilitative treatment, Blade proceeds to shoot a vampire and then violently slice off the heads of half a dozen more. This occurs even after one of the vampires suggests talking over their conflict and negotiating a truce. Instead, Blade chooses a no-holds-barred mass execution. And when he succeeds in assassinating the last vampire in the group he exclaims, "Crackhead piece of trash! The hell he get off offering me a truce?" In this case, a softer response to people sick with porphyria is not even given consideration.

When there is some hint of rehabilitation, it is usually cast aside as folly. In *Arkham Asylum*, Jeremiah Arkham sets out to construct a new Arkham Aslyum with a new creed: "rehabilitation, not incarceration." He clearly states his intentions: "I will rebuild Arkham, not as a prison, not as a hospital, but as a true asylum—a place of sanctuary for those whose unique qualities have made [them] outcasts." However, Jeremiah's vision of rehabilitation at Arkham is explicitly based "on the principles of Jeremy Bentham's panopticon," with a tower constructed in the middle of the facility providing surveillance of the prisoners. In addition to the totalizing surveillance, inmates are implanted with remote chips in their brains that may be activated at any moment to maintain order. Jeremiah's attempts at a rehabilitative model for Arkham are short-lived and by the end of the story arc, Jeremiah's own insanity became evident as he was revealed to be the villainous Black Mask. His mental condition had deteriorated to a state as problematic as those he was attempting to assist.

Rehabilitation also proves elusive in *Birds of Prey: Endrun*. Early in the book Oracle, (a.k.a. Barbara Gordon) refers to Brian Durlan (a.k.a. Savant) as "one of the few successfully rehabilitated Gotham supercriminals." Yet in the following issue, his rehabilitation appears to be a sham when Savant kidnaps Oracle and confronts her about her betrayal that led to his torture at the hands of the supervillain Calculator. Throughout the story arc, Oracle repeatedly expresses her disappointment at being unable to successfully rehabilitate Savant. Eventually, psychologically damaged by reliving the torture every day, Savant attempts suicide in the presence of Oracle. She continues to hold out hope for rehabilitation, stating that there's a "therapist who specializes in people . . . like us . . . I'm not letting you go again, Savant," but the implication is that it is hopeless.

Wonder Woman also dismisses rehabilitation as an option in favor of retributive punishment. For example, after expressing empathy for the atrocities that Captain Nazi faced as a child, including physical abuse and a murderous father, Wonder Woman declares that these horrors suffered as a

Arkham Asylum reopens in anticipation of providing a safe retreat for the criminally insane, but the hopes for rehabilitation are short-lived. (*Arkham Reborn* #1, David Hine and Jeremy Haun, DC, 2009)

youngster are not relevant to the deserved punishment of today. She states, "and even for him, I follow the Amazon code when facing a vanquished foe: punishment for the adult . . . empathy for the child" (*Wonder Woman: The Circle*). Similarly, the rehabilitation of Typhoid Mary, a mentally ill villain with telekinetic and pyrokinetic powers, is treated skeptically by Daredevil (#509). She describes for him the "recombinant personality assimilation" she underwent in order to unite her three dissociative identities. She tells Daredevil, "I joined the Initiative [government superhero team]. They treated me. Helped me address my—my issues. I'm all better now." Daredevil replies, "And you expect me to believe that?"

The dismissive approach to rehabilitation in comics is probably due to a number of factors, including the comic book formula itself, which, in a quest to have endless serial stories to tell, leaves little room for "curing" the supervillains that readers love to hate. More importantly, the consideration of rehabilitation as futile may be viewed within a larger social context. Criminal justice scholars have traced the rejection of rehabilitation back to the 1970s, a time when therapy and other programs were deemed failures. Robert Martinson's controversial findings presented in the 1974 article titled "What Works? Questions and Answers about Prison Reform" helped usher in skepticism among the general public as well as criminal justice professionals.[4] Martinson reviewed 231 evaluation studies examining the effectiveness of various rehabilitation programs and found that few programs had any appreciable affect on recidivism rates.

The fallout from the article and subsequent media appearances by Martinson led to the overall perception that "nothing works" with regard to rehabilitation. In fact, the "nothing works" catchphrase was erroneous in that some rehabilitative programs are effective for some types of offenders.[5] Nonetheless, the idea that "nothing works" helped in part to shape public opinion about the value of rehabilitation as a policy goal and preceded a "get-tough-on-crime" era that still resonates today.[6] Here, the actual efficacy of the rehabilitative programs was not as important as the rhetoric surrounding rehabilitation. Neoconservative scholar James Q. Wilson's *Thinking about Crime* added to this discourse by arguing that human nature does not lend itself to rehabilitation.

It requires not merely optimistic but heroic assumptions about the nature of man to lead one to suppose that a person, finally sentenced after (in most cases) many brushes with the law, and having devoted a good part of his youth and young adulthood to misbehavior of every sort, should, by either the solemnity of prison or the skillfulness of a counselor, come to see the error of his ways and to experience a transformation of his character.[7]

However, more recent scholarship on factors that contribute to desistance suggests that behavior can change as people mature through the life course.[8] Unfortunately, for the most part, our sample of comic books does not confront desistance as a possibility.

Absent Restorative Justice

Storylines that touch on the potential for restorative-justice approaches to crime, such as victim-offender mediation, are almost entirely absent. Restorative justice is a movement in criminal justice scholarship that gained ground with John Braithwaite's seminal work *Crime, Shame, and Reintegration.*[9] In the book, Braithwaite argues for the use of shaming by family members, friends, and the community as a means of strengthening the moral bond between the offender and the community. It serves to sanction an offender's wrong while also affording the means through which the offender can ultimately be restored to the community. The focus in this form of justice is not abstract notions of law and morality in the context of the state, but the practical need for the victim who has been wronged to confront the offender in the context of the community. Nils Christie advocated for this type of participatory justice in *Limits to Pain*, arguing that when punishments are more personal and the community participates, meaningful justice emerges for all involved. Moral bonds weakened by the relinquishing of criminal justice to state actors and behavior specialists can be restored.[10]

One way restorative or participatory justice is actualized is through restorative justice conferencing, which consists of a meeting among offenders, victims, and both parties' family and friends. The participants explore the consequences of the crime and decide together how to repair the harm. Proponents argue that conferencing is a victim-sensitive problem-solving process that shows how individuals can resolve problems when a suitable community forum is available—and it has a proven track record of reducing recidivism.[11]

Victim-offender mediation is another restorative approach to justice in which the victim and offender discuss the crime and the potential responses to it with a third-party mediator. Considered most appropriate for non-violent, low-level crimes, the approach has also been used in some cases for violent crime. However, because talking out conflicts in comic books is often eschewed in favor of action—or in many cases, the story involves situations that have allegedly moved beyond the willingness of the parties to talk—victim-offender mediation is an approach that is usually outside the narrative formula. Whereas numerous examples of explicit devaluation of rehabilitation as a policy response are present in comics, restorative justice themes are conspicuously absent. For example, for Blade, in the previously mentioned *Ultimate Avengers 3* (#1), engaging in dialogue as a means of conflict resolution is simply off the table in terms of approaches to vampires, even when they explicitly indicate their willingness to negotiate a truce. In *Ultimate Spider-Man* #52, Spider-Man is caught in the middle of a fight between Black Cat and Elektra, unsure of which side he should take. He asks Elektra, "What exactly can we do to make you stop and go away? Or would you at all be interested in calmly explaining who sent you and what exactly you want?" When Elektra responds with a high kick to his face, Spider-Man quips, "So, that's a no?"

Similarly, in *New Avengers* (#3), while creatures from another dimension are attacking Earth, Spider-Man and the Thing find themselves in a fierce battle to protect the planet. They engage in this facetious dialogue,

> SPIDER-MAN: Maybe we should open a dialogue with these fine fellows and see if we can come to some sort of peaceful accord.
> THE THING: Meh. Not my style.

Restorative justice in this context may be viewed as less emotionally satisfying for the readers. As quoted in a previous chapter, one focus group participant commented,

> [B]ut sometimes [the hero] doesn't have time to be diplomatic. There's no more talking, no more words, there's no one there to stop [the violence] and those times, I think the hero just has to do it. And I'm not saying there are not repercussions for it, because there are.[12]

Repercussions in comic books, though, are few and far between. In fact, heroes are expected to administer justice violently, and resolution through nonviolent means is rare. The starting point for many comic books, as we have argued, is a point of crisis that often by definition has moved beyond a talking-it-out phase and necessitates more extreme measures.

Lukewarm Overtures to Deterrence

In *Justice*, Batman and Superman discuss the concept of deterrence in their conversation regarding the fear criminals have of "being found out and getting caught." Batman reveals that one of Superman's greatest strengths is in his omnipresence—the idea that Superman could literally be anywhere at any time, striking fear in the heart of criminals. Batman says to Superman, "[Y]ou take the power out of the shadows. You steal away a criminal's safety in the dark. You make them afraid." Deterrent principles are far more common in comic book narratives than rehabilitation or restorative justice. However, according to our focus groups, fans often appreciate the appeal of deterrence within the context of the dominant rationales of incapacitation and retribution. Many times, rationales for retribution in comics also shifted into a corollary purpose of violence as deterrence—acting violently against crime sends a powerful message about the consequences would-be criminals could face.[13]

Deterrence theory originated in the classical school of criminology when philosophers such as Cesare Beccaria (seventeenth century) and Jeremy Bentham (eighteenth century) argued that self-interested individuals can be deterred from crime if the costs of the crime outweigh the benefits. If sentencing laws are crafted so that they ratchet up the consequences of crime to the point of equilibrium at which most people will think it not worth the potential reward, crime can be deterred. Individuals learn about the consequences of crime either through the examples of the costs of crime to other members of society, known as general deterrence, or as a result of personally experiencing a sanction, called specific deterrence. In this way, deterrence is a utilitarian theory—forms of punishment are constructed solely on the basis of their function as a deterrent.

In comics, however, contemplating what doesn't occur, because it has been deterred, is often without suitable action and violence for a dramatic plot line. If villains do not at least attempt fantastic crimes, there is little around which to construct the comic book narrative. As a result, deterrence is not the dominant solution to crime presented by mainstream comic books. When deterrence does come into play, it is often contained within the larger policy response of incapacitation.

Apocalyptic Incapacitation

For contemporary American comic books, "true justice" most often occurs in the form of incapacitation with the veneer of individualized, retributive punishment. In essence, many of the storylines involve a tease of sorts: How far will the hero go toward retribution? Vengeance? Violence is the preferred response—violence that incapacitates temporarily yet most often does not kill the offender. But the seduction of retribution is always present and many plots involve the heroes wrestling with their own emotional desire for retribution. This combination of incapacitation and retribution, or what we call apocalyptic incapacitation, allows the perpetual yearning for utopia to continue. The villains are incapacitated, but never ultimately put to rest. In "Entertainment and Utopia," film critic Richard Dyer writes that entertainment does not provide a model of a utopian world; rather, "the utopianism is contained in the feelings it embodies . . . what utopia would feel like rather than how it would be organized."[14] Here, in these continual ongoing sagas, the violent nature of the incapacitation provides for the emotional satisfaction that retribution offers.

In their seminal work on incapacitation, criminologists Franklin Zimring and Gordon Hawkins describe how incapacitation rose to prominence in the twentieth century as a justification for imprisonment. Incapacitation refers to the practice of restraining criminals so they are physically unable to engage in criminal behavior.[15] Imprisonment is the most visible form of incapacitation in the criminal justice system—while imprisoned, individuals are physically unable to commit crime outside the facility. Zimring and Hawkins point out that incapacitation gained favorability, not due to empirical evidence touting its success in reducing recidivism, but rather due to the disappointment with other rationales for punishment.[16]

Spider-Man's incapacitation orientation is made explicit in *Ultimate Spider-Man* #50, in which he tells Mary Jane that he may retire from crime fighting because the retribution people demand is not fulfilling to him. Spider-Man feels a responsibility to protect those he can, but his character typically refuses to go beyond neutralizing a threat. Yorick in *Y the Last Man* also shows a preference for incapacitation. When asked why he didn't kill his sister, Hero, after she killed an innocent woman at the direction of a violent ultra-feminist, he replies, "Because my mother—*our* mother, taught Hero and me that no one should die for their crimes. Better to let them rot in prison for the rest of their miserable lives."

Likewise, in *Superman: Sacrifice*, the policy implication is that some people are monsters and irredeemable, thereby potentially deserving death as a means of warding off serial criminality. However, Superman falls short of killing his foes, preferring to incapacitate them even when an argument for death can be made. When the cyborg OMACs (a.k.a. Omni Mind and Community) threaten the lives of millions, Superman expresses a desire to kill, until he finds that the machines are harboring human beings inside their shells. And, in the opening pages of *Criminal: Lawless*, the narrator explains, "Tracy knew he didn't have to kill him, but some people deserve to die." In the story, Tracy, a reformed criminal and war veteran, is on a mission to find out who killed his brother and why. Yet, the story is ultimately not resolved with a retributive killing of his brother's murderer despite this being used in the plot to maintain suspense.

Focus group participants explained the importance of incapacitation to their own notions of comic book justice, "I think there are plenty of times that Batman should have killed the Joker . . . and I understand why Batman doesn't do it, but . . . there are some individuals who are too damaged [and need] a total removal from society without it being a further burden on society."[17] Frequently, incapacitation is balanced against a sole alternative—killing to neutralize the threat. Many participants indicated that killing villains advances justice and that *not* killing is tantamount to negligence: "This is one of the reasons I don't like Batman: When are you going to take out the Joker? This guy's like ruined the lives of your best friends and when are going to do something about it?"[18] Another participant stated, "You can't save everybody, that includes the villains. You can't save someone who doesn't want to, who will always put into jeopardy everyone else's life. That's why I think there are some heroes that, in honesty . . . become villainized by *not* killing someone, know what I mean?"[19]

While fans revel in the emotional delight of vengeance, they most often express admiration for heroes who are unwilling to kill in their quest for justice. As one focus group participant says about Superman, "You have an individual who will suffer, who has the right to give back vengeance . . . a guy who has all the power in the world and will still . . . you know, he won't kill them."[20] Incapacitation serves as a viable solution for Superman and other heroes who most often adhere to the "no kill" policy.

Comic book narratives routinely include the use of incapacitation as a means of (temporarily) halting criminal behavior. Though the majority of those incarcerated in the United States are housed in medium- and minimum-level secure facilities, these types of prisons are not represented in contemporary, mainstream American comic books. In comic books, there appear to be few criminals appropriate for a minimum or medium facility; virtually all represent a dire threat to society and many, a threat reaching apocalyptic proportions—the dangers of which a less secure facility cannot contain.

Despite the effort to construct facilities designed to contain super-powered predators, the prisons are notoriously ineffective in their efforts to incapacitate. Prison breakouts and riots occur on a regular basis, implying that incapacitation through incarceration is simply a foolish and downright dangerous policy.

Prisons are often a spin on real-life facilities such as "Stryker's Island," the largest facility in Metropolis, home of Clark Kent (a.k.a. Superman), Marvel's "Ryker's Island" and DC's "Alcatraz Island." Prison facilities may be built to contain street criminals, the mentally ill, or "meta" or super-powered individuals—whether supervillains or superheroes gone bad. As a result, the prisons must be constructed with security in mind that extends beyond mere "maximum" security. For example, in *New Avengers: Breakout*, the Raft is introduced as "Ryker's *maximum-maximum* security installation." Jessica Drew (a.k.a. Spider-Woman) describes the facility that contains eight levels filled with villains who have been "cut off from any and all human contact." They are monitored via live broadcasts of their cells, which are reinforced with steel and "adamantium" (a fictional indestructible metal), housed underwater, and guarded by "highly trained, fully armed S.H.I.E.L.D. officers" (*New Avengers: Breakout*).

Similarly, in *Osborn: Evil Incarcerated*, Norman Osborn is held at the Raft. Here, the government officials considered the Raft an inadequate facility to hold the unpredictably dangerous Osborn, so a transfer to a "Special Containment Center" (SCC) at an undisclosed location was authorized. The SCC

The prison is imagined in "maximum-maximum" proportions in the *New Avengers*. (*The New Avengers: Breakout*, Brian Michael Bendis and David Finch, Marvel, 2006)

holds "supervillains so dangerous, they've been locked away out of sight and mind for years, even decades." However, shortly after transfer, Osborn and his allies orchestrate an escape, unleashing a prison riot in the process.

One of the more interesting uses of incapacitation is found in the *Fantastic Four* as Reed Richards (a.k.a. Mr. Fantastic) detains villains in a suspended state in individual, tube-like tanks. When his wife queries, "Is this even legal?" Reed responds, "[I]t's arguably the most humane form of punishment. They're doing nothing more than dreaming." Reed acknowledges that the tanks are only temporary, and that what is required is the "apprehension and imprisonment of every single one of our enemies." Given the limitations of the current prisons, Reed is determined to create a new, better, escape-proof facility. The plan involves using the "negative zone" as a prison—an outer, negatively charged dimension with a single portal. In *Fantastic Four: Foes*, Reed explains,

> [I]t is inhabited only by plant life and some primitive insects. There're plenty of open spaces. . . . This planetoid is perfect. . . . It would be dangerous for them to escape. . . . Escape from this prison would mean being stranded in a realm of harsh unfamiliarity—with no way of getting home.

Unfortunately, before construction was even completed on the negative zone prison, a breakout plot was in motion.

The Negative Zone Prison Alpha (a.k.a. Fantasy Island, Project 42) was also used in *Civil War* to house "for life" superheroes that refused to register with the government. Tony Stark (a.k.a. Iron Man) shrugs off concerns about the potential unconstitutionality of the facility and states, "This place is outside the jurisdiction of local and federal courts. . . . American laws don't touch here. American lawyers don't come here. Once non-registrants come here they're legal non-entities. Occupants. Prisoners." Readers could easily find parallels to the post-9/11 actions of the United States government in detaining enemy combatants in the military Guantanamo Bay facility. The blog post titled "The Negative Zone Gulag" contains a lively discussion debating the constitutional issues surrounding the establishment of a gulag outside of United States territory and detaining citizens indefinitely, with many readers interpreting this story as a critique of the overreach of governmental power in a post-9/11 context.[21]

Retributive Tease

The tenets of retribution are frequently voiced in comic book narratives. When a threat of apocalyptic proportions presents itself, retribution is often explicitly tied in with messianic justice. In the DC universe, the Spectre is the mythical embodiment of God's wrath, ready to step in when all other avenues have failed. In *Final Crisis: Revelations*, Crispus Allen, deceased Gotham City police detective, has been chosen by God to take on the mantle of the Spectre. The Spectre confronts offenders, declares his/her sins, and administers the final judgment. He states to the villain Libra, "You are a murderer. You have committed genocide. The blood of the last martian [Manhunter] was spilled by your hand . . . and so your blood shall be spilled by my hand." In swirls of fire and lightning, bodies of rapists and murderers disintegrate before Allen. However, Allen expresses discontent with his role as the deliverer of God's justice. He distinguishes between vengeance and justice,

> Vengeance has nothing to do with balance. Justice is about balance. Vengeance is about payback. It's about pain and suffering . . . about hurting the other guy back. That's not justice. It never will be. . . . Here's the difference between vengeance and justice. Vengeance comes from the heart, it's driven by emotion. Justice comes from the head, it's driven by reason.

Retribution reflects the principle of *lex talionis*, or the law of retaliation, requiring that punishment be proportionate to the harm incurred and underlying the concept of retributive justice. In *Doing Justice,* Andrew von Hirsch distinguishes between the concepts of retribution and desert. The use of the term "retribution" (defined as "recompense for, or requital of evil done; return of evil") is discarded for the preferred term "desert" (i.e., "those who violate others' rights deserve punishment").[22] For von Hirsch, the case for punishment rests on considerations of both desert and deterrent principles. Punishment is justified because it is deserved, and though punishment inflicts human suffering, it is believed to work in the best interest of the greater good by potentially preventing more harm than is caused by the punishment's infliction of human suffering. The author states, "[T]he benefits accruing to society simply do not justify depriving anyone (even violators) of their fundamental rights: that it is essential to the very existence of the criminal sanction that the violator deserves to be punished."[23] Or, as Immanuel Kant would suggest, punishment is obligatory, a moral imperative.[24] Von Hirsch's concept of just deserts is presented in *Doing Justice* as a model for sentencing policy.

In mainstream comic books, retribution is most often expressed as an "eye for an eye" or the killing of the villain (or at least the potential killing). One of the most notable purveyors of retributive justice is the Punisher. Frequently called out by other heroes in the Marvel universe, the Punisher maintains his commitment to violent retribution. In one issue, the criminal Inskipp is begging for his life as the Punisher catches up to him. "I am begging you in the name of God—" he says, and the Punisher replies, "You can beg the sun not to come up in the morning, Inskipp. But it always does anyway." He proceeds to throw the criminal off a skyscraper (*The Punisher* #37). In another issue, the Punisher is seen blowing away the foot soldiers in a criminal organization, his machine guns raging at full blast, bodies being blown back by bullets, with the Punisher's narration, "Yes. Oh yes. Burn in hell you worthless bastards" (*The Punisher* #34). Fans of the Punisher, for example, often explain that what they like about the character is that he is not afraid to act with retribution and even vengeance, fulfilling the promise of the comic book tease. As one focus group participant explained, "One of my favorites has always been the Punisher for the simple reason that (a) he doesn't take any crap and (b) whatever he comes across, that's it. There's no if's and's or but's about it."[25] Another said, "Sometimes we over-think this stuff and sometimes bad people deserve to get spanked. They deserve a beating equivalent to the crime they've committed. . . . [S]ometimes the bad guys just need to be thrown around."[26] And another commented, "[B]ut I'm not opposed to violence either. . . . [E]very now and again you just kinda have to take the hammer to the handle."[27] More frequently, though, retribution is merely a tease, as heroes incapacitate villains in spectacularly violent ways that pack the emotional punch of retribution, but fall short of the "eye for an eye" symmetry associated with retribution. As one focus group participant explained, referring to the death of Gwen Stacy at the hands of the Green Goblin in the classic Spider-Man story,

> I think at this more than any other time Spider-Man could have killed the Green Goblin. He [understood] who the Green Goblin was, which was his best friend's father. And even though he beat the mess out of the guy, he didn't kill him. So that speaks a lot to his character and what lines he is not willing to cross.[28]

However, comic fans appear to have no limit to the amount of physical damage, short of killing, that the hero may inflict on the villain. Torture has evolved to be a preferred form of retribution that is short of killing and does not preclude ultimately imposing incapacitation. Bullseye was tortured by Daredevil in *Ultimate Elektra: Devil's Due*. In *Irreedemable*, the superhero Qubit tortures a minion of Plutonian in order to find out his location. The female victim is strapped onto a metal structure with several metal tendrils that poke and prod her mercilessly (*Irredeemable* #9).

For some, the pornographic quality of the violence leading up to the lack of killing completely overshadows the absence of the ultimate vengeance a killing would represent. In *Moon Knight: The Bottom*, Moon Knight battles the Committee, a group of villains bent on his destruction and that of his friend and allies. He is disabled in fighting the villain Bushman, whose face Moon Knight literally cuts off in the process. Later in the story, Marlene Alraune, his ex-girlfriend, asks what he plans to do about the Committee and he says, "Vengeance!" She replies, "Don't give them a second chance." Yet, the resolution of the plot, for all its tough talk and even tougher fighting scenes, ends in a showdown with the villain Taskmaster during which Moon Knight beats Taskmaster and slices his costume. Moon Knight's wrath alone is enough to terrorize Taskmaster, who manages to escape. Profile, another villain witnessing the scene, vomits out of fear of Moon Knight, who once again manages to stay alive despite multiple assassination attempts. Here, Moon Knight does not kill despite the chance to do so, and instead stops short by creating enough fear in his opponents to end the fight. Yet, the tease of violence is what fans focus on in touting Moon Knight stories. One blog commentator said, "He's the living embodiment of vengeance. He regards the very concept of it as spiritual, holy. To him, busting heads and cutting bitches, no matter how inconsequential or petty, is like going to evening mass."[29]

Similarly, the X-Men live by a code of not killing their enemies, yet this code is constantly in danger of being violated by characters overcome by the apocalyptic circumstances. Wolverine is most frequently portrayed as chomping at the bit to kill foes in such titles as *Astonishing X-Men: Ghostbox* and *Psylocke*, among others. In *The Punisher* (#34), Daredevil attempts to talk Wolverine out of killing the Punisher after the Punisher elbows him in the face during a dispute over crime-fighting strategy. Wolverine says to Darevil, "Outta th' way, do-gooder! Gonna teach this looney-tune a lesson he won't ferget [sic], once an' fer [sic] all!" Luckily Spider-Man and Daredevil are able to hold Wolverine back from the retributive brink.

Psylocke is another mutant who pushes the envelope of violence. In the opening scene of *Psylocke*, the villain Mister Sack threatens the borders of Utopia and is taking hostages. Once apprehended, Psylocke tells her mutant allies that he should be killed in order to prevent future problems. Reminded of the X-Men code by Cessily, she instead orders him to the cell block. As the drama continues, Psylocke embarks on a revenge mission to kill Matsu'o Tsurayaba, the villain who had swapped her into an Asian body in a classic Psylocke story arc, and to whom she showed mercy. Meanwhile, Wolverine has been keeping Matsu'o alive despite a painful condition in which his hands and many body parts were destroyed. Rather than allowing him to die, Wolverine lets the pain of his condition torture him as revenge for poisoning and ultimately killing his lover, Mariko Yashida. When Psylocke asks why he doesn't kill him, he replies, "Because that is too easy. Me and Matsu'o, we're gonna live with what he did. We're both gonna suffer." In the end, Psylocke does kill Matsu'o, but the killing is considered merciful because he wanted to die in order to end the pain of his disease. In fact, he had set the events of her revenge mission in motion as an elaborate suicide wish. Psylocke narrates, "[T]he man I killed today, I killed him for the right reasons. If there is such a thing."

Comic books as retributive tease sometimes make good on the violent foreplay. In the two-page-spread title page of *Azrael: Death's Dark Knight*, Azrael, a recruit of the Order of Purity, a splinter group of the Order of St. Dumas, is charged with carrying out God's will. Azrael stands as a "soldier of God" above a kneeling undercover cop. The bound officer admits to beating "many, many people," or "punks," in the line of duty. Before severing the cop's head with a flaming sword, Azrael states his claim to a greater justice: "I serve God's justice!"

Dismayed that Azrael has committed murder, the Order of Purity begins to recruit a new avenging angel, Michael Lane. However, wearing the Azrael "suit of sorrows" brings burdens that are ultimately too great for the wearer to bear. The suit eventually induces insanity and when the wearer goes "over the edge," the suit must be reclaimed. Lane accepts the suit—and the inevitable drain on his soul—in hopes of serving the greater good. In the final panels of issue #3, the new Azrael (Michael Lane) stands above a man that was caught on camera kicking someone to death during a riot. Rather than killing the criminal, Azrael leaves vengeance to the Lord, demanding, "[Y]ou committed your sins with your legs . . . so that's the price you have to pay. An eye for an eye, a tooth for a tooth. Gotham City is finally ready for *true justice.*"

Vigilante Incapacitation

When a tsunami threatens the Gulf Coast in the short comic called "Thumb on the Pulse" within the *Age of Heroes* series, the Avengers are there to hold back the wave and break it up, thereby saving lives. Following on the heels of the events of *Siege*, in which the superheroes were unable to prevent the destruction of the city of Asgard, the successful tsunami response represents a revitalization of citizen support for superheroes with depictions of everyday-looking guys in Yankees hats fist pumping the air and yelling, "Awright! Go! Go!" and "They are back! They are so back! Man! Someone finally back on our side!" Similar to the depiction of these citizens in the Marvel universe, focus group discussants also longed to live in a world in which heroes exist to stand up for the little guy or save people from danger in the nick of time. This yearning for protectors seems to be one of the most important themes in comic books that makes their fantasy worlds so satisfying to fans. As two participants discussed,

Azrael calls for biblical retribution in Gotham City. (*Azrael: Death's Dark Knight* #3, Fabian Nicieza and Frazer Irving, DC, 2009)

PARTICIPANT 1: I want to live in a world where . . . if a woman is about to be raped and she screams, the [perpetrator] is like, "oh no!" and he runs away. I wish that was—

PARTICIPANT 2: In other words, you want to live in a world where there are superheroes

PARTICIPANT 1: Yes, you're not going to let Lex Luthor loose, you know . . . [Y]ou're not going to let these really big bad guys live.[30]

Our focus group participants often explained that vigilante justice in comic books was an exaggeration of what was possible in the real world. One focus group participant asked the potent question, "Why aren't there more real-life costumed vigilantes?" This was the premise of Mark Millar's popular comic book series and motion picture *Kick-Ass* (2010). Dave Lizewski is a nerdy high school kid and comics fanboy who decides to don a green and yellow costume, calls himself Kick-Ass, and takes to the streets of New York as a vigilante superhero. The harsh realities of actualizing the superhero mythology set in as his first encounter with a graffiti gang leaves him hospitalized. Nonetheless, he soldiers on, bolstered by being made famous for his exploits on YouTube. He meets up with a father-daughter team of like-minded costumed vigilantes on a crusade against an organized crime group. Again he is beaten up and then violently tortured by his foes. Kick-Ass's beat-downs are shown in graphic detail, with blood dripping profusely from his and his compadres' bodies. The blood seems to ooze and drip from every part of these vigilantes' bodies, driving home how physically demanding and unpleasant real vigilante crime fighting might be. Similarly, focus group participants cited fear of bodily harm as the main reason why real people do not often become costumed crime fighters, preferring to leave the superhero motif to fantasy or merely dressing up as their favorite hero for Comic Con without taking on a crime-fighting agenda.

In the real world, it's rare, but not unheard of, for someone to actually act out a superhero fantasy. For example, Shadow Hare, a spandex-clad "superhero" armed with accoutrements such as handcuffs, a taser, and pepperspray, patrols the streets of Cincinnati. Shadow Hare is a member of a larger group, the Allegiance of Heroes, who communicate online and assist police in their respective cities. Along with Shadow Hare, the other members, Wall Creeper, Master Legend, Mr. Extreme, and Apocalyptico, operate within the law, making citizen arrests if they witness a crime.[31]

Kick-Ass takes a beating at the hands of enemies who wonder why he sacrifices himself as a self-proclaimed superhero when the personal costs are so high. (*Kick-Ass*, Mark Millar and John Romita Jr., Icon, 2010)

In San Diego, a self-proclaimed crime fighter named Mr. Xtreme wears a mask and a jersey bearing his Xtreme Justice League (XJL) logo while patrolling local neighborhoods with a first-aid kit, a flashlight, and a stun gun. He regularly hands out granola bars and orange juice to the homeless and claims that he has broken up a potentially violent road-rage dispute. He also participates in volunteer searches for missing children or suspects when they occur in San Diego County. Although described by the *San Diego Reader* as having a "thin" crime-fighting resume, his engagement in looking out for fellow citizens was applauded by the journalist.[32]

Retribution Fantasyland

Depictions of punishment in our sample of contemporary American comic books overwhelmingly privilege incapacitation coupled with a retributive tease. For fans, one of the major attractions to comic books is the emotional resonance of retributive justice—the visceral response to the violent narratives and graphic imagery. Simultaneously, the fans expect heroes to adhere to a moral compass, one that most often disallows the killing of others.

However, the realization of retributive justice may occur through a hyperviolent resolution. Here, fans engage in contextualized justice where the appropriateness of the punishment meted out by the hero is determined not on the characteristics of the crime but rather on the characteristics of the hero. For some heroes, killing is not only desired, but expected. The fans relish the transgressive consumption of comic books, but are quick to point out that this desire is only appropriate in a fantasy context—that is, few advocate vigilante justice in "real life."

The focus on retribution and incapacitation in comic books, to the exclusion of other rationales for punishment, mirrors the broader retributive discourse in American society that David Garland describes as dominating social responses to crime.[33] There is little room for alternatives to incapacitation or retribution as a response to crime, with rehabilitation and restorative justice virtually absent from the narratives. Such omissions are partially due to the constraints of the superhero genre that necessitate a suspenseful, violent climax rendered in splashy graphics. After all, the public also readily embraces deterrence as a justification for punishment, but as discussed, this perspective is merely alluded to in passing rather than a major focus of the comic books we sampled.

We suggest that comic books form part of a larger popular cultural discourse about issues of crime and justice. They are part of the narratives that, as David Green mentions, are fed and regurgitated, feeding the public's imagination and ultimately contributing potential solutions to the crime problem, particularly as it is presented as an apocalyptic threat. Comic books are often filled with plots that build with suspense toward the promise of retribution. Unfortunately, readers' desires often remain unrequited in that their heroes frequently deal short-term blows of incapacitation to their enemies, as opposed to full-blown payback. The rhetoric of retribution is the emotionally attractive component, rather than the implementation of retribution itself. The emotional tease of retribution satisfies consumers' imaginations, contributing to a quintessentially American type of tough talk that resonates widely despite often being all bark and no bite.

10

CONCLUSION

ULTIMATE JUSTICE

During the September 8, 2011, Republican presidential primary, Texas governor and candidate Rick Perry underscored his commitment to capital punishment by saying,

> In the state of Texas, if you come into our state and you kill one of our children, you kill a police officer, you're involved with another crime and you kill one of our citizens, you will face the ultimate justice in the state of Texas, and that is you will be executed.[1]

This expression of "ultimate justice" elicited the biggest applause of the night and dominated headlines in the hours following. However, in his study of the death penalty, sociologist and legal studies scholar David Garland points out that the death penalty is no longer about actually carrying out executions; rather, it is "primarily a communication system . . . about threats rather than actual executions," a "performance of discourse and debate."[2] Yet, this "peculiar institution" continues to capture the imaginations of Americans across the country. Actual executions are relatively rare, concentrated in specific geographical areas, and heavily influenced by local political interests; however, this in no way reduces the power of the death penalty as an important mechanism for expressing American values about punishment.³ Notwithstanding that Texas is a state that does, with some frequency, carry out the death penalty, we suggest that the sentiment behind Governor Perry's statement elicited such a boisterous response from the audience because it reflects public fascination with the idea of retribution more than the acts of execution themselves. Such calls for retribution rile up many members of the public, suggesting that tough-talking rhetoric around the death penalty is emotionally satisfying to many Americans.

Similarly, the preference for retributive talk by protagonists in comic books represents one of the most seductive thrills of these books, even as retribution was rarely the ultimate outcome of a storyline. We found that in our broad sample of comic books, retributive ideological messages consistently surfaced. Our sample showed that protagonists favored a kind of retributive brinkmanship that led to restraint and incapacitation of any threats, even those reaching apocalyptic proportions.

Although a retributive policy message is not a surprising finding to even casual comic book readers, we argue that comic books present a special kind of retribution in which the rhetorical ramping up of threats is just as important as, if not more important than delivering the punch. This is evident in the larger American culture as well. During the first decade of the millenium, the United States government overtly relied on simplistic, comic book–style rhetoric to rally support for military action against enemies of the United States in the name of national security. Most notably, former President G. W. Bush used slogans such as "wanted dead or alive" and "smoke em' out" to describe his administration's response to Al Qaeda and employed the rhetoric of "good versus evil" to justify America's pursuit of those responsible for the 9/11 attacks. The rhetoric works because it taps into sentiments and symbols of tough-talking Americanisms already embedded in popular consciousness through a variety of media, including comic books.

In our study we found that comic books consistently employ the rhetoric of retribution despite actually fulfilling the goal of incapacitation—what we call apocalyptic incapacitation. Here, the villains are incapacitated, but retribution ultimately remains incomplete while the perpetual yearning for utopia continues. As superhero Barbara Gordon says in *Oracle: The Cure*, "[P]art of me likes the idea of an eye for an eye." What is notable about our findings is that the presence of this retributive sentiment alone is satisfying to readers. There is no requirement that it be carried through to completion. We suggest that this is, in part, a product of the medium itself—visual, often graphic, depictions of violence and suspenseful action sequences that take place within a particular continuity in the context of enduring dystopia. Apocalyptic incapacitation often has the emotional quality of vengeance that is realized through action-oriented, extra-legal plot developments. In essence, our sample of comic books frequently talked tough, looked bloody, but ultimately contained threats of retribution rather than full execution of it.

At the same time, our sample tended to devalue nonviolent conflict resolution and was devoid of any critical or radical explanations for criminal behavior. As in virtually all other media accounts, criminal behavior is most frequently reduced to simplistic, individualized explanations without regard to the larger social structure in which the individual operates. Criminality is often written on the face, or the body, of the villain, creating a physical rendering of evil itself. The readers' transgressive engagement with the comic books is evident as they report that they enjoy the villains as much as the heroes, all the while acknowledging that to do so is "so wrong."[4] What is significant is the emotional connection that the reader *feels*—the readers thoroughly enjoy consuming the transgressions in a vicarious manner, but at a cognitive level may reject the behavior as contemptible. Through this connection, these iconic villains then become symbols of larger-than-life evil.

We found that comic books provide readers with a means of processing existential dilemmas in an age of anxiety about threats that reach global proportions, such as terrorism or genocide, that may be construed as apocalyptic in nature. Such crises often demand vigilante responses when law enforcement cannot protect citizens from the impending doom. At times, the books create an opportunity for resistance to this status quo formula by providing scenarios in which the use of extralegal tactics as a solution to the crime problem is rendered problematic. For example, in *Cry for Justice*, when Green Lantern confronts Green Arrow about his excessive use of force, readers are forced to consider what type of behavior they are willing to accept in the quest for justice. In fact, during our research, one thing that readers were keen to point out is the way, as with any other form of literature, they use comic book narratives to work through their own understandings of the world. When the heroes violently "interrogate" suspects as a means of gathering intelligence, readers use those narratives as a means of making sense of what they would, or would not, approve of in real-world settings. That these judgments are contextualized, by virtue of their being applied on the basis of the character of the hero rather than simply the crime itself, lends insight into the way readers perceive of the concept of justice. Further, this process sheds light on policies that may be supported or rejected by readers as a solution to crime in the real world.

By raising these issues, comic books show that they are more than capable of presenting complex issues about the debate between public safety and individual rights. Ultimately, the books provide readers an opportunity to move beyond knee-jerk reactions and explore the consequences of power and authority. Readers are thoughtful, and serious, about their interpretations of the criminal justice process. When readers rail against the storyline in *Cry for Justice* because it implicitly condones torture, and indicate that they are "depressed" at the notion that "in these half-dozen pages, all I see is a half-dozen superheroes taking Vice President Dick Cheney's side of the real world," they are demonstrating the process of reading comic books as a ritual moral exercise.[5] That is, readers are actively engaging in the material as a means of confronting moral dilemmas and expressing moral indignation. While reading is a solitary act, the expression of these moral sentiments certainly is not. Readers themselves indicate that expressing their views on moral issues is an important part of the immersion into mainstream comic book culture. Further, even those fans who do not consciously consider crime and justice a primary reason for indulging in comic books often find themselves in debate over whether or not the hero did the "right" thing.

Many of the participants in our focus groups, though not necessarily political conservatives in the voting booth, had some conservative ideas about crime and tended to be tough talkers when it came to neutralizing criminal threats. Like criminologist Frederic Thrasher, we believe it would be too reductionist to argue that reading comic books necessarily produces the conservative perspectives we encountered.[6] Rather, we believe these books reflect a general and enduring American social conservatism and fear of crime that are palpable in many other media and reflect the larger social context. And in that comic books are cultural touchstones that readers consume, there is a potential dialectic in play, in which comic book constructions and the kinds of musings that fans engage in on podcasts and Internet discussion boards contribute to shaping perspectives about crime and justice as well. Cultural criminologists such as Jeff Ferrell, Keith Hayward, and Jock Young have come to similar conclusions in exploring the role of media representations in Western, industrialized societies as Thrasher once did in combating Frederic Wertham's blanket condemnation of comic books: it is too simplistic to say that cultural artifacts solely contribute to a given attitude or behavior, but not off the mark to posit that these artifacts, in conjunction with other influences, provide symbolic scripts that can be seen reflected and reiterated in real life, whether consciously or unconsciously.[7]

We acknowledge that, as with other forms of popular culture, a reader's interpretation of comic book narratives is a product of his or her social location and is influenced by socioeconomic status, race, gender, sexual orientation, and other social factors. However, readers drawn to mainstream superhero comic books consume stories that generally reflect a broad, tough-on-crime orientation. Alternative constructions, though they do exist, are rarely best-sellers and are ideologically drowned out by another rhetorical ass-kicking from a time-honored superhero. This makes mainstream comic books, though diverse in one sense, also more prone to status quo ideological messages, which maintain existing power structures and celebrate America's hegemonic place in the world. In other words, the conservative ideological orientation sells, but at the same time, one could still dig deeper at one's local comic books store and dust off something less popular, but more liberal in plot possibilities and ideological messages.

Our findings show that indeed readers feel intensely connected to the stories they consume. From a criminological perspective, we are most interested in the ways in which themes of crime and justice are interwoven into these narratives. We interrogate the explicit images of graphic violence and implicit suggestions of violence, and find they are an integral part of the reading experience. In fact, according to fans, this is one of most satisfying aspects of these stories. However, this is not an appreciation of violence for violence' sake. The violence is tied to specific, American notions of justice. It is a response to a crisis that necessitates action that operates outside the boundaries of constitutional law and the criminal justice system. Whether or not that violence is satisfying is contextual. We find that readers judge the hero as he or she navigates the path to justice, but not in a classical criminological tradition. For example, rather than making a determination of whether the punishment as meted out by the hero fits the crime, the reader determines whether the punishment is just according to the *character of the hero*. We see this most starkly in our analysis of deathworthiness. On the path to justice, whether to kill villains or merely incapacitate them is a frequently occurring obsession among heroes. Likewise, the traditional Christian-influenced American retributive context has long been about sorting good from evil. In the same way that the expression of retribution is more important than the execution of it, the sorting of persons into categories of good versus evil is also more important than the consequences of that decision.

We began our analysis in a post-9/11 context—a world in which it was declared that "everything had changed." Our findings, as well as those of other scholars, attest that 9/11 did in fact create a fissure in the comic book industry, prompting an overall reexamination of the hero in contemporary society and an opportunity for more diverse representations of the "other," particularly those of Middle Eastern descent. However, as we noted in our chapters on gender, sexual orientation, and race, these books remain the domain of white heterosexual creators and characters. Our analysis includes an examination of difference, including the ways in which race and sexual orientation are portrayed in comic books. Our findings suggest that heroes operate in a primarily patriarchal, heterosexual world that is disguised as race-neutral. This analysis is essential as it relates to larger cultural assumptions regarding the type of person our society considers heroic and the type of person considered villainous.

This cultural ambivalence about accepting heroes of difference came to the fore when, in 2012, DC Comics announced they would be reintroducing a popular male superhero as gay. "One Million Moms," the group created by the vehemently antigay American Family Association, dedicated to protecting children from the "filthy" segments of our society, responded by embarking on a public relations assault against the comic industry.[8] Their method of attack included a Facebook page "warning" parents that Green Lantern (a.k.a. Alan Scott) would be reintroduced as gay. However, shortly thereafter, readers reacted with overwhelming pro-gay sentiments, "flooding" the Facebook comments section. Soon, the page mysteriously disappeared, presumably removed by one of the one million moms involved in the organization.[9]

The notion that Americans cannot tolerate gay heroes is belied by the fact that many of our real-life heroes are, in fact, gay. For example, New

York Fire Department chaplain Mychal Judge heroically rushed to the aid of victims of the World Trade Center during the attacks of 9/11, and was killed as a result. *New York* magazine declared him the "first and most famous victim" of the attacks.[10] He was marked "Victim 0001" by officials as tributes poured in by fellow New Yorkers and others around the world to commemorate his bravery. His life's work is described by journalist Amy Goodman as that of "peace, tolerance, and reconciliation."[11] Another gay hero, airline passenger Mark Bingham, was aboard Flight 93 on September 11, 2011. Bingham was instrumental in assisting other passengers as they took down the hijacked flight over Pennsylvania, ultimately avoiding further casualties. He was immediately deemed a hero by the media and, as details emerged, his openly gay status became widely known.[12] Revelations such as these challenge Americans to confront the hegemonic conception of a hero that traditionally excludes gays and other minorities.

In August 2011, Marvel comics introduced Miles Morales to the Ultimates universe. The controversy surrounding the character was not due to the notion that a new Spider-Man would be populating the Ultimates universe but rather to Morales's ethnic heritage: half-Latino and half African American. When *USA Today* ran a story about the character, the site received impassioned comments from readers, ranging from cheers (e.g., "This is a good thing.") to jeers (e.g., "Why does everything have to be politically correct?" "Well, that nails it. Spidey[']s dead to me.").[13]

These comments demonstrate that culturally, we have not passed into a postracial environment where race/ethnicity no longer matters in our conceptions of who may be considered heroic. Instead, there continues to remain resistance around heroes of difference. This is especially true with regard to characters facing double marginality—those that are racial/ethnic minorities and gay and/or female. Or, as one commenter posted in response to the suggestion that Morales may also be gay, and that eventually this revelation would, and should, be considered normal and met with little fanfare: "Equating being black to being gay . . . thanks for insulting blacks everywhere."[14] These prejudiced sentiments are fueled by popular political pundits such as Glenn Beck, who commented on the introduction of Morales on his *Glenn Beck Radio Program*. After declaring that he does not care one bit about the race/ethnicity of the character, Beck revealed that his single concern is that the introduction of Morales was the result of a nefarious plot by First Lady Michelle Obama to "change the traditions" of this country.[15] Through his bizarre conspiracy theory, along with his supposed denial of "caring" about the racial/ethnic identity of the character, Beck reveals that he is threatened. He has demonstrated that changes in the identities of superheroes are no less than attacks on conservative American values. This is one reason we, as well as a majority of our focus group participants, feel it is so vitally important to increase the representation of minorities within the pages of mainstream comic books. The promise of an America as a just place for all its inhabitants starts with its popular mainstream imaginations.

While the past decade or so has opened up possibilities for heroes of difference, there remains a tendency for comic book characters' race and sexual orientation to reflect those of their creators—primarily straight, white males. This is significant because our findings suggest that readers are eager for their beloved fictional heroes to represent "them" in their diversity. As it stands, the industry lags behind in providing fully dimensional heroes of diversity. Until that happens, the question of whether gay, black, or female heroes are "believable" or "relatable" will continue to be posed.

Alternatively, the lack of diversity could make these books more comfortable for readers who remain in privileged positions within white hegemony and patriarchy. In recruiting participants for focus groups, we only managed to include one woman. In the vast majority of comics-related meet-ups we attended, we were the only female attendees. In larger contexts, such as Comic Cons, men frequently outnumber women. At one point in the review of various discussion boards and podcasts, we sensed that some male fans might be more socially comfortable around hypothetical aliens and zombies than around females, particularly "strong" females. On the other hand, we found a strong representation of male fans of color, suggesting that racial and ethnic inclusiveness may be less important for men in a genre that celebrates traditional notions of masculinity.

Readers may be attracted to comic books precisely for the conservative ideological content—from retribution to white hegemony. The apocalyptic incapacitation that is violently enacted, for example, acts as a transgressive voyeuristic pleasure in which readers may explore getting tougher on crime than perhaps their off-page selves would find reasonable. Many of our focus group participants indicated they were drawn to the dystopic settings, or "the dreary sense of crime" as one participant called it.[16] Further, the assumption of whiteness or maleness may elicit a certain transgressive thrill in a contemporary globalized world, particularly when coupled with the kinds of American nostalgia the books often evoke.

In our study, we were struck by the vibrant comic book subculture, which continues to grow at a rapid pace, as evidenced by attendance at various annual comic conventions around the United States. We suggest that the impact of comic books is greater than it may first appear. Though individual sales of floppies may be low compared to, say, dollar grosses on motion pictures or may reach fewer viewers than a summer blockbuster, we suggest that the floppies and the stories they contain are greater than the sum of their parts. While the latest issue of Batman may have sold only tens of thousands of copies, most Americans "know" who Batman is; many flock to the theaters to see the latest Batman-inspired movie. There are probably countless people who have tattooed logos of Batman, Superman, or Wonder Woman on their bodies yet have never read even a single issue of a comic book. Nonetheless, the characters originate in the comic books, and the industry continues to primarily drive the mythology even as it absorbs scripts and plot lines from successful movie adaptations.

Despite the influence of the industry in American popular culture, we found the fan culture to exhibit a high degree of cultural intimacy. Not only do complicated Marvel and DC continuities exist to sort out the true fans from the mere tourists, but a relatively closeted pride in the medium's conservative orientation also characterizes insiders. Drawing on anthropologist Michael Herzfeld's notion of cultural intimacy, an attitude that may cause shame or embarrassment externally serves the internal function of providing cohesion among subcultural group members.[17] Herzfeld describes this as the "social poetics" of a context, in which essentialized cultural meaning becomes a semiotic illusion performed and reified within the social group, until it reaches the status of being natural, not interpretative. Aspects of the world of comic books such as its apocalyptic constructions, its pornification of the female superhero, and its dystopic worldview, may have, for many readers, become self-evident facts hardly worthy of investigation while also serving as points of cohesion and identity within the subculture.

In this way, we are aware that comic book fans themselves may be unhappy with our treatment of their favorite medium. Some may fear that exposure of this may threaten the comfortable insularity of the world of comic books, an insularity that has been maintained despite the fact that these plots and characters have been blown up on the Hollywood big screen. As participant-observers in this world, we are not insiders to the extent of having mastered the Marvel or DC continuities, but we took seriously those continuities because of their importance to fans, as the social poetics of the context, and learned as much as we could during the course of our study. But far from being mere tourists in the world of comic books, we came to the study having personally followed particular titles. Somewhere in the middle of these two extremes—the die-hards and the tourists—we brought a critical and cultural criminological sensibility to an oft-neglected subculture, paying close attention to the crime and justice messages that resonate from the books.

Future studies into comic books and their avid readers must continue to confront the notion that comic books are a kind of cultural sleeper cell for conservative, tough-on-crime American nostalgia and retributive brinkmanship. Criminologists may explore how the medium impacts the message, for example, by examining how the transition from comic book to big screen transforms the notions of crime and justice. It is our hope that in any case, comic books will continue to be studied by criminologists as an important source for understanding quintessentially American notions of crime and justice. It is one of the many important cultural influences that contribute to American considerations of the moral ramifications of criminal justice policies in the real world.

APPENDIX: SAMPLE AND METHODOLOGY

Table A.1

Series	Publisher	"Popular" *
100 Bullets	DC-Vertigo	
52 Weeks	DC	Popular
9-11 Emergency Relief	Alternative Comics	
9/11 Report: A Graphic Representation	Hill & Wang	
A Moment of Silence	Marvel	
Abandon: First Vampire	UpDown Studios	
After 9/11: America's War on Terror (2001-)	Hill & Wang	
Age of Heroes	Marvel	
All-Star Batman and Robin	DC	Popular
All-Star Superman	DC	Popular
Amazing Spider-Man	Marvel	Popular
American Vampire	DC-Vertigo	
American Widow	Villard	
Arab in America	Last Gap	
Arkham Reborn	DC	
Arkham Asylum	DC	
Astonishing X-Men	Marvel	Popular

Series	Publisher	"Popular" *
Azrael: Death's Dark Knight	DC	
Batgirl	DC	
Batman	DC	Popular
Batman and Robin	DC	Popular
Batman: Battle for the Cowl	DC	Popular
Batman: Streets of Gotham	DC	
Batman: The Brave and the Bold	DC	
Batwoman	DC	
Birds of Prey	DC	
Black Adam: The Dark Age	DC	
Black Cat: The Amazing Spiderman Presents	Marvel	
Black Panther	Marvel	
Black Widow: The Things They Say About Her	Marvel	
Blackest Night	DC	Popular
Blue Beetle	DC	
Books of Doom	Marvel	
Brightest Day	DC	
Buddha	Virgin	
Buffy the Vampire Slayer	Dark Horse	Popular
Cairo	DC-Vertigo	
Captain America	Marvel	Popular
Captain America: Reborn	Marvel	Popular
Case Files: Sam & Twitch	Marvel	
Catwoman: When in Rome	DC	
Cinderella: From Fabletown with Love	DC-Vertigo	
Civil War	Marvel	Popular
Civil War: Confession	Marvel	Popular
Civil War: Frontline	Marvel	Popular
Civil War: Initiative	Marvel	Popular
Civil War: Return	Marvel	Popular
Comics' 9-11: Artists Respond	Dark Horse	
Countdown to Infinite Crisis	DC	Popular
Coup d'Etat	Wildstorm	
Crime Bible	DC	
Criminal	Icon	

Series	Publisher	"Popular" *
Criminal Macabre	Dark Horse	
Daredevil	Marvel	
Dark Avengers	Marvel	Popular
Dark Avengers/Uncanny X-Men: Utopia	Marvel	Popular
Dark Reign	Marvel	
Dark Tower: Gunslinger Born	Marvel	Popular
Dark Tower: Long Road Home	Marvel	Popular
Dark Wolverine	Marvel	
DC Universe #0	DC	
DC Universe: Brave New World	DC	Popular
Deadshot	DC	
Detective Comics	DC	
Emma Frost	Marvel	
Ex Machina	Wildstorm	
Fables	DC	Popular
Fallen Son: Death of Captain America	Marvel	Popular
Fantastic Four: Foes	Marvel	
Fell	Image	
Final Crisis	DC	Popular
Flash	DC	
Flash: Rebirth	DC	Popular
Garuda	Virgin	
Girl Comics	Marvel	
Gotham Central	DC	
Gotham Gazette	DC	
Green Arrow	DC	
Green Arrow/Black Canary: A League of Their Own	DC	
Green Lantern	DC	
Green Lantern Rebirth	DC	Popular
Hellblazer	DC-Vertigo	
Heroes for Hire	Marvel	
House of M	Marvel	Popular
Human Target	DC-Vertigo	
Identity Crisis	DC	Popular
In the Shadow of No Towers	Pantheon	

Series	Publisher	"Popular" *
Incorruptible	Boom!	
Incredible Hulk	Marvel	Popular
Infinite Crisis	DC	Popular
Iron Man: Extremis	Marvel	
Irredeemable	Boom!	
Jalila	AK Comics	
JLA/The 99	DC	
Joker	DC	Popular
Jonah Hex: Special Edition	DC-Vertigo	
Justice	DC	Popular
Justice League of America	DC	Popular
Justice League: Cry for Justice	DC	
Justice League of America/Avengers	Marvel	Popular
Justice Society of America	DC	Popular
Kick-Ass	Marvel-Icon	
League of Extraordinary Gentlemen	DC	Popular
Lex Luthor: Man of Steel	DC	
Lucifer	DC-Vertigo	
Magneto: Testament	Marvel	
Marvel 1602	Marvel	Popular
Marvel Divas	Marvel	
Marvel Zombies	Marvel	Popular
Midnighter	DC-Wildstorm	
Mighty Avengers	Marvel	Popular
Milestone Forever	DC	
Moon Knight	Marvel	
New Avengers	Marvel	Popular
New Mutants	Marvel	
Nightwing: The Great Leap	Marvel	
Northlanders: Sven the Returned	DC-Vertigo	
Oracle: The Cure	DC	
Osborn: Evil Incarcerated	Marvel	
Persepolis	Pantheon	
Planetary: Systems	Wildstorm	
Powergirl	DC	

Series	Publisher	"Popular" *
Powers	Image	
Pride of Baghdad	DC-Vertigo	Popular
Project Superpowers	Dynamite	
Punisher	Marvel	
Punisher Max	Marvel	
Punisher vs. Bullseye	Marvel	
Punisher War Zone	Marvel	
Queen & Country	Marvel	
Ra's al Ghul (one-shot)	DC	
Rawhide Kid: Slap Leather	Marvel	
Red Robin	DC	
Rose & Thorn	DC	
Route 666	CrossGen	
Runaways	Marvel	
Scalped	DC-Vertigo	
Secret Avengers	Marvel	
Secret Invasion	Marvel	Popular
Secret Six	DC	
Secret War	Marvel	Popular
Secret Warriors: Nick Fury, Agent of Nothing	Marvel	
Serenity	Dark Horse	Popular
Shadowland	Marvel	
She-Hulk: Jaded	Marvel	
Shooting War	Grand Central Publishing	
Siege	Marvel	
Silver Surfer: Requiem	Marvel	
Sleeper: All False Moves	Marvel	
Spider-Man/Black Cat: The Evil That Men Do	Marvel	
Spider-Woman: Origin	Marvel	
The Boys	Dynamite	Popular
The Stand: Captain Trips	Marvel	Popular
Supergirl	DC	
Superman	DC	Popular
Superman: Earth One	DC	
Superman: Kansas Sighting	DC	

Series	Publisher	"Popular" *
Superman/Batman	DC	Popular
Teen Titans	DC	
Terra Obscura: Volume 2	America's Best Comics	
The 99	Tashkeel	
The Authority: Transfer of Power	DC-Wildstorm	
The Call of Duty: The Brotherhood	Marvel	
The Girl from H.O.P.P.E.R.S.	Fantagraphics	
The Life and Times of Savior 28	IDW	
The Losers	DC-Vertigo	
The Question: Pipeline	DC	
The World's Finest Comic Book Writers and Artists Tell Stories to Remember	Image	
Thunderbolts	Marvel	
Ultimate Avengers	Marvel	Popular
Ultimate Elektra	Marvel	
Ultimate Iron Man	Marvel	Popular
Ultimate Spider-Man	Marvel	Popular
Ultimates	Marvel	Popular
Ultimates 3	Marvel	Popular
Umbrella Academy: Apocalypse Suite	Dark Horse	Popular
Uncanny X-Men	Marvel	Popular
Vigilante	DC	
Villains United	DC	Popular
Walking Dead	Image	Popular
Waltz with Bashir	Metropolitan Books	
Wolverine	Marvel	Popular
Wolverine Weapon X	Marvel	
Wonder Woman	DC	
World War Hulk	Marvel	Popular
X-Factor	Marvel	Popular
X-Force	Marvel	Popular
X-Force and Cable: The Legend Returns	Marvel	
X-Men	Marvel	Popular
X-Men: Age of Apocalypse	Marvel	Popular
X-Men: Messiah Complex	Marvel	Popular

Series	Publisher	"Popular" *
X-Men Origins: Wolverine	Marvel	
Y the Last Man	DC-Vertigo	Popular
Year One: Batgirl	DC	
Year One: Batman/Ra's al Ghul	DC	
Year One: Batman/Scarecrow	DC	
Year One: Two Face	DC	

* "Popular" is based on the Michaels' Index calculated from March 2003 – August 2009.

Our units of analysis were story arcs appearing in the series mentioned in the sampling list. For our purposes, we defined a series according to the book title. Thus a large-scale crossover event such as "Civil War" has several titles, such as *Civil War, Civil War: Chronicles, Civil War: Frontline,* and *Civil War: X-Men.* Rather than consider these as a single series, even if we might analyze them, in some cases, as part of a unified story arc, we elected to refer to them separately. Thus, because of the measure of popularity we used (explained below) one-shots and short series that were widely popular tend to be more heavily represented than longer-running, more commonly known comic book series in our comparison to popular titles. We accepted this slight bias in the sampling because such series-level subpackages within crossovers and large universe-wide events are often what capture the imagination and stimulate conversation among readers.

To confirm that our sample captures content from among the best-selling comic books, we utilized the ICv2 monthly best-seller lists for the period between March 2003 and August 2009. Even though our sample covers the period from 2001 to 2010, we elected to use the ICv2 list starting in March 2003 because changes in the way the sales figures were calculated in 2003 meant that data before that time were not comparable. We stopped obtaining sales data from ICv2 in August 2009, though we continued to read some titles through 2010.

To determine a title's popularity over time, rather than merely monthly, we decided not to use the so-called Diamond Index, a value that might better be called the Batman Index, as that is the only title used to calculate it. For the Diamond Index, all other sales are compared to the sales of the "Batman" title to produce the index each month. While Batman is a popular title, it makes a poor barometer of overall comic book popularity. Some months the Batman series may be exceptionally popular, even as overall comic sales are down. Therefore, the Diamond Index varies too much by the ups and downs of Batman, rather than capturing what is happening more generally with comic books.

As an alternative we calculated an index using a method developed by sociology graduate student Matt Michaels. The Michaels Index is calculated on the basis of comics that match two criteria: (1) they were published consistently throughout the period of the data set, and (2) they had a low variance relative to the total population of comic books as an estimated quantity sold each month. In our sample, sixteen series met the criteria and were used to form the index appearing below.

1. HELLBLAZER
2. WITCHBLADE
3. FABLES
4. SPAWN
5. PUNISHER
6. WONDER WOMAN
7. ACTION COMICS
8. DAREDEVIL
9. DETECTIVE COMICS
10. FANTASTIC FOUR
11. SUPERMAN
12. GREEN LANTERN
13. ULTIMATE SPIDER-MAN
14. WOLVERINE
15. BATMAN
16. UNCANNY X-MEN

From the index, we used an average estimated quantity sold for each series for each month. The index value is produced by dividing the amount a particular title sold in a month by the average sales of these sixteen titles in that month. The resulting Michaels Index is less prone to being skewed by an individual title selling particularly poorly or particularly well in a single month.

We then used the Michaels Index to calculate popularity of a series. The average of the index value for a comic book series indicates, on average, how well a series title sells relative to its competitors each month. On the basis of this measure, we identified the one hundred most popular comic series during the period, from among the top three hundred best-selling comics from each month.

For our sample, graphic novel (GN) popularity was calculated differently. Sales are not as heavily weighted to the initial distribution. Consequently, popular GNs often have relatively low amounts bought in a given month, but over time are sold in quite high volume; relative month-to-month measures of sales do not tell much about the popularity of any given GN. Also, we do not have full three-hundred-title lists for each month for the period we examined data for. Between March 2003 and January 2004 the list available from ICv2 reflects the top fifty GNs. Between February 2004 and October 2008 the list has the top one hundred GNs for each month. From November 2008 to August 2009 the lists contain the most popular three hundred GNs. The measure we used for graphic novels was based on the total of the estimated sales for a GN over the entire time period of the data set. From this we identified the one hundred GNs that sold best during the period.

The latter approach has several limitations. First, since we only selected a limited number of top GNs from each month, we miss the possibility of a GN selling in small numbers consistently over the time that precedes or succeeds our data period. To be sure, this is really only likely to affect the months where we were only using a top-fifty list. The one hundred covers all of the GNs selling more than one thousand comics a month, and the top three hundred typically includes all the comics that sell a few hundred copies or more. Second, the beginning and end periods means that some comics may seem less popular than they are because the overall sales for that comic book did not fall in the time period. Since we did not use this as a method of selection, but rather only to assess the value of our sample, we do not consider this much of a problem; our sample clearly captured many popular GNs.

NOTES

CHAPTER 1

1. Josh Kurtz, "New Growth in a Captive Market"; Gail A. Caputo, *Intermediate Sanctions in Corrections.*

2. The influence and quality of comic books have not gone unnoticed by academics who have published literary critiques such as *Arguing Comics: Literary Masters on a Popular Medium* (2004), *The Sandman Papers* (2006), and *The Best American Comics Criticism*, among others. College professors, particularly in the humanities, have moved toward the inclusion of comic books and graphic novels in course syllabi. Further, scholarly interest has expanded to include the development of courses available in colleges and universities specifically devoted to the sequential art medium. For example, John Jay College of Criminal Justice offers a literature course entitled "Comic Books." Developed and taught by Dr. Jonathan Gray, the course is described as an

> introduction to the Graphic Novel as a literary form. The course investigates the three dominant genres in graphic narrative: superhero tales, autobiographical narratives, and political reportage. The best graphic novels . . . revolve around the themes of justice, morality and minority rights in dystopian societies, making this course especially apt for a college dedicated to criminal justice. (John Jay College of Criminal Justice, 2009, Course offerings: LIT 298)

In addition, a class on sequential art that includes both comic books and cartoon strips was offered by Seattle Central Community College in 2007. Ben Fowle, cofounder of the National Association of Comics Art Educators, told one journalist reporting on comics-related college classes that interest in the academic study of comic books has grown nationally since the early 2000s. And, a 2003 article in *The Chronicle of Higher Education* explores comic books as a pedagogical tool that can help bridge the cultural and generational gap between student and teacher. This increased interest has spawned a vibrant comics scholars listserv out of the University of Florida, heavily populated by scholars sharing academic discourse and pedagogical resources for comics studies courses. Christine Frey, "Funny What Colleges Teach These Days: Donald Duck, Superman Subjects for Serious Study," *Seattle Post-Intelligencer*, April 26, 2007, http://www.seattlepi.com/local/313189_comics26.html; P. Buhle, "The New Scholarship of Comics," *Chronicle of Higher Education*, May 16, 2003; Comix-Scholars Discussion List, *University of Florida*, n.d., http://www.english.ufl.edu/comics/scholars.

3. Stephanie Kane, "The Unconventional Methods of Cultural Criminology," 316.

4. Esther B. Fein, "Holocaust as a Cartoonist's Way of Getting to Know His Father," C19.

5. Scott McCloud, *Reinventing Comics: How Imagination and Technology Are Reinventing an Art Form*, 1.

6. In *The Power of Comics: History, Form, Culture,* Randy Duncan and Matthew J. Smith provide a chapter on the engagement of the reader with the comic book, describing the process of decoding the words and images. They write,

> It is not possible for a reader to passively receive meaning from a comic book. Even comprehending what each picture represents and what each word means requires some effort, and moving beyond image comprehension to understating the panel as a whole and how it fits into the overall narrative requires comic book readers to make inferences about the functions of images and the relationships between images. (168)

For a more comprehensive analysis of the consumption and processing of sequential images, see Neil Cohn, "The Limits of Time and Transitions: Challenges to Theories of Sequential Image Comprehension"; Robin Varnum and Christina T. Gibbons, *The Language of Comics*; Thierry Groensteen, *The System of Comics*.

7. Kathryn H. Fuller, *At the Picture Show: Small-Town Audiences and the Creation of Movie Fan Culture*; Carine Harrington, *Soap Fans: Pursuing Pleasure and Making Meaning in Everyday Life*; Henry Jenkins, *Textual Poachers*; Matthew J. Pustz, *Comic Book Culture: Fanboys and True Believers*.

8. Brian Eason, "The Life and Death and Life of Jason Todd."

9. Matthew Wolf-Meyer, "The World Ozymandias Made: Utopias in the Superhero Comic, Subculture, and the Conservation of Difference."

10. David Garland, *The Culture of Control: Crime and Social Order in Contemporary Society*.

11. Jared Lovell, "Step Aside Superman . . . This Is a Job for [Captain] America! Comic Books and Superheroes Post September 11"; Amy K. Nyberg, "Of Heroes and Superheroes"; Nickie Phillips and Staci Strobl, "Cultural Criminology and Kryptonite: Constructions of Crime and Justice in Comic Books in America."

12. Henry Jenkins, "Captain America Sheds His Mighty Tears: Comics and September 111"; Bradford W. Wright, *Comic Book Nation: The Transformation of Youth Culture in America*.

13. Jack G. Shaheen, "Arab Images in American Comic Books."

14. Manga and child-marketed publications were excluded from the sample because they represent a distinct market with their own conventions. For a full discussion of the history and cultural significance of manga, see Paul Gravett's *Manga: 60 Years of Japanese Comics*.

15. Two major companies comprise the vast majority of the comic book industry sales: DC (formerly known as National Allied Publishing) and Marvel (formerly known as Timely Publications and Atlas Comics).

16. ICv2 provides an index of the best-selling top three hundred monthly comics and top three hundred graphic novels. It should be noted that these are direct market sales—to comic book specialty stores—not sales to individuals. We acknowledge that there are other ways of determining "best-selling" comics that would yield a sample more inclusive of alternative titles and that using the ICv2 somewhat biases our sample toward superhero comics published by DC and Marvel. We acknowledge that there is a world of alternative and independently published comic books both in comic book stores and in other venues. However, other bestseller lists, such as Amazon and the *New York Times*, do not provide accounts of monthly floppies.

17. For a more comprehensive take on the origins of cultural criminology, see Jeff Ferrell, "Cultural Criminology"; Jeff Ferrell and C. Sanders, eds., *Cultural Criminology*; Jeff Ferrell, Keith Hayward, and Jock Young, *Cultural Criminology: An Invitation*.

18. Ferrell, Hayward, and Young, *Cultural Criminology*, 130; Ferrell, "Cultural Criminology"; Keith Hayward and Jock Young, "Cultural Criminology: Some Notes on the Script," 259.

19. Dominic Strinati, "The Big Nothing? Contemporary Culture and the Emergence of Postmodernism."

20. Jean Baudrillard, *Simulacra and Simulation*.

21. Nickie Phillips and Natasha Frost, "Crime in Prime Time."

22. John Storey, *Cultural Theory and Popular Culture: An Introduction*, p. 189.

23. Nicole Rafter, "Crime, Film, and Criminology," 416.

24. Jock Young, "Constructing the Paradigm of Violence: Mass Media, Violence, and Youth," 3.

25. Jack Katz, "What Makes Crime News?" 64.

26. Ibid.

27. David Garland, *Punishment and Modern Society: A Study in Social Theory*, 62.

28. Mike Presdee, *Cultural Criminology and the Carnival of Crime*. Here, we are considering Mike Presdee's study of the "carnival of crime" and the ways in which transgressions may manifest in contained space and time. We may think of the annual Comic-Cons themselves as carnivalesque—an annual celebration and socially acceptable outlet where adults may engage in cosplay (fans dressing up as their favorite superheroes, villains, or manga characters).

29. Focus Group #1 (2010).

30. Ibid.

31. Ibid.

32. Azn Badger, "Moon Knight, Thank You for Being So Freakin' Crazy."

33. Umberto Eco, *The Role of the Reader: Explorations in the Semiotics of Texts*. Philosopher Peregrine Dace counters Umberto Eco's contention. Instead, Dace contends that, for example, Frank Miller's *Dark Knight Returns* is replete with themes rendering the work subversive. Here, the aging Batman does not reinforce the status quo by legitimizing law enforcement efforts; rather, he goes underground to gather a group of potential crime fighters training for social change. Peregrine Dace, "Nietzsche contra Superman: An Examination of the Work of Frank Miller," *South African Journal of Philosophy* 26, no. 1 (2007): 98-106.

34. Jeff Williams, "Comics: A Tool of Subversion?"

35. John Fiske, *Understanding Popular Culture*, 123.

36. Steven Bryan, "The San Diego Comic-Con Wraps Up for 2008"; Calvin Reid, "Soldout in San Diego: Another Booming Comic-Con"; Heidi MacDonald and Calvin Reid, "Fans Wild for New York Comic Con 2010."

37. Jenkins, *Textual Poachers*, 23.

38. Ibid.

39. Pustz, *Comic Book Culture*.

40. Duncan and Smith, *The Power of Comics*.

41. Pustz, *Comic Book Culture*.

42. However, in early 2011, DC Comics announced the return of the DC letters pages. Matt Moore, "At DC Comics, Readers' Letters to Make a Return."

43. Douglas Wolk, *Reading Comics: How Graphic Novels Work and What They Mean*.

44. Roz Kaveney, *Superheroes! Capes and Crusaders in Comics and Films*, 202.

45. This is most apparent in the Disney acquisition of Marvel and DC Comics' transition to DC Entertainment in an effort to focus on more varied forms of entertainment; see Brad Trechak, "DC Comics Is Now DC Entertainment"; Brooks Barnes, "Disney to Buy Marvel and Its 5,000 Characters for $4 Billion."

46. ICv2, "Comic and Graphic Novel Sales Down in 2009."

47. Garyn Roberts, "Understanding the Sequential Art of Comic Strips and Comic Books and Their Descendants in the Early Years of the New Millennium." Both Marvel and DC offer digital comics for consumption on various devices, including computers and mobile devices. With the success of mobile applications (such

as those used with iOS and Android devices), publishers have aligned themselves with software creators to make their content available in various formats for e-book readers and the iPad.

48. Diamond Publishers, "Publisher Market Shares: 2009."

49. M. P. McAllister, E. H. Sewell, and I. Gordon, *Comics and Ideology.*

50. There is some debate over the usefulness of the term "graphic novel," with some using the term to refer to bound copies of previously published comic books and others reserving the term for self-contained stories. For example, Lopes defines the "graphic novel" as "long-arced narratives with complex story lines." *Demanding Respect: The Evolution of the American Comic Book.* Duncan and Smith define graphic novels as "longer than the typical comic book and most often featur[ing] self-contained, rather than continuing stories." *The Power of Comics,* 4. Others find fault with the term "novel," as many so-called graphic novels are not fiction.

51. Duncan and Smith, *The Power of Comics.*

52. For an in-depth analysis of the development of the superhero genre, see Peter Coogan's *Superhero: The Secret Origin of a Genre.*

53. Henry Jenkins, "Man without Fear: David Mack, Daredevil, and the Bounds of Difference (Part One)."

54. Valerie D'Orazio, "Occasional Superheroine."

55. Paul Simpson, Helen Rodiss, and Michaela Bushell, *The Rough Guide to Superheroes;* Movieweb, "All-Time Top 100 Grossing Films." Titles include *The Dark Knight, Spider-Man, Spider-Man 3, Iron Man, Iron Man 2, Batman, X-Men: Last Stand,* and *The Incredibles.*

56. *The Dark Knight* was a critical, as well as commercial, success with the late Heath Ledger winning an Academy Award and Golden Globe for best supporting actor for his portrayal of Batman's arch-nemesis, the Joker.

57. MSNBC, "Video Sales Overtaking Music." EDGE, "The 60 Best-Selling Games in the Last 12 Months." In 2007, Spider-Man was the fifteenth best-selling video game, with 3.4 million copies sold. Among the top video games sold in 2008 were Lego Batman (2.8 million sold), Iron Man (2.3 million sold), and Mortal Kombat vs. DC Universe (1.5 million sold).

58. Geoff Boucher, "Nick Fury No More? Samuel L. Jackson Says "Maybe I Won't be Nick Fury," *Los Angeles Times,* January 14, 2009, http://herocomplex.latimes.com/2009/01/14/nick-fury-no-mo.

59. Roz Kaveney, *Superheroes! Capes and Crusaders in Comics and Films,* 141.

CHAPTER 2

1. Bradford W. Wright, *Comic Book Nation: The Transformation of Youth Culture in America,* 36.

2. For a comprehensive cultural history of comic books see Jean-Paul Gabilliet, *Of Comics and Men: A Cultural History of American Comic Books.*

3. Mike Benton, *Crime Comics: The Illustrated History,* 3.

4. Ibid., 15.

5. Danny Fingeroth, *Superman on the Couch: What Superheroes Really Tell Us about Ourselves and Our Society*; Wright, *Comic Book Nation*. Superman, created by Jerry Siegel and Joe Shuster, is generally considered the origin of the superhero genre, though other scholars note that the roots of the genre reach back further into mythical and legendary gods and heroes that represent our "collective cultural unconsciousness." Gina Misiroglu, *The Superhero Book*; Matthew J. Pustz, *Comic Book Culture: Fanboys and True Believers*; Chris Knowles, *Our Gods Wear Spandex: The Secret History of Comic Book Heroes*. Peter Coogan, *Superhero: The Secret Origin of a Genre*, 125. Superman's origin story is described in "The Origin of Superman" by Len Wein. He writes, "Realizing his beloved homeworld was doomed, a scientist named Jor-El sent his infant son Kal-El (a.k.a. Superman) rocketing in the direction of our Earth mere instants before Krypton exploded."

6. Wright, *Comic Book Nation*.

7. David Hajdu, *The Ten Cent Plague: The Great Comic-Book Scare and How It Changed America*, 30; Thomas Andrae, "From Menace to Messiah: The History and Historicity of Superman"; Fingeroth, *Superman on the Couch*.

8. Wright, *Comic Book Nation*, 24.

9. Frank Plowright, *The Slings and Arrows Comic Guide: A Critical Assessment*, 179.

10. The tone of the Batman stories changed over the decades with a move from pulp inspiration to science fiction by the 1960s. The 1960s television show *Batman* introduced the audience to a campy and lighthearted Batman and Robin. By 1970, the dynamic duo were restored to their roots as dark vigilante avengers by creators Dennis O'Neil and Neal Adams. Decades later, a more grim and gritty Batman surfaced with Frank Miller's *Batman: The Dark Knight Returns*. Roz Kaveney, *Superheroes! Capes and Crusaders in Comics and Films*; Pat, "Batman and Guns"; Andrae, "From Menace to Messiah: The History and Historicity of Superman."

11. The term "ages," referring to various comic eras, is used with the acknowledgment that comics scholars are not entirely in agreement on what time period or designation constitutes each age. Categories, or "ages," are designations used by comics fans as well as those in the comics industry (particularly vendors) to highlight general narrative shifts and tonal changes over the lifespan of the medium (see Benjamin Woo, "An Age-Old Problem: Problematics of Comic-Book Historiography," *International Journal of Comic Art* 10, no. 1 (2008): 268–79). Some scholars prefer their own system of classification. For example, Randy Duncan and Matthew J. Smith prefer a classification of eight eras based on "major changes in comic book content or industry practices." *The Power of Comics: History, Form, and Culture*, 22. In contrast, Paul Lopes prefers the use of two categories: the industrial age and the heroic age. Paul Douglas Lopes, *Demanding Respect: The Evolution of the American Comic Book*.

12. Pustz, *Comic Book Culture*.

13. Wright, *Comic Book Nation*, 42.

14. Ibid., 41, 45.

15. Comics.org, "Action Comics #58."

16. Wright, *Comic Book Nation*, 123.
17. Pustz, *Comic Book Culture*; Wright, *Comic Book Nation*.
18. Hajdu, *The Ten Cent Plague*, 5.
19. Gabilliet, *Of Comics and Men*.
20. Pustz, *Comic Book Culture*, 27.
21. Amy Kiste Nyberg, "Comic Books and Juvenile Delinquency: An Historical Perspective"; Wright, *Comic Book Nation*; Hajdu, *The Ten Cent Plague*. Interestingly, Hajdu (*The Ten Cent Plague*) writes that though the writer Charles Biro takes credit for the scripts, most were ghostwritten by college graduate Virginia Hubbell.
22. Hajdu, *The Ten Cent Plague*, 110, 189.
23. Wright, *Comic Book Nation*, 77.
24. Wright, *Comic Book Nation*.
25. Al Feldstein, *Crime SuspenStories*.
26. Fredric Wertham, *Seduction of the Innocent*.
27. Amy Kiste Nyberg, *Seal of Approval: The History of the Comics Code*. See also Wright, *Comic Book Nation*; Hajdu, *The Ten Cent Plague*.
28. Nyberg, *Seal of Approval*; Wright, *Comic Book Nation*; Hajdu, *The Ten Cent Plague*; Cary Atkinson, "The Amazing Spider-Man and the Evolution of the Comics Code: A Case Study in Cultural Criminology"; Benton, *Crime Comics*.
29. Hajdu, *The Ten Cent Plague*; Nyberg, *Seal of Approval*; Wright, *Comic Book Nation*.
30. Nyberg, *Seal of Approval*, 35.
31. Subcommittee to Investigate Juvenile Delinquency, "Hearings Before the Subcommittee to Investigate Juvenile Delinquency of the Committee on the Judiciary, United States, Eighty-third Congress, Second Session, Pursuant to S. 190."
32. Hajdu, *The Ten Cent Plague*; Wright, *Comic Book Nation*.
33. Hajdu, *The Ten Cent Plague*: Amy Kiste Nyberg, "Comic Books and Juvenile Delinquency: An Historical Perspective"; Nyberg, *Seal of Approval*; Amy Kiste Nyberg, "Of Heroes and Superheroes"; Wright, *Comic Book Nation*; Atkinson, "The Amazing Spider-Man and the Evolution of the Comics Code"; Subcommittee to Investigate Juvenile Delinquency, "Hearings Before the Subcommittee to Investigate Juvenile Delinquency."
34. Hajdu, *The Ten Cent Plague*; Nyberg, *Seal of Approval*; Wright, *Comic Book Nation*.
35. Subcommittee to Investigate Juvenile Delinquency, "Hearings Before the Subcommittee to Investigate Juvenile Delinquency."
36. Frederic Thrasher, "The Comics and Delinquency: Cause of Scapegoat"; U.S. Congress, Senate, Committee on the Judiciary, Juvenile Delinquency, "Comic Books and Juvenile Delinquency."
37. Hajdu, *The Ten Cent Plague*, 151. Roundly accused of "including extraneous facts and statements" along with overgeneralizations, Wertham's various articles and books condemning the comic book industry strike many social scientists as

bunk. Hajdu, *The Ten Cent Plague*; Wright, *Comic Book Nation*, 259. However, Nyberg points out that while Wertham's methodology may have been flawed, he was genuinely interested in exploring the social causes of delinquency, particularly the impact of the mass media. See also Bart Beaty, *Fredric Wertham and the Critique of Mass Culture*. Though he was a psychiatrist, he was interested in a more interdisciplinary approach toward delinquency that took into consideration cultural meaning with an approach that is well respected today. That is, Wertham was interested in how meaning is constructed in comic books and interpreted by readers. Nyberg writes that Wertham believed that the "effects of comic books could be best understood by analyzing how the readers themselves made sense of what they were reading." Nyberg, *Seal of Approval*, 96.

38. Hajdu, *The Ten Cent Plague*; Wright, *Comic Book Nation*; Atkinson, "The Amazing Spider-Man and the Evolution of the Comics Code."

39. Wright, *Comic Book Nation*, 172.

40. "The Comics Code Authority."

41. Hajdu, *The Ten Cent Plague*.

42. Pustz, *Comic Book Culture*.

43. Hajdu, *The Ten Cent Plague*, 5, 326.

44. Hajdu, *The Ten Cent Plague*, 314; Nyberg, *Seal of Approval*; Wright, *Comic Book Nation*, 181.

45. Atkinson, "The Amazing Spider-Man and the Evolution of the Comics Code"; Nyberg, *Seal of Approval*, 158.

46. Plowright, *The Slings and Arrows Comic Guide: A Critical Assessment*.

47. Wright, *Comic Book Nation*, 184.

48. Ibid., 186.

49. Atkinson, "The Amazing Spider-Man and the Evolution of the Comics Code."

50. Wright, *Comic Book Nation*, 199.

51. Ibid., 215, 241.

52. Jeffrey S. Lang and Patrick Trimble, "Whatever Happened to the Man of Tomorrow? An Examination of the American Monomyth and the Comic Book Superhero."

53. Tom DeFalco et al., *Marvel Chronicle*, 81.

54. Gerald Clarke, "The Comics on the Couch."

55. Nyberg, *Seal of Approval*; Wright, *Comic Book Nation*. This was not the first time, nor the last, that the government would influence comic book content. In 1936, the comic strip "War on Crime" was created at the request of J. Edgar Hoover with the intent of shaping readers' attitudes about the competence and effectiveness of federal agents. Later, in 2000, the government under the Clinton administration gave $2.5 million to Marvel Comics for an antidrug Spider-Man story arc.

56. Atkinson, "The Amazing Spider-Man and the Evolution of the Comics Code."

57. Wright, *Comic Book Nation*; Nyberg, *Seal of Approval*; DeFalco et al., *Marvel Chronicle*; Atkinson, "The Amazing Spider-Man and the Evolution of the Comics Code." Though all mainstream comic book publishers adhered to

the code, there was a vibrant underground comic book counterculture. Most notably, Robert Crumb's *Zap Comix* was first published in 1968 and often imitated.

58. Nyberg, *Seal of Approval*, 170; Wright, *Comic Book Nation*.

59. Nyberg, *Seal of Approval*, 141.

60. DeFalco et al., *Marvel Chronicle*.

61. Focus Group #2 (2010).

62. Ibid.

63. Coogan, *Superhero*; DeFalco et al., *Marvel Chronicle*; Duncan and Smith, *The Power of Comics*.

64. DeFalco et al., *Marvel Chronicle*; Wright, *Comic Book Nation*; Misiroglu, *The Superhero Book*.

65. Jordana Greenblatt, "I for Integrity: (Inter)Subjectivities and Sidekicks in Alan Moore's *V for Vendetta* and Frank Miller's *Batman: The Dark Knight Returns*."

66. In terms of the administration of the Code, Nyberg writes that with the initiation of the first version of the Code, "the association hired office staff to review the comics." Ibid., 105. Later, during the 1950s, a group of women were hired to review the comics—in part because of the belief that protecting the children was a woman's responsibility. However, by 1994, one person served "as both the CMAA secretary and code administrator. . . . She reviewed between 125 and 150 comic books a month for member publishers. While Munter did most of the reviewing herself, occasionally other staff members at the management office were called upon to assist her." Ibid., 151.

67. Nyberg, *Seal of Approval*, 154.

68. For more on the cultural legitimacy of comic books, independent publishing, and the significance of underground comics, see Jean-Paul Gabilliet, *Of Comics and Men: A Cultural History of American Comic Books*.

69. Greenblatt, "I for Integrity," 1; Aeon Skoble, "Superhero Revisionism in *Watchmen* and *The Dark Knight Returns*"; Roz Kaveney, *Superheroes! Capes and Crusaders in Comics and Films*.

70. Kaveney, *Superheroes!*; Nyberg, *Seal of Approval*. DC Comics formally terminated submission of their books to the Comic Code Authority in 2011 and replaced the code with their own rating system. Marvel ceased submission to the code in 2001. Michael Doran and Albert Ching, "DC Replaces Comics Code Approval with Own Rating System."

71. Jason Bainbridge, "'This Is the Authority: This Planet Is under Our Protection'; An Exegesis of Superheroes' Interrogations of Law."

72. Atkinson, "The Amazing Spider-Man and the Evolution of the Comics Code"; Misiroglu, *The Superhero Book*.

73. Coogan, *Superhero: Secret Origins of a Genre*, 216.

74. Greenblatt, "I for Integrity"; Graham J. Murphy, "Gotham (K)Nights: Utopianism, American Mythology, and Frank Miller's Bat(-topia)."

75. Wright, *Comic Book Nation*, 267.

76. Kaveney, *Superheroes!* 150.

77. Murphy, "Gotham (K)Nights."

78. Kaveney, *Superheroes!* 158.

79. Rogers, "Legendary Comics Writer Alan Moore on Superheroes, the League, and Making Magic."

80. Both would since be revived.

CHAPTER 3

1. Sid Jacobson and Ernie Colon, *The 9/11 Report: A Graphic Adaptation*, x.

2. James Mulholland, "Teaching and Learning the 9/11 Novel."

3. Susan Faludi, *The Terror Dream*.

4. Henry Jenkins, "Captain America Sheds His Mighty Tears: Comics and September 11"; Alex Evans, "Superman Is the Faultline: Fissures in the Monomythic Man of Steel"; Amy K. Nyberg, "Of Heroes and Superheroes"; Jared Lovell, "Step Aside Superman . . . This Is a Job for [Captain] America! Comic Books and Superheroes Post September 11"; Scott Cord, "Written in Red, White, and Blue: A Comparison of Comic Book Propaganda from World War II and September 11"; Justine Toh, "The Tools and Toys of (the) War (on Terror): Consumer Desire, Military Fetish, and Regime Change in Batman Begins"; Julian Sanchez, "The Revolt of the Comic Books"; Nickie Phillips, "The Dark Knight: Constructing Images of Good vs. Evil in an Age of Anxiety"; Jason Bainbridge, "'This Is the Authority: This Planet Is under Our Protection'; An Exegesis of Superheroes' Interrogations of Law."

5. Jenkins, "Captain America Sheds His Mighty Tears"; Nyberg, "Of Heroes and Superheroes"; Lovell, "Step Aside Superman."

6. Faludi, *The Terror Dream*; Nyberg, "Of Heroes and Superheroes."

7. Lovell, "Step Aside Superman," 166.

8. *9/11 Emergency Relief* (Alternative Comics, 2002), 20.

9. "Son of Star Wars" is a reference to a real-life anti-missile defense program. BBC News, "U.S. Missile Defence."

10. Jenkins, "Captain America Sheds His Mighty Tears," 78.

11. Ibid., 95.

12. Sanchez, "The Revolt of the Comic Books."

13. Ibid.; John Shelton Lawrence and Robert Jewett, *The Myth of the American Superhero*.

14. S. Woods, "Graphic Violence."

15. Lovell, "Step Aside Superman."

16. Nyberg, "Of Heroes and Superheroes."

17. Michael Medved, "Captain America, Traitor?"

18. Michael Lackner, "Hate America 'Superhero'?"

19. Phillips, "The Dark Knight."

20. Andrew Klaven, "Opinion: What Bush and Batman Have in Common," *Wsj. com*, July 25, 2008, sec. Commentary (U.S.), http://online.wsj.com/article/ SB121694247343482821.html.

21. Jack G. Shaheen, "Arab Images in American Comic Books."
22. Ibid.
23. L. Keys, "Drawing Peace in the Middle East: Super Men Replace Superman as the Israeli-Palestinian Conflict Invades Comics."
24. Lovell, "Step Aside Superman."
25. R. Lee, "Superheroes with a Muslim Message: 99 Islamic Superheroes Find Success on Newsstands."
26. Not all are thrilled with the representation of Muslim superheroes as depicted in *JLA/The 99.* One Muslim American commenter expresses dissatisfaction with the portrayal of Muslim superheroes in the *JLA/The 99* crossover on a comic-related blog. Muneer states,

> This [*JLA/The 99*] proves that superheroes can only be based on the values of Western Liberalism, and a real Muslim superhero could only ever be portrayed as a lame supervillain and global terrorist trying to spread a fascist agenda who proceeds to be quickly jailed by the likes of any DC comics hero. (Desire The Mayhem, "The 99: Muslim Justice League of Avengers Assemble!")

27. C. Keyes, "Comic Book Publisher Praised for Reflecting 'Tolerance of Islam.'"
28. Keys, "Drawing Peace in the Middle East."
29. A. Khan, "Middle East Heroes: Drawn to a Fair Future."
30. Naif Al-Mutawa, *The 99.*
31. Bill Ashcroft, Gareth Griffiths, and Helen Tiffin, *The Empire Writes Back: Theory and Practice in Post-Colonial Literature.*
32. D. Williams, "Arab Superheroes Leap Pyramids in a Single Bound," C1.
33. Williams, "Arab Superheroes Leap Pyramids in a Single Bound."
34. Jonathan Curiel, "'The 99,' an Allah-inspired Comic Wildly Popular in the Islamic World, Is Set to Make Its TV Debut."
35. Homi Bhabha, *The Location of Culture*; Gayatri Chakravorty Spivak, "World Systems and the Creole."
36. Edward Said, "Homage to Joe Sacco," 10.
37. Kristaan Versluys, "Art Spiegelman's *In the Shadow of No Towers*: 9/11 and the Representation of Trauma."
38. *9/11 Emergency Relief*, 78.
39. Versluys, "Art Spiegelman's *In the Shadow of No Towers*," 991.
40. Ibid., 992.
41. Jeff Birkenstein, Anna Froula, and Karen Randell, *Reframing 9/11: Film, Popular Culture, and the "War on Terror*," 77–78.

CHAPTER 4

1. Despite the initial success of *The Authority,* at the end of 2010 DC ceased operation of Wildstorm with the intention of reintroducing characters from *The*

Authority, and other licensed characters, into the DC Universe. Andy Khouri, "Generation WildStorm: Growing Up in Jim Lee's Universe"; Jonah Weiland, "'Coup D'etat: Sleeper' and 'Afterword' Sold Out at DC."

2. Mike Alsford, *Heroes and Villains*; Nickie Phillips and Staci Strobl, "Cultural Criminology and Kryptonite: Constructions of Crime and Justice in Comic Books in America."

3. Paul Simpson, Helen Rodiss, and Michaela Bushell, *The Rough Guide to Superheroes*; Bradford W. Wright, *Comic Book Nation: The Transformation of Youth Culture in America.*

4. David Bleich, *Utopia: The Psychology of a Cultural Fantasy,* 24; F. Manuel, "Toward a Psychological History of Utopias," 319.

5. Focus Group #1 (2010).

6. Focus Group #2 (2010).

7. Etienne Wenger, *Communities of Practice: Learning, Memory, and Identity.*

8. Alsford, *Heroes and Villains.*

9. Benedict Anderson, *Imagined Communities: Reflections on the Origin and Spread of Nationalism.*

10. Arjun Appadurai, *Modernity at Large: Cultural Dimensions of Globalization.*

11. Y. Kanno and B. Norton, "Imagined Communities and Educational Possibilities: Introduction," 247–48.

12. According to the Marvel database, S.H.I.E.L.D. (Supreme Headquarters International Espionage Law-Enforcement Division) is described as "an extra-government intelligence and security organization dedicated to protecting the nations and peoples of Earth from all threats, terrestrial or extraterrestrial" (http://marvel.com/universe/S.H.I.E.L.D.).

13. Phillips and Strobl, "Cultural Criminology and Kryptonite."

14. Richard Dyer, "Entertainment and Utopia," 9080–84.

15. Ibid., 9226–80.

16. Danny Fingeroth, *Superman on the Couch: What Superheroes Really Tell Us about Ourselves and Our Society*; John Shelton Lawrence and Robert Jewett, *The Myth of the American Superhero.*

17. Phillips and Strobl, "Cultural Criminology and Kryptonite."

18. Jock Young, *The Exclusive Society: Social Exclusion, Crime, and Difference in Late Modernity,* 81.

19. Jock Young, "Moral Panic: Its Origins in Resistance, Ressentiment, and the Translation of Fantasy in to Reality," 14.

20. Daniele Hervieu-Leger, *Religion as a Chain of Memory,* 123.

21. Matthew Wolf-Meyer, "The World Ozymandias Made: Utopias in the Superhero Comic, Subculture, and the Conservation of Difference."

22. Zygmunt Bauman, *Liquid Times: Living in an Age of Uncertainty,* 103.

23. Todd McFarlane, *Spawn Origins Volume 1.*

24. Alsford, *Heroes and Villains.*

25. Lawrence and Jewett, *The Myth of the American Superhero*, 6.

26. Susan Sontag, *Illness as Metaphor and AIDS and Its Metaphors*, 73.

27. Jimmy Stamp, "On Influence: Batman, Gotham City, and an Overzealous Architecture Historian with a Working Knowledge of Explosives."

28. Brett Patterson, "No Man's Land: Social Order in Gotham City and New Orleans."

29. Ibid., 44.

30. CNN, "Big Easy a Lost Cause? Did Idaho Senator Hide Gay Behavior? Castro Endorses Hillary-Obama."

31. CBS, "McCain to Tour Katrina."

32. Robert Jay Lifton, *Destroying the World to Save It: Aum Shinrikyo, Apocalyptic Violence, and the New Global Terrorism*.

33. Greg Garrett, *Holy Superheroes! Exploring the Sacred in Comics, Graphic Novels, and Film*, 36.

34. Robert Jewett and John Lawrence, *Captain America and the Crusade against Evil: The Dilemma of Zealous Nationalism*.

35. Ibid., 14, 135.

36. Ibid., 8.

37. Garrett, *Holy Superheroes!*; Chris Knowles, *Our Gods Wear Spandex: The Secret History of Comic Book Heroes*.

38. Keith J. Hayward, *City Limits: Crime, Consumer Culture, and the Urban Experience*.

CHAPTER 5

1. Mike Alsford, *Heroes and Villains*, 110.

2. Mike Presdee, *Cultural Criminology and the Carnival of Crime*, 30.

3. Focus Group #1 (2010).

4. Ibid.

5. Peter Coogan, *Superhero: The Secret Origin of a Genre*, 76.

6. Manuel Perez-Rivas, "Bush Vows to Rid the World of 'Evil-doers.'"

7. Meet the Press, "Meet the Press Transcript Sunday September 14, 2003.

8. BBC News, "Text of Bush's Act of War Statement."

9. CNN, "'You Are Either with Us or Against Us.'"

10. Perez-Rivas, "Bush Vows to Rid the World of 'Evil-doers.'"

11. The fear tactics waged by the Bush administration were successful, in part, because they tapped into existential anxieties prevalent in our modern society. The Bush administration was well aware of the potential value of constructing media images that serve to shape public perceptions and attitudes and, as a result, policy decisions. This tactic was explicitly discussed with Ron Suskind in his interview with an anonymous Bush aide in 2004. The aide dismissed those who make decisions based on an evaluation of the facts at hand or, as he put it, through a "judicious study of discernible reality" (Suskind, "Faith, Certainty, and

the Presidency of George W. Bush"). Rather, the aide stated that the administration operates in a different kind of world:

> [W]e're an empire now, and when we act, we create our own reality. And while you're studying that reality—judiciously, as you will—we'll act again, creating other new realities, which you can study too, and that's how things will sort out. We're history's actors . . . and you, all of you, will be left to just study what we do. (Suskind, "Faith, Certainty, and the Presidency of George W. Bush")

This postmodern context of contemporary society sheds light on why the administration was particularly preoccupied with image over substance and why they utilized the idea of mythic monsters to bolster support for a never-ending war. Though the Bush administration was not the first to recognize the value of perpetuating media myths, they were particularly adept at managing spectacle (e.g., the landing of the aircraft carrier) (Neal Gabler, *Life: The Movie; How Entertainment Conquered Reality*; Media Matters, "Mission Accomplished: A Look Back at the Media's Fawning Coverage of Bush's Premature Declaration of Victory in Iraq").

12. Ray Surette, *Media, Crime, and Criminal Justice: Images, Realities, and Policies*.
13. Su Epstein, "The New Mythic Monster," 73.
14. Epstein, "The New Mythic Monster."
15. Ibid., 77.
16. Victims, on the other hand, are frequently portrayed as entirely innocent, wholesome beings. In media accounts certain victims marked by race and gender are privileged over others. For example, scholars have noted that accounts of missing white women are prominent in the media while missing women of color are marginalized. Robert Bing, *Race, Crime, and the Media*. A history of media portrayals of criminals as mythic monsters juxtaposed against pure, innocent victims creates an easily digestible formula for justice.
17. Cesare Lombroso, *Criminal Man*; Scott Vollum and Cary Adkinson, "The Portrayal of Crime and Justice in the Comic Book Superhero Mythos."
18. Lombroso, *Criminal Man*, 51.
19. Lombroso, *Criminal Man*; Nicole Rafter, *The Criminal Brain: Understanding Biological Theories of Crime*.
20. Wayne Morrison, "Lombroso and the Birth of Criminological Positivism: Scientific Mastery or Cultural Artifice?" 68.
21. Gina Misiroglu, *Supervillain Book: The Evil Side of Comics and Hollywood*.
22. Ibid., 387.
23. Phillip Lamar Cunningham, "The Absence of Black Supervillains in Mainstream Comics," 53.
24. Cunningham, "The Absence of Black Supervillains in Mainstream Comics."

25. Coogan, *Superhero*, 83.
26. Sigmund Freud, *The Interpretation of Dreams*.
27. J. Reid Meloy, *The Psychopathic Mind: Origins, Dynamics, and Treatment*, 5.
28. Meloy, *The Psychopathic Mind*.
29. Robert Hare, *Without Conscience: The Disturbing World of Psychopaths among Us*, 1.
30. Hervey M. Cleckley, *The Mask of Sanity: An Attempt to Clarify Some Issues about the So-Called Psychopathic Personality*.
31. Characteristics of antisocial personality disorder are found in the APA Diagnostic Manual. These include "a pervasive pattern of disregard for and violation of the rights of others occurring since age 15" and at least three or more of the following: failure to conform to social norms, deceitfulness, impulsivity, aggressiveness, irresponsibility, lack of remorse, and reckless disregard for the safety of others. John S. McIntyre and the American Psychological Association, *Quick Reference to the Diagnostic Criteria from DSM-IV*, 279.
32. Meloy, *The Psychopathic Mind*, 68; Katarina Wahlund and Marianne Kristiansson, "Aggression, Psychopathy, and Brain Imaging: Review and Future Recommendations."
33. Meloy, *The Psychopathic Mind*, 70.
34. R. James Blair, "The Emergence of Psychopathy: Implications for the Neuropsychological Approach to Developmental Disorders," 421.
35. Hare, *Without Conscience*, 113.
36. Louis Schlesinger, "The Potential Sex Murderer: Ominous Signs, Risk Assessment."
37. Abbie Stein, *Prologue to Violence: Child Abuse, Dissociation, and Crime*.
38. Ibid., 73,75.
39. Derek Cornish and Ronald Clarke, "The Rational Choice Perspective."
40. Jeremy Bentham, *An Introduction to the Principles of Morals and Legislation*, 1.
41. Cornish and Clarke, "The Rational Choice Perspective."
42. Frances Cullen and Robert Agnew, *Criminological Theory: Past and Present*; Stephen Brown, Finn-Aage Ebensen, and Gilbert Geis, *Criminology: Explaining Crime and Its Context*.
43. Robert J. Sampson and William Julius Wilson, "Toward a Theory of Race, Crime, and Urban Inequality."
44. Kenneth D. Tunnell, "Socially Disorganized Rural Communities."
45. Cullen and Agnew, *Criminological Theory: Past and Present*; Brown, Ebensen, and Geis, *Criminology: Explaining Crime and Its Context*; Michael J. Lynch, Raymond J. Michalowski, and W. Byron Groves, *The New Primer in Radical Criminology: Critical Perspectives on Crime, Power, and Identity*.
46. Jeffrey Reiman, *The Rich Get Richer and the Poor Get Prison*.

CHAPTER 6

1. Richard Quinney, "The Way of Peace: On Crime, Suffering, and Service," 12.
2. Frances Cullen and Robert Agnew, *Criminological Theory: Past and Present*.

3. The origin of superheroes, or the "heroic myth," predates comic books as we know them, yet our culture continues to be fascinated with the reimagining of age-old stories incorporating the "hero's journey." Joseph Campbell, *The Power of Myth*; Joseph Campbell, *The Hero with a Thousand Faces*; Danny Fingeroth, *Superman on the Couch: What Superheroes Really Tell Us about Ourselves and Our Society*; John Shelton Lawrence and Robert Jewett, *The Myth of the American Superhero*. We are enchanted with tales in which an individual is seemingly compelled to action, rises to the challenges along the way, and emerges a better person. Superheroes are usually defined as those who embody goodness, are selfless, and are willing to sacrifice and follow ethical principles. He or she may have special powers or abilities acquired supernaturally or through extensive training. Superheroes may be characterized in a number of different ways, such as by their powers, their mission, and their identity (Peter Coogan, *Superhero: The Secret Origin of a Genre*), or they may be grouped according to their historical antecedents such as messiahs, wizards, amazons, and golems (Chris Knowles, *Our Gods Wear Spandex: The Secret History of Comic Book Heroes*). For the purposes of our study, we focus on the heroes' path to justice as it relates to criminal justice/criminology.

4. Nickie Phillips and Staci Strobl, "Cultural Criminology and Kryptonite: Constructions of Crime and Justice in Comic Books in America"; Scott Vollum and Cary Adkinson, "The Portrayal of Crime and Justice in the Comic Book Superhero Mythos"; Bradford Reyns and Billy Henson, "Superhero Justice: The Depiction of Crime and Justice in Modern-Age Comic Books and Graphic Novels"; Graeme Newman, "Batman and Justice: The True Story."

5. F. Tallon and A. Walls, "Superman and Kingdom Come: The Surprise of Philosophical Theology."

6. Fingeroth, *Superman on the Couch*, 17.

7. Greg Garrett, *Holy Superheroes! Exploring the Sacred in Comics, Graphic Novels, and Film*.

8. Phillips and Strobl, "Cultural Criminology and Kryptonite"; Newman, "Batman and Justice."

9. Focus Group #1 (2010).

10. Manuel Perez-Rivas, "Bush Vows to Rid the World of 'Evil-doers.'"

11. Reyns and Henson, "Superhero Justice."

12. Vollum and Adkinson, "The Portrayal of Crime and Justice in the Comic Book Superhero Mythos," 101.

13. Reyns and Henson, "Superhero Justice;" Vollum and Adkinson, "The Portrayal of Crime and Justice."

14. Mike Alsford, *Heroes and Villains*.

15. George Bush, "President Declares 'Freedom at War with Fear.'"

16. Wolf Blitzer, "Search for the 'Smoking Gun.'"

17. 11 O'Clock Comics Podcast, "11 O'Clock Comics Episode 114."

18. Augie De Blieck Jr., "Criminal: An Appreciation."

19. Mark Waid, "Mark Waid Talks 'Irredeemable.'"
20. Comic-Con Magazine, "Comic-Con International: The Bendis-Fraction Conversation."
21. Robert Jewett and John Lawrence, *Captain America and the Crusade against Evil: The Dilemma of Zealous Nationalism*, 131.
22. *Miranda v. Arizona* (1966).
23. Ibid.
24. S.H.I.E.L.D. (Supreme Headquarters International Espionage Law-Enforcement Division) is described as "an extra-government intelligence and security organization dedicated to protecting the nations and peoples of Earth from all threats, terrestrial or extraterrestrial" (http://marvel.com/universe/S.H.I.E.L.D.).
25. Focus Group #3 (2010).
26. Ibid.
27. Brookings Institute, "The Impact of September 11 on Public Opinion: Increased Patriotism, Unity, Support for Bush; More Interest in News."
28. Brian Ross and Richard Esposito, "CIA's Harsh Interrogation Techniques Described"; Stephanie Condon, "Cheney: Ending Enhanced Interrogations 'Unwise in the Extreme'"; Stephanie Condon, "Debate Continues over Role of Waterboarding in Gathering Bin Laden Intel."
29. Condon, "Cheney: Ending Enhanced Interrogations."
30. We see this sentiment played with great effect in other forms of popular culture such as television's counterterrorism-focused drama *24*, which celebrated the use of enhanced interrogation techniques. The show has been quoted by Supreme Court Justice Antonin Scalia as evidence that, at times, it is necessary to operate outside the law (Peter Lattman, "Justice Scalia Hearts Jack Bauer," *Blogs.wsj.com*, June 20, 2007, http://blogs.wsj.com/law/2007/06/20/justice-scalia-hearts-jack-bauer). Similarly, Dahlia Lithwick reports that John Yoo, author of the infamous "torture memos," cited the show in his book titled *War by Other Means*, which essentially outlines the redefinition of torture and defends enhanced interrogation (Dahlia Lithwick, "Our Torture Policy Has Deeper Roots in Fox Television Than the Constitution," *Slate.com*, July 26, 2008, http://www.slate.com/articles/news_and_politics/jurisprudence/2008/07/the_bauer_of_suggestion.html).
31. Aeon Skoble, "Superhero Revisionism in *Watchmen* and *The Dark Knight Returns*."
32. Douglas Wolk, *Reading Comics: How Graphic Novels Work and What They Mean*, 103.
33. Phyllis Crocker, "Concepts of Culpability and Deathworthiness: Differentiating between Guilt and Punishment in Death Penalty Cases," 83.
34. Crocker, "Concepts of Culpability and Deathworthiness."
35. *Gregg v. Georgia* (1976).
36. Donohue John and Justin Wolfers, "The Death Penalty: No Evidence for Deterrence"; Jeffrey Fagan, "Death and Deterrence Redux: Science, Law, and Causal Reasoning on Capital Punishment"; David Garland, *Peculiar Institution: America's*

Death Penalty in an Age of Abolition; Robert Weisberg, "The Death Penalty Meets Social Science: Deterrence and Jury Behavior under New Scrutiny."

37. Karl Keys, "State Capital Cases Relief Denied: *State v. Timmendequas* (NJ)."

38. Raging Bullets Podcast #220.

39. Though it is later revealed that Daredevil has been overtaken by a demon "Beast," he readily takes responsibility for his actions. Daredevil states,

> Because that first step over the line, that decision to take the life of a murderer and become one myself, that was all me. And everything that followed on from it—the insanity, the darkness and death—that's the burden I have to carry down a long and lonely road paved with good intentions.

40. review2akill, "The Devil's Dare."

41. "The Negative Zone Gulag."

42. However, some fans point out that killing is not unfamiliar to Wonder Woman. Brian Cronin, "Lorendiac's 'Timeline of Wonder Woman's Killings, Post-Crisis': Comics Should Be Good!"

43. IGN, "Defending Wonder Woman"; IGN, "Defending Maxwell Lord: Comics Feature at IGN."

44. Focus Group #1 (2010).

45. Silver2467, "Wonder Woman Maxwell Lord."

46. Greg Kirkorian, "5 Lacking Parts of the Wonder Mythos and How JMS's Run May Fix Them."

47. Focus Group #2 (2010).

48. Focus Group #1 (2010).

CHAPTER 7

1. Norma Percora, "Superman/Superboys/Supermen: The Comic Books Hero as Socializing Agent," in *Men, Masculinity, and the Media* (Newbury Park, CA: Sage Publications., 1992), 61–77.

2. Amy Kiste Nyberg, *Seal of Approval: The History of the Comics Code*, 175.

3. Andrew Karmen, *Crime Victims: An Introduction to Victimology* (Independence, KY: Cengage Learning, 2009).

4. Richard L. Fox, Robert W. Van Sickel, and Thomas L. Steiger, *Tabloid Justice: Criminal Justice in an Age of Media Frenzy*, second ed. (Boulder, CO: Lynne Rienner, 2007); Gary W. Potter and Victor E. Kappeler, *Constructing Crime: Perspective on Making News And Social Problems*.

5. R. Reiner, "Media-Made Criminality: The Representation of Crime in the Mass Media," *Oxford Handbook of Criminology* 3 (2002): 376–418.

6. Fox, Sickel, and Steiger, *Tabloid Justice*; Potter and Kappeler, *Constructing Crime*.

7. *Identity Crisis* is the storyline containing the rape presumably referred to in D'Orazio's Occasional Superheroine blog. Sarah Stillman, "'The Missing White

Girl Syndrome': Disappeared Women and Media Activism," *Gender and Development* 15, no. 3 (2007): 491–502; Nancy Signorelli, *Violence in the Media* (Santa Barbara, CA: ABC-CLIO, 2005).

8. Focus Group #2 (2010).

9. George Gustines, "A Comic Book Gets Serious on Gay Issues: A Major Character Becomes a Victim of a Hate Crime," *New York Times*, August 13, 2002, http://www.nytimes.com/2002/08/13/arts/comic-book-gets-serious-gay-issues-major-character-becomes-victim-hate-crime.html?pagewanted=all&src=pm; Associated Press, "Green Lantern Fights Gay-Bashing," *Freerepublic.com*, August 13, 2002, http://www.freerepublic.com/focus/f-news/732674/posts; Lawrence Ferber, "Shining a Lantern on Hate Crimes," *Advocate*, September 17, 2002.

10. *Green Lantern: Brother's Keeper* (DC Comics, 2003).

11. Valerie Palmer-Mehta and Kellie Hay, "A Superhero for Gays? Gay Masculinity and Green Lantern," *Journal of Popular Culture* 28, no. 4 (2005): 390–404.

12. Judith Butler, *Gender Trouble: Feminism and the Subversion of Identity*, tenth anniversary edition (New York: Routledge, 2006).

13. James Messerschmidt, *Crime as Structured Action: Gender, Race, Class, and Crime in the Making* (Thousand Oaks, CA: Sage, 1997).

14. R. Connell, *Gender and Power: Society, the Person, and Sexual Politics* (Stanford, CA: Stanford University Press, 1987), 183.

15. Connell, *Gender and Power*, 183.

16. Ibid., 184–85.

17. Ibid., 84.

18. Arnold Blumberg, "The Night Gwen Stacy Died," *Reconstruction: Studies in Contemporary Culture*, n.d., http://reconstruction.eserver.org/034/blumberg.htm.

19. Ibid.

20. Douglas Wolk, *Reading Comics: How Graphic Novels Work and What They Mean*, 70.

21. Mitra Emad, "Reading Wonder Woman's Body," *Journal of Popular Culture* 39, no. 6 (2006): 971.

22. Emad, "Reading Wonder Woman's Body."

23. Charlie Anders, "Supergirls Gone Wild: Gender Bias in Comics Shortchanges Superwomen," *Mother Jones*, July 30, 2007, http://motherjones.com/media/2007/07/supergirls-gone-wild-gender-bias-comics-shortchanges-superwomen.

24. Comic Book Page Podcast, "Comic Book Page Podcast #123," December 16, 2009, http://www.comicbookpage.com/Podcast/?p=368.

25. Sean Whelan and Jim Segulin, *Raging Bullets*, Podcast, vol. 235, 2010, http://ragingbullets.libsyn.com/raging-bullets-episode-235-a-dc-comics-fan-podcast.

26. Focus Group #2 (2010).

27. Ibid.

28. For an analysis of hypermasculinity and hyperfemininity as a challenge to hegemonic constructions of maleness and femaleness, see Aaron Taylor, "'He's Gotta

Be Strong, and He's Gotta Be Fast, and He's Gotta Be Larger Than Life': Investigating the Engendered Superhero Body," *Journal of Popular Culture* 40, no. 2 (2007): 344–60. He states, "Admiration for the excessive body is a refusal to credit the hegemonies that construct the desirability of 'normal' body boundaries, and may even be a means of empowerment for readers who seek to deny such normalizing discourses" (358).

29. Contemporary comic books have also examined the fluidity of gender in ways difficult for other mediums. In one of the more interesting portrayals of gender as it relates to sexual orientation, Marvel Comics introduced Xavin, a shape-shifting alien Skrull, in *Runaways*. The *Runaways* are a multicultural group of teens who, to their horror, learn that their parents belonged to a clandestine criminal society. Once aware of the true nature of their parents' activities, the kids go on the run. When Xavin, a male, proposes marriage to Karolina, a member of the Runaways, she reveals that she cannot marry him because she is gay. Xavin responds by simply shapeshifting into a female and declares that for Skrulls, gender is amorphous. Karolina states, "I can't marry you . . . I can't do it because it'd be a lie. I . . . I like girls." Xavin responds, "Is that all that's stopping you? Karolina, Skrulls are shapeshifters, for us, changing gender . . . is no different than changing hair color." For the Runaways, neither sexual orientation, race, ethnicity, nor national origin are perceived as barriers to the team's ability to fight crime.

30. Palmer-Mehta and Hay, "A Superhero for Gays?"

31. Judd Winick, introduction to *Green Lantern: Brother's Keeper* (DC Comics, 2003).

32. CNN, "Marvel Comics to Unveil Gay Gunslinger," News, *CNN*, December 9, 2002, http://archives.cnn.com/2002/SHOWBIZ/12/09/rawhide.kid.gay.

33. Frank Bramlett, "The Confluence of Heroism, Sissyhood, and Camp in *The Rawhide Kid: Slap Leather*," *ImageTexT: Interdisciplinary Comics Studies* 5, no. 1 (2008), http://www.english.ufl.edu/imagetext/archives/v5_1/bramlett.

34. Ibid.

35. Amnesty International, "USA: Stonewalled; Police Abuse and Misconduct against Lesbian, Gay, Bisexual, and Transgender People in the U.S.," *Amnesty International*, September 21, 2005, http://www.amnesty.org/en/library/info/AMR51/122/2005; John D'Emilio, *Making Trouble: Essays on Gay History, Politics, and the University* (New York: Routledge, 1992); Martin Bauml Duberman, *Stonewall* (New York: Plume, 1994).

36. Urvashi Vaid, *Virtual Equality: The Mainstreaming of Gay and Lesbian Liberation* (New York: Anchor, 1996).

37. Susan Ehrlich Martin and Nancy Jurik, *Doing Justice, Doing Gender: Women in Law and Criminal Justice Occupations* (Thousand Oaks, CA: Sage, 1996), 72.

38. Ibid., 49.

39. Connell, *Gender and Power*, 187.

40. Bramlett, "The Confluence of Heroism, Sissyhood, and Camp in *The Rawhide Kid*." Meda Chesney-Lind and Michele Eliason, "From Invisible to Incorrigible: The Demonization of Marginalized Women and Girls," *Crime, Media, Culture* 2, no. 1 (2006): 31.

41. Les Daniels, *Batman: The Complete History* (San Francisco: Chronicle Books, 2004); Gina Misiroglu, *The Superhero Book*.

42. Lonely Gods, "No Place for a Girl: Batman Comics of the 1950s," *Lonely Gods,* n.d., http://www.lonelygods.com/w/bat2.html; Mike Madrid, *The Supergirls: Fashion, Feminism, Fantasy, and the History of Comic Book Heroines* (Minneapolis, MN: Exterminating Angel Press, 2009).

43. Caroline Hedley, "Lesbian Batwoman Is DC Comics' First Gay Superhero," *Telegraph,* February 11, 2009, http://www.telegraph.co.uk/news/newstopics/howaboutthat/4587541/Lesbian-Batwoman-is-DC-Comics-first-gay-superhero.html.

44. Ibid.

45. Laura Mulvey, "Visual Pleasure and Narrative Cinema," in *Film Theory and Criticism: Introductory Readings*, ed. Leo Braudy and Marshall Cohen, 833-44 (New York: Oxford University Press, 1999), 837.

46. Madrid, *The Supergirls*, 281.

47. Foucault, *Discipline and Punish*.

48. Anneke Smelik, "Lara Croft, Kill Bill, and the Battle for Theory in Feminist Film Studies," in *Doing Gender in Media, Art, and Culture*, ed. Rosemarie Buikema and Iris Van der Tuin, 178-92 (New York: Routledge, 2009).

49. Focus Group #3 (2010).

50. Focus Group #1 (2010).

51. Ibid.

52. Matt Brady, "Power Girl's Power Girl: Amanda Conner," *Newsarama.com*, n.d., http://www.newsarama.com/comics/050906-Power-Amanda.html.

53. Sam Eihorn, "Retconning My Brain: Wednesday Haul! Lots of Girls, a Few Zombies, and a Woman," October 21, 2009, http://retconningmybrain.blogspot.com/2009/10/wednesday-haul-lots-of-girls-few.html.

54. iFanboy, "iFanboy Episode #225: Batman and Robin #10," *Ifanboy.com*, March 14, 2010, http://ifanboy.com/podcasts/03-14-2010-episode-225-batman-and-robin-10.

55. Madrid, *The Supergirls*, vi.

56. Comic Book Page Podcast, "Comic Book Page Podcast #123."

57. Douglas Wolk, p. 98; Gail Simone, "Women in Refrigerators," *Women in Refrigerators*, 1999, http://www.unheardtaunts.com/wir/index.html. Wonder Woman's creator, William Moulton Marston, has been described as an eccentric character, involved in a polyamorous relationship with his wife and fascinated with sadomasochism and bondage, which influenced his characterization of Wonder Woman. Bob Greenberger, *Wonder Woman: Amazon. Hero. Icon.* (New York: Rizzoli/Universe, 2010); Trina Robbins, *The Great Women Superheroes*

(Northampton, MA: Kitchen Sink Press, 1996); Lillian S. Robinson, *Wonder Women: Feminisms and Superheroes* (New York: Routledge, 2004). Mike Madrid wrote that although Marston created Wonder Woman as a role model for girls and believed essentially that "women were superior to men" (Madrid, *The Supergirls*, 35), he wrote the Wonder Woman character with a "healthy, or unhealthy, dose of bondage. Wonder Woman's bizarre, kinky rogue's gallery of villains was constantly finding new and elaborate ways to restrain the Amazon, which she always overcame with great resolve. She was tied up, chained up, buried underground, sealed in tanks of water, and tied to railroad tracks" and simultaneously "exhorted the virtues of 'loving submission,' an Amazon version of dominance" (Madrid, *The Supergirls*, 45). Marston was also an accomplished psychologist and the creator of the polygraph.

58. Steven Padnick, "Why the Cover for *Heroes for Hire* #13 Is Wrong," *The Roar of Comics*, May 23, 2007, http://roar-of-comics.blogspot.com/2007/05/why-cover-for-heroes-for-hire-13-is.html.

59. Perry Moore, "Who Cares about the Death of a Gay Superhero Anyway? A History of Gays in Comics," *Perry Moore Stories*, 2004, http://www.perrymoorestories.com/content/hero.asp?id=superheroes.

60. Tim Barribeau, "The 15 Dumbest Superhero Retcons of All Time," *Www.io9.com*, November 17, 2009, http://io9.com/5405696/the-15-dumbest-superhero-retcons-of-all-time.

61. goodcomics.blogspot.com, "Comics Should Be Good: Update on the Whole Meltzer Rape Thing I Am Always Yammering On About," March 7, 2006, http://goodcomics.blogspot.com/2006/03/update-on-whole-meltzer-rape-thing-i.html.

62. Anders, "Supergirls Gone Wild."

63. "Project Girl Wonder, *Girl-Wonder.org*, n.d. http://girl-wonder.org/robin/projectgirlwonder.html.

CHAPTER 8

1. Marc Singer, "'Black Skins' and White Masks: Comic Books and the Secret of Race," 107.

2. Singer, "'Black Skins' and White Masks"; Rebecca Wanzo, "Wearing Hero-Face: Black Citizens and Melancholic Patriotism in *Truth: Red, White, and Black*."

3. James Messerschmidt, *Masculinities and Crime*; Thorsten Sellin, *Culture, Conflict, and Crime*; Jock Young, "Radical Criminology in Britain: The Emergence of a Competing Paradigm"; Ian Taylor, Paul Walton, and Jock Young, *The New Criminology: For a Social Theory of Deviance*; William J. Chambliss, *Power, Politics, and Crime*.

4. Robert Bing, *Race, Crime, and the Media*; Ted Chiricos and Sarah Eschholz, "Racial and Ethnic Typification of Crime and the Criminal Typification of Race and Ethnicity in Local Television News"; Ray Surette, *Media, Crime, and Criminal Justice: Images, Realities, and Policies*; Kelly Welch, "Black Criminal Stereotypes and Racial Profiling"; Melissa Barlow, "Race and the Problem of Crime in *Time*

and *Newsweek* Cover Stories, 1946 to 1995"; Coramae Richey Mann, Marjorie S. Zatz, and Nancy Rodriguez, *Images of Color, Images of Crime: Readings*; Delores Jones-Brown, "Forever the Symbolic Assailant: The More Things Change, the More They Remain the Same."

5. Jones-Brown, "Forever the Symbolic Assailant."

6. See also Bing, *Race, Crime, and the Media*; Chiricos and Eschholz, "Racial and Ethnic Typification of Crime"; Surette, *Media, Crime, and Criminal Justice*; Mann, Zatz, and Rodriguez, *Images of Color, Images of Crime*.

7. Katheryn Russell-Brown, *The Color of Crime: Racial Hoaxes, White Fear, Black Protectionism, Police Harassment, and Other Macroaggressions*, 4.

8. Dana E. Mastro and Amanda L. Robinson, "Cops and Crooks: Images of Minorities on Primetime Television."

9. Jeffrey A. Brown, "Comic Book Masculinity and the New Black Superhero," 28.

10. bell hooks, *Black Looks: Race and Representation*.

11. Brown, "Comic Book Masculinity and the New Black Superhero," 30.

12. Russell-Brown, *The Color of Crime*; Mastro and Robinson, "Cops and Crooks."

13. Phillip Lamar Cunningham, "The Absence of Black Supervillains in Mainstream Comics," 51.

14. Stuart Hall, "What Is This 'Black' in Black Popular Culture?" 377.

15. Lord Darkseid, "Blackfolk: Black Superheroes."

16. Dwayne McDuffie, "Another Black Superhero Is Now Dead."

17. Focus Group #2 (2010).

18. Naomi R. Rockler, "Race, Whiteness, 'Lightness,' and Relevance: African American and European American Interpretations of *Jumpstart* and *The Boondocks*," 401.

19. Singer, "'Black Skins' and White Masks," 111.

20. Dwain C. Pruitt, "Adding Color to a Four-Color World: Recent Scholarship on Race and Ethnicity in Comic Books"; Danny Fingeroth and Stan Lee, *Disguised as Clark Kent: Jews, Comics, and the Creation of the Superhero*; Mark Evanier, *Kirby: King of Comics*; Arie Kaplan, *From Krakow to Krypton: Jews and Comic Books*; Lawrence Baron, "X-Men as J Men: The Jewish Subtext of a Comic Book Movie"; Simcha Weinstein, *Up, Up, and Oy Vey: How Jewish History, Culture, and Values Shaped the Comic Book Superhero*.

21. Weinstein, *Up, Up, and Oy Vey*, 16.

22. Weinstein, *Up, Up, and Oy Vey*.

23. Pruitt, "Adding Color to a Four-Color World."

24. Baron, "X-Men as J Men."

25. Helena Frankil Schlam, "Contemporary Scribes: Jewish American Cartoonists," 101.

26. Brown, "Comic Book Masculinity and the New Black Superhero."

27. Cunningham, "The Absence of Black Supervillains in Mainstream Comics," 54.

28. Gina Misiroglu, *The Superhero Book*, 241. The Green Lanterns are essentially considered an intergalactic police force, and most often face intergalactic threats.

In the early 1990s, Stewart was briefly featured as the title character in *Green Lantern: Mosaic*, where he was instrumental in forging a cohesive society from the fragments of communities from various planets and in maintaining peace. Despite its popularity among fans, the series was canceled after eighteen issues. In an interview, Rik Offenberger of *Comics Bulletin* asked Cully Hamner, the artist for *Green Lantern: Mosaic*, "What did you think of the concept that John Stewart had to keep peace on a patchwork world?" Hamner stated the following with regard to the series cancellation:

> Well, I thought it was interesting, and would have afforded us a cool opportunity to comment on society, but there were a few things that were against it: First, the industry went and changed on us, and an introspective book like this just wasn't welcome in the midst of the Image Revolution. It was a concept that was hard to shoehorn into work-for-hire super-hero comics at the time. Second, as I was told at the time, it didn't fit with DC editorial vision (whatever that means). Sales didn't matter, fan support didn't matter; the first issue sold about 210,000 copies and my last issue sold about 70,000, so there was plenty of support for the book. It was marked for cancellation when issue #5 came out, and they allowed Gerry Jones a year to wrap it up, but there was no doubt that it was being cancelled because somebody upstairs just didn't care for it. (Rik Offenberger, "Getting Down with Cully Hamner")

29. Bob Lendrum, "The Super Black Macho, One Baaad Mutha: Black Superhero Masculinity in 1970s Mainstream Comic Books"; Wanzo, "Wearing Hero-Face."
30. Tom DeFalco et al., *Marvel Chronicle*.
31. Ibid.
32. Ibid.
33. Adilifu Nama, *Super Black: American Pop Culture and Black Superheroes*, 509 Kindle Edition.
34. Ibid., 523.
35. Wanzo, "Wearing Hero-Face," 357.
36. Ibid., 350.
37. Ibid., 341.
38. Anonymous, "Why Spawn Isn't Black."
39. Marc Snetiker, "Avengers Files: Nick Fury."
40. Emily Wight and Genevieve Roberts, "Online Anger Erupts over Blockbuster's 'Racelifting.'"
41. gregyo, "Are Some People Still Angry That Nick Fury Is Black?"
42. niggaz4life, "Nick Fury Is Black OMG."
43. paime77, "STAG for Urbanity2002."
44. Tony Whitt, "Nick Fury: Does It Matter If He's Black or White?"

45. boxofficemojo, "Iron Man (2008)."
46. Anonymous, "Sam Jackson Reups as Nick Fury."
47. David Walker, "Why Aren't There More Black Superheroes?"
48. Nama, *Super Black*, 568.
49. For a more comprehensive analysis of Milestone and fan culture, see Jeffrey A. Brown, *Black Superheroes, Milestone Comics, and Their Fans.*
50. Brown, "Comic Book Masculinity and the New Black Superhero."
51. Walker, "Why Aren't There More Black Superheroes?"
52. Alastair Dougall, *The Marvel Encyclopedia: The Definitive Guide to the Characters of the Marvel Universe.*
53. Focus Group #4 (2010).
54. Dougall, *The Marvel Encyclopedia.*
55. Jeff Yang et al., *Secret Identities: The Asian-American Superhero Anthology*, 62.
56. Baron, "X-Men as J Men."
57. Beta Magnus, "Nerd Rage #1: Cassandra Cain as Batgirl."
58. Andrew Wheeler, "No More Mutants by Andrew Wheeler #3: The Secret Asians."
59. Ibid.
60. Karen McGrath, "Gender, Race, and Latina Identity: An Examination of Marvel Comics' Amazing Fantasy and Arana."
61. Ross E. Lockhart, "The Transcendent Image: Jaime Hernandez's *The Death of Speedy*."
62. Ibid.
63. McGrath, "Gender, Race, and Latina Identity," 268.
64. Baron, "X-Men as J Men."
65. Dougall, *The Marvel Encyclopedia.*
66. Ibid.
67. Vaneta Rogers, "Jason Aaron: Sticking with 'Scalped.'"
68. William Rozier, "'Scalped': Not an Everyday Crime Story."

CHAPTER 9

1. David A. Green, "Feeding Wolves," 518.
2. Stuart Hall, "Encoding-Decoding."
3. Samuel Walker, *Sense and Nonsense about Crime, Drugs, and Communities*, 251.
4. David Garland, *The Culture of Control: Crime and Social Order in Contemporary Society*; Robert Martinson, "What Works? Questions and Answers about Prison Reform," 22–54.
5. Garland, *The Culture of Control*; Walker, *Sense and Nonsense.*
6. Sasha Abramsky, *American Furies: Crime, Punishment, and Vengeance in the Age of Mass Imprisonment*; Garland, *The Culture of Control*; Mark A. R. Kleiman, *When Brute Force Fails: How to Have Less Crime and Less Punishment*; The Sentencing Project and Marc Mauer, *Race to Incarcerate*; Walker, *Sense and Nonsense.*
7. James Q. Wilson, *Thinking about Crime*, 170.

8. David P. Farrington, *Integrated Developmental and Life-Course Theories of Offending*; Shadd Maruna, *Making Good: How Ex-Convicts Reform and Rebuild Their Lives*.

9. John Braithwaite, *Crime, Shame, and Reintegration*.

10. Nils Christie, *Limits to Pain*.

11. Hennessey Hayes, "Assessing Reoffending in Restorative Justice Conferences."

12. Focus Group #3 (2010).

13. Focus Group #1 (2010).

14. Richard Dyer, "Entertainment and Utopia," 9082–90.

15. Franklin E. Zimring and Gordon Hawkins, *Incapacitation: Penal Confinement and the Restraint of Crime*.

16. Ibid.

17. Focus Group #1 (2010).

18. Focus Group #2 (2010).

19. Focus Group #1 (2010).

20. Ibid.

21. "The Negative Zone Gulag."

22. Andrew von Hirsch, *Doing Justice: The Choice of Punishments; Report of the Committee for the Study of Incarceration*, 45, 54.

23. Ibid., 53.

24. H. L. A. Hart, *Punishment and Responsibility: Essays in the Philosophy of Law*.

25. Focus Group #2 (2010).

26. Focus Group #1 (2010).

27. Focus Group #3 (2010).

28. Focus Group #2 (2010).

29. Azn Badger, "Moon Knight, Thank You For Being So Freakin' Crazy."

30. Focus Group #1 (2010).

31. Graham Smith, "Self-Proclaimed Superhero 'Shadow Hare' Declares War on Crime . . . Although at 5ft 7ins Tall He Might Need a Little Help."

32. Ollie, "San Diego's Superhero."

33. Garland, *The Culture of Control*.

CHAPTER 10

1. Arlette Saenz, "Death Penalty: Applause for Rick Perry's 'Ultimate Justice' at Republican Debate."

2. David Garland, *Peculiar Institution: America's Death Penalty in an Age of Abolition*, 312.

3. Garland, *Peculiar Institution*.

4. Focus Group #1 (2010).

5. Caleb Mozzocco, "Every Day Is Like Wednesday: Cry for Justice Continues to Make Me Laugh . . . and Cry, Alternately, Depending on the Page."

6. Frederic Thrasher, "The Comics and Delinquency: Cause of Scapegoat."

7. Jeff Ferrell, Keith Hayward, and Jock Young, *Cultural Criminology: An Invitation*.

8. "One Million Moms."

9. David Badash, "Exclusive: One Million Moms Deletes 'Green Lantern Is Gay' Post after Flood of Pro-Gay Comments."

10. Jennifer Senior, "The Firemen's Friar."

11. Ibid.

12. Michael Jensen, "United 93, Mark Bingham, and Why It Matters That He Was Gay."

13. Brian Truitt, "Half-Black, Half-Hispanic Spider-Man Revealed."

14. Ibid.

15. Media Matters, "Beck Ties New 'Half-Black Half-Hispanic Gay Spider-Man' to Michelle Obama Saying That 'We're Gonna Have to Change Our Traditions.'"

16. Focus Group #1 (2010).

17. M. Herzfeld, *Cultural Intimacy: Social Poetics in the Nation-State.*

BIBLIOGRAPHY

Abramsky, Sasha. *American Furies: Crime, Punishment, and Vengeance in the Age of Mass Impris-onment*. Boston: Beacon Press, 2008.

Alsford, Mike. *Heroes and Villains*. Waco, TX: Baylor University Press, 2006.

Altheide, David. "Ethnographic Content Analysis." *Qualitative Sociology* 10, no. 1 (1987): 65–77.

Amnesty International. "USA: Stonewalled: Police Abuse and Misconduct against Lesbian, Gay, Bisexual, and Transgender People in the U.S." *Amnesty International*, September 21, 2005. http://www.amnesty.org /en/library/info/AMR51/122/2005.

Anders, Charlie. "Supergirls Gone Wild: Gender Bias In Comics Shortchanges Super-women." *Mother Jones*, July 30, 2007. http://motherjones.com/media/2007/07/ supergirls-gone-wild-gender-bias-comics-shortchanges-superwomen.

Anderson, Benedict. *Imagined Communities: Reflections on the Origin and Spread of Nation-alism*. New ed. London: Verso, 2006.

Andrae, Thomas. "From Menace to Messiah: The History and Historicity of Superman." In *American Media and Mass Culture*, edited by Donald Lazere, 124–38. Berkeley: Univer-sity of California Press, 1987.

Anonymous. "Sam Jackson Reups as Nick Fury." *Indy.com*, February 25, 2009. http:// www.google.com/#hl=en&q=2010+not+1910+nick+fury&aq=f&aqi=&aql=&oq= &gs_rfai=&fp=c401d881a5ff002f.

———. "Why Spawn Isn't Black." *Blue Corn Comics*, February 8, 2001. http://www.bluecorn-comics.com/deadher2.htm.

Appadurai, Arjun. *Modernity at Large: Cultural Dimensions of Globalization*. Minneapolis: University of Minnesota Press, 1996.

Ashcroft, Bill, Gareth Griffiths, and Helen Tiffin. *The Empire Writes Back: Theory and Prac-tice in Post-Colonial Literature*. London: Routledge, 1990.

Associated Press. "Green Lantern Fights Gay-Bashing." *Freepublic*, August 13, 2002. http://www.freepublic.com/focus/f-news/732674/posts.

Atkinson, Cary. "The Amazing Spider-Man and the Evolution of the Comics Code: A Case Study in Cultural Criminology." *Journal of Criminal Justice and Popular Culture* 15, no. 3 (2008): 241–59.

Badash, David. "Exclusive: One Million Moms Deletes 'Green Lantern Is Gay' Post after Flood of Pro-Gay Comments." *The New Civil Rights Movement*, June 1, 2012. http://thenewcivilrightsmovement.com/exclusive-one-million-moms-deletes-green-lantern-is-gay-post-after-flood-of-pro-gay-comments/politics/2012/06/01/40420.

Badger, Azn. "Moon Knight, Thank You for Being So Freakin' Crazy." *Azn Badger's Blog*, May 30, 2010. http://aznbadger.wordpress.com/2010/05/30/moon-knight-thank-you-for-being-so-freakin-crazy.

Bainbridge, Jason. "'This Is the Authority: This Planet Is under Our Protection'; An Exegesis of Superheroes' Interrogations of Law." *Law, Culture, and the Humanities* 3, no. 3 (October 1, 2007): 455–76.

Barak, Gregg. *Media, Process, and the Social Construction of Crime: Studies in Newsmaking Criminology*. New York: Routledge, 1995.

Barlow, Melissa. "Race and the Problem of Crime in *Time* and *Newsweek* Cover Stories, 1946 to 1995." *Social Justice* 25, no. 2 (1998): 149–83.

Barnes, Brooks. "Disney to Buy Marvel and Its 5,000 Characters for $4 Billion." *New York Times*, August 31, 2009. http://www.nytimes.com/2009/09/01/business/media/01disney.html.

Baron, Lawrence. "X-Men as J Men: The Jewish Subtext of a Comic Book Movie." *Shofar* 22, no. 1 (2003): 44–52.

Baudrillard, Jean. *Simulacra and Simulation*. Ann Arbor: University of Michigan Press, 1995.

Bauman, Zygmunt. *Liquid Times: Living in an Age of Uncertainty*. Cambridge, UK: Polity, 2007.

BBC News. "US Missile Defence." *BBC*, February 23, 2007. http://news.bbc.co.uk/2/hi/americas/696028.stm.

———. "Text of Bush's Act of War Statement." *BBC*, September 12, 2001. http://news.bbc.co.uk/2/hi/americas/1540544.stm.

Beaty, Bart. *Fredric Wertham and the Critique of Mass Culture*. Jackson: University Press of Mississippi, 2005.

Bentham, Jeremy. *An Introduction to the Principles of Morals and Legislation*. N.p.: Herzberg Press, 1781.

Benton, Mike. *Crime Comics: The Illustrated History*. Dallas, TX: Taylor Publishing, 1993.

Bhabha, Homi. *The Location of Culture*. London: Routledge, 1994.

Bing, Robert. *Race, Crime, and the Media*. New York: McGraw-Hill Humanities/Social Sciences/Languages, 2009.

Birkenstein, Jeff, Anna Froula, and Karen Randell. *Reframing 9/11: Film, Popular Culture, and the "War on Terror."* New York: Continuum, 2010.

Blair, R. James. "The Emergence of Psychopathy: Implications for the Neuropsychological Approach to Developmental Disorders." *Cognition* 101, no. 2 (September 2006): 414–42.

Bleich, David. *Utopia: The Psychology of a Cultural Fantasy*. Ann Arbor, MI: UMI Research Press, 1984.

Blitzer, Wolf. "Search for the 'Smoking Gun.'" *CNN.com*, January 10, 2003. http://articles.cnn.com/2003-01-10/us/wbr.smoking.gun_1_smoking-gun-nuclear-weapons-hans-blix?_s=PM:US.

Blumberg, Arnold. "'The Night Gwen Stacy Died': The End of Innocence and the Birth of the Bronze Age." *Reconstruction*, n.d. http://reconstruction.eserver.org/034/blumberg. htm.

Boucher, Geoff. "Nick Fury No More? Samuel L. Jackson Says 'Maybe I Won't Be Nick Fury.'" *Los Angeles Times*, January 14, 2009. http://herocomplex.latimes/2009/01/14/ nick-fury-no-more.

boxofficemojo. "Iron Man (2008)." *Box Office Mojo*, June 6, 2012. http://boxofficemojo.com/ movies/?id=ironman.htm.

Brady, Matt. "Power Girl's Power Girl: Amanda Conner." *Newsarama*, May 6, 2009. http:// www.newsarama.com/comics/050906-Power-Amanda.html.

Braithwaite, John. *Crime, Shame, and Reintegration.* Cambridge, UK: Cambridge University Press, 1989.

Bramlett, Frank. "The Confluence of Heroism, Sissyhood, and Camp in The Rawhide Kid: Slap Leather." *ImageTexT: Interdisciplinary Comics Studies* 5, no. 1. (2008). http://www. english.ufl.edu/imagetext/archives/v5_1/bramlett/.

Brookings Institute. "The Impact of September 11 on Public Opinion: Increased Patriotism, Unity, Support for Bush; More Interest in News. *Brookings.edu*, March 27, 2002. http:// www.brookings.edu/events/2002/0327terrorism.aspx.

Brown, Jeffrey A. *Black Superheroes, Milestone Comics, and Their Fans.* Jackson: University Press of Mississippi, 2001.

———. "Comic Book Masculinity and the New Black Superhero." *African American Review* 33, no. 1 (1999): 25–42.

Brown, Stephen, Finn-Aage Ebensen, and Gilbert Geis. *Criminology: Explaining Crime and Its Context.* Fourth ed. Cincinnati, OH: Anderson Publishing, 2001.

Bryan, Steven. "The San Diego Comic-Con Wraps Up for 2008." *Yahoo! Voices*, July 29, 2008. http://voices.yahoo.com/the-san-diego-comic-con-wraps-2008-1740289.html.

Bush, George. "President Declares 'Freedom at War with Fear.'" *The White House: President George W. Bush*, September 20, 2001. http://georgewbush-whitehouse.archives.gov/ news/releases/2001/09/20010920-8.html.

Butler, Judith. *Gender Trouble: Feminism and the Subversion of Identity.* New York: Routledge, 2006.

Campbell, Joseph. *The Hero with a Thousand Faces.* Third ed. Novato, CA: New World Library, 2008.

———. *The Power of Myth.* New York: Anchor, 1991.

Caputo, Gail A. *Intermediate Sanctions in Corrections.* Denton: University of North Texas Press, 2004.

Cavender, Gray. "Media and Crime Policy: A Reconsideration of David Garland's *The Culture of Control.*" *Punishment and Society* 6, no. 3 (2004): 335–48.

CBS. "McCain to Tour Katrina." *CBS*, April 24, 2008. http://www.cbsnews.com/ blogs/2008/04/24/politics/fromtheroad/entry4040391.shtml.

Chambliss, William J. *Power, Politics, and Crime.* Boulder, CO: Westview Press, 2000.

Chesney-Lind, Meda, and Michele Eliason. "From Invisible to Incorrigible: The Demonization of Marginalized Women and Girls." *Crime, Media, Culture* 2, no. 1 (2006): 29–47.

Chiricos, Ted, and Sarah Eschholz. "Racial and Ethnic Typification of Crime and the Criminal Typification of Race and Ethnicity in Local Television News." *Journal of Research in Crime and Delinquency* 39 (2002): 400–420.

Christie, Nils. *Limits to Pain.* N.p.: M. Robertson, 1982.

Clarke, Gerald. "The Comics on the Couch." *Time*, December 13, 1971. http://www.time.com/time/magazine/article/0,9171,910181,00.html.

Cleckley, Hervey M. *The Mask of Sanity: An Attempt to Clarify Some Issues about the So-Called Psychopathic Personality.* Fifth ed. N.p.: William A. Dolan, 1988.

CNN. "Big Easy a Lost Cause? Did Idaho Senator Hide Gay Behavior? Castro Endorses Hillary-Obama." *CNN*, August 29, 2007. http://transcripts.cnn.com/TRAN-SCRIPTS/0708/29/gb.01.html.

———. "'You Are Either with Us or against Us.'" *CNN*, November 6, 2001. http://archives.cnn.com/2001/US/11/06/gen.attack.on.terror.

Cohn, Neil. "The Limits of Time and Transitions: Challenges to Theories of Sequential Image Comprehension." *Studies in Comics* 1, no. 1 (April 2010): 127–47.

Comic-Con Magazine. "Comic-Con International: The Bendis-Fraction Conversation." *Comic-Con Magazine*, Winter 2010. http://www.comic-con.org/common/2010_bendis_fraction.php.

Comics.org. "Action Comics #58." *Comics.org*, January 6, 2010. http://www.comics.org/issue/2764.

Condon, Stephanie. "Cheney: Ending Enhanced Interrogations 'Unwise in the Extreme'; Political Hotsheet." *CBS*, May 21, 2009. http://www.cbsnews.com/8301-503544_162-5030892-503544.html.

———. "Debate Continues over Role of Waterboarding in Gathering Bin Laden Intel." *CBS*, May 3, 2011. http://www.cbsnews.com/8301-503544_162-20059438-503544.html.

Connell, R. *Gender and Power: Society, the Person, and Sexual Politics.* First ed. Palo Alto, CA: Stanford University Press, 1987.

Coogan, Peter. *Superhero: The Secret Origin of a Genre.* Austin, TX: MonkeyBrain Books, 2006.

Cord, Scott. "Written in Red, White, and Blue: A Comparison of Comic Book Propaganda from World War II and September 11." *Journal of Popular Culture* 40, no. 2 (2007): 325–43.

Cornish, Derek, and Ronald Clarke. "The Rational Choice Perspective." In *The Essential Criminology Reader*, edited by Stuart Henry and Mark Lanier, 18–29. Boulder, CO: Westview Press, 2005.

Crocker, Phyllis. "Concepts of Culpability and Deathworthiness: Differentiating between Guilt and Punishment in Death Penalty Cases." *Fordham Law Review* 66 (1997): 21–86.

Cronin, Brian. "Lorendiac's 'Timeline of Wonder Woman's Killings, Post-Crisis': Comics Should Be Good!" *Comic Book Resources*, November 11, 2008. http://goodcomics.comicbookresources.com/2008/11/11/lorendiacs-timeline-of-wonder-womans-killings-post-crisis.

Cullen, Frances, and Robert Agnew. *Criminological Theory: Past and Present.* Third ed. Los Angeles: Roxbury, 2006.

Cunningham, Phillip Lamarr. "The Absence of Black Supervillains in Mainstream Comics." *Journal of Graphic Novels and Comics* 1, no. 1 (2010): 51.

Curiel, Jonathan. "'The 99,' an Allah-Inspired Comic Wildly Popular in the Islamic World, Is Set to Make Its TV Debut." *MinnPost*, September 2, 2009.

Daniels, Les. *Batman: The Complete History.* San Francisco: Chronicle Books. 2004.

De Blieck Jr., Augie. "Criminal: An Appreciation." *Comic Book Resources*, March 20, 2007. http://www.comicbookresources.com/?page=article&id=15519.

DeFalco, Tom, Peter Sanderson, Tom Brevoort, and Matthew Manning. *Marvel Chronicle.* London: DK Adult, 2008.

D'Emilio, John, *Making Trouble: Essays on Gay History, Politics, and the University*. New York: Routledge, 1992.

Desire The Mayhem. "The 99; Muslim Justice League of Avengers Assemble!" *Desire The Mayhem*, June 30, 2010. http://dizaydammahom.blogspot.com/2010/06/99-muslim-justice-league-of-avengers.html.

Deuze, Mark. "Media Life." *Culture and Society* 33, no. 1 (2011): 137–48.

Diamond Publishers. "Publisher Market Shares: 2009." *Diamond Comics*. 2010. http://www.diamondcomics.com/public/default.asp?t=1&m=1&c=3&s=5&ai=90742.

Doran, Michael, and Albert Ching. "DC Replaces Comics Code Approval with Own Rating System." *Newsarama.com*, January 20, 2011. http://www.newsarama.com/comics.

D'Orazio, Valerie. "Occasional Superheroine." *Occasionalsuperheroine.blogspot.com*, November 16, 2006. http://occasionalsuperheroine.blogspot.com/2006/11/goodbye-to-comics-7-we-need-rape-my.html.

Dougall, Alastair. *The Marvel Encyclopedia: The Definitive Guide to the Characters of the Marvel Universe*. New York: DK Publishing, 2006.

Duberman, Martin Bauml. *Stonewall*. New York: Plume. 1994.

Duncan, Randy, and Matthew J. Smith. *The Power of Comics: History, Form, and Culture*. New York: Continuum, 2009.

Dyer, Richard. "Entertainment and Utopia." In *The Cultural Studies Reader*. Second ed. Kindle for iPad. London: Routledge, 1999.

Eason, Brian. "The Life and Death and Life of Jason Todd." *Comic Book Resources*, June 11, 2007. http://www.comicbookresources.com/?page=article&id=10464.

Eco, Umberto. *The Role of the Reader: Explorations in the Semiotics of Texts*. Bloomington: Indiana University Press, 1984.

EDGE. "The 60 Best-Selling Games in the Last 12 Months." *EDGE: Global Game Industry Network*, 2009. http://www.edge-online.com/features/the-60-biggest-selling-games-last-12-months?page=0%2C0.

Eihorn, Sam. "Wednesday Haul! Lots of Girls, a Few Zombies, and a Woman." *Retconning My Brain*, October 21, 2009. http://retconningmybrain.blogspot.com/2009/10/Wednesday-haul-lots-of-girls-few.html.

11 O'Clock Comics Podcast. "11 O'Clock Comics Episode 114." *11 O'Clock Comics Podcast*, June 24, 2010. http://bullpenbulletins.libsyn.com/2010/06.

Emad, Mitra. "Reading Wonder Woman's Body." *Journal of Popular Culture* 39, no. 6 (2006): 954.

Epstein, Su. "The New Mythic Monster." In *Cultural Criminology*, edited by Jeff Ferrell and C. Sanders, 66–79. Boston: Northeastern University Press, 1995.

Evanier, Mark. *Kirby: King of Comics*. New York: Abrams, 2007.

Evans, Alex. "Superman Is the Faultline: Fissures in the Monomythic Man of Steel." In *Reframing 9/11: Film, Popular Culture, and the "War on Terror,"* edited by Jeff Birkenstein, Anna Froula, and Karen Randell, 1872–2025. Kindle for iPad. New York: Continuum, 2010.

Fagan, Jeffrey. "Death and Deterrence Redux: Science, Law, and Causal Reasoning on Capital Punishment." *SSRN eLibrary*, 2006. http://papers.ssrn.com/sol3/papers.cfm?abstract_id=935102.

Faludi, Susan. *The Terror Dream*. Kindle ed. New York: Holt, 2008.

Farrington, David P. *Integrated Developmental and Life-Course Theories of Offending (Advances in Criminological Theory)*. Piscataway, NJ: Transaction Publishers, 2008.

Fein, Esther B. "Holocaust as a Cartoonist's Way of Getting to Know His Father." *New York Times*, December 10, 1991, sec. Books. http://www.nytimes.com/1991/12/10/books/holo-caust-as-a-cartoonist-s-way-of-getting-to-know-his-father.html?pagewanted=1.

Feldstein, Al. *Crime SuspenStories*. Timonium, MD: Gemstone Publishing, 2007.

Ferber, L. "Shining a Lantern on Hate Crimes." *Advocate*, September 17, 2002.

Ferrell, Jeff. "Cultural Criminology." *Annual Review of Sociology* 25, no. 1 (1999): 295–418.

Ferrell, Jeff, Keith Hayward, and Jock Young. *Cultural Criminology: An Invitation*. Thousand Oaks, CA: Sage Publications, 2008.

Ferrell, Jeff, and C. Sanders, eds. *Cultural Criminology*. Boston: Northeastern University Press, 1995.

Fingeroth, Danny. *Superman on the Couch: What Superheroes Really Tell Us about Ourselves and Our Society*. New York: Continuum, 2004.

Fingeroth, Danny, and Stan Lee. *Disguised as Clark Kent: Jews, Comics, and the Creation of the Superhero*. New York: Continuum Books, 2007.

Fiske, John. *Understanding Popular Culture*. Reprint. New York: Routledge, 2006.

Focus Group #1 (2010, July 28). New York City.

Focus Group #2 (2010, August 11). New York City.

Focus Group #3 (2010, September 24). New York City.

Focus Group #4 (2010, November 24). New York City.

Foucault, Michel. *Discipline & Punish: The Birth of Prison*. 2nd Edition. New York: Vintage, 1995.

Fox, Richard L., R.W. Van Sickel, and T.L. Steiger, *Tabloid Justice: Criminal Justice in an Age of Media Frenzy*, Second ed. Boulder, CO: Lynne Reiner, 2007.

Freud, Sigmund. *The Interpretation of Dreams: The Complete and Definitive Text*. Translated by James Strachey. First trade paper ed. New York: Basic Books, 2010.

Fuller, Kathryn H. *At the Picture Show: Small-Town Audiences and the Creation of Movie Fan Culture*. Charlottesville: University of Virginia Press, 2001.

Gabilliet, Jean-Paul. *Of Comics and Men: A Cultural History of American Comic Books*. Translated by Bart Beaty and Nick Nguyen. Jackson: University Press of Mississippi, 2010.

Gabler, Neal. *Life: The Movie; How Entertainment Conquered Reality*. First ed. New York: Vintage, 2000.

Garland, David. *Peculiar Institution: America's Death Penalty in an Age of Abolition*. Cambridge, MA: Belknap Press of Harvard University Press, 2010.

———. *Punishment and Modern Society: A Study in Social Theory*. Chicago: University of Chicago Press, 1993.

———. *The Culture of Control: Crime and Social Order in Contemporary Society*. Chicago: University of Chicago Press, 2002.

Garrett, Greg. *Holy Superheroes! Exploring the Sacred in Comics, Graphic Novels, and Film*. Revised and expanded ed. Louisville, KY: Westminster John Knox Press, 2008.

Gravett, Paul. *Manga: 60 Years of Japanese Comics*. London: Laurence King, 2004.

Green, David A. "Feeding Wolves." *European Journal of Criminology* 6, no. 6 (November 1, 2009): 517–36.

Greenberger, Bob, and G. Perez. *Wonder Woman: Amazon. Hero. Icon*. New York: Rizzoli Universe Promotional Books, 2010.

Greenblatt, Jordana. "I for Integrity: (Inter)Subjectivities and Sidekicks in Alan Moore's *V for Vendetta* and Frank Miller's *Batman: The Dark Knight Returns*." *ImageTexT: Interdisciplinary Comics Studies* 4, no. 3 (2008). http://www.english.ufl.edu/imagetext/archives/v4_3/greenblatt.

Gregg v. Georgia, 428 U.S. 153 (1976).

gregyo. "Are Some People Still Angry That Nick Fury Is Black?" *Comic Book Resources*, June 1, 2012. http://forums.comicbookresources.com/showthread. php?414764-Are-Some-People-Still-Angry-that-Nick-Fury-is-Black.

Groensteen, Thierry. *The System of Comics*. Jackson: University Press of Mississippi, 2009.

Gustines, George Gene. "A Comic Book Gets Serious on Gay Issues: A Major Character Becomes a Victim of a Hate Crime." *New York Times*, August 13, 2002, http://www. nytimes.com/2008/08/13/arts/comic-book-gets-serious-gay-issues-major-character-becomes-hate-crime-victim.html?pagewanted=all&src=pm.

Hajdu, David. *The Ten Cent Plague: The Great Comic-Book Scare and How It Changed America*. New York: Picador, 2008.

Hall, Stuart. "Encoding-Decoding." In *Crime and Media: A Reader*, edited by Chris Greer, 44–55. New York: Routledge, 2010. http://www.routledge.com/books/ details/9780415422390.

———. "What Is This 'Black' in Black Popular Culture?" In *Cultural Theory and Popular Culture: A Reader*, edited by John Storey, 374–82. Fourth ed. Harlow, UK: Longman, 2009.

Hare, Robert. *Without Conscience: The Disturbing World of Psychopaths among Us*. New York: Pocket, 1995.

Harrington, Carine. *Soap Fans: Pursuing Pleasure and Making Meaning in Everyday Life*. Philadelphia: Temple University Press, 1995.

Hart, H. L. A. *Punishment and Responsibility: Essays in the Philosophy of Law*. New York: Oxford University Press, 1968.

Hayes, Hennessey. "Assessing Reoffending in Restorative Justice Conferences." *Australian and New Zealand Journal of Criminology* 38, no. 1 (2005): 77–102.

Hayward, Keith J. *City Limits: Crime, Consumer Culture, and the Urban Experience*. Abingdon, UK: Psychology Press, 2004.

Hayward, Keith, and Jock Young. "Cultural Criminology: Some Notes on the Script." *Theoretical Criminology* 8, no. 3 (2004): 259–73.

Hedley, Caroline. "Lesbian Batwoman is DC Comics' First Gay Superhero." *Telegraph.co.uk*, February 11, 2009. http://www.telegraph.co.uk/news/newstopics/howaboutthat/4587541/ Lesbian-Batwoman-is-DC-Comics-first-gay-superhero.html.

Hervieu-Leger, Daniele. *Religion as a Chain of Memory*. New Brunswick, NJ: Rutgers University Press, 2000.

Herzfeld, M. *Cultural Intimacy: Social Poetics in the Nation-State*. New York: Routledge, 1997.

hooks, bell. *Black Looks: Race and Representation*. Toronto: Between the Lines, 1992.

ICv2. "Comic and Graphic Novel Sales Down in 2009," *ICv2*, April 16, 2010. http://www. icv2.com/articles/news/17291.html.

IGN. "Defending Maxwell Lord: Comics Feature at IGN." *IGN*, August 9, 2005. http://comics.ign.com/articles/640/640461p1.html.

———. "Defending Wonder Woman: Comics Feature at IGN." *IGN*, August 1, 2005. http:// comics.ign.com/articles/638/638186p1.html.

Jacobson, Sid, and Ernie Colon. *The 9/11 Report: A Graphic Adaptation*. New York: Hill and Wang, 2006.

Jenkins, Henry. "Captain America Sheds His Mighty Tears: Comics and September 11." In *Terror, Culture, Politics: Rethinking 9/11*, edited by Daniel J. Sherman and Terry Nardin, 69–102. Bloomington: Indiana University Press, 2006.

———. "Man without Fear; David Mack, Daredevil, and the Bounds of Difference (Part One)." *Confessions of an Aca-Fan*, June 18, 2010. http://henryjenkins.org/2010/06/man_without_fear.html.

———. *Textual Poachers*. New York: Routledge, 1992.

Jensen, Michael. "United 93, Mark Bingham, and Why It Matters That He Was Gay." *AfterElton.com*, May 2, 2006. http://www.afterelton.com/archive/elton/people/2006/5/bingham.html.

Jewett, Robert, and John Lawrence. *Captain America and the Crusade against Evil: The Dilemma of Zealous Nationalism*. Grand Rapids, MI: Eerdmans, 2002.

Jewkes, Yvonne. *Media and Crime*. Los Angeles: Sage, 2009.

John, Donohue, and Justin Wolfers. "The Death Penalty: No Evidence for Deterrence." *The Economists' Voice* 3, no. 5 (2006). http://www.bepress.com/ev/vol3/iss5/art3.

Jones-Brown, Delores. "Forever the Symbolic Assailant: The More Things Change, the More They Remain the Same." *Criminology and Public Policy* 6 (February 2007): 103–21.

Kane, Stephanie. "The Unconventional Methods of Cultural Criminology." *Theoretical Criminology* 8, no. 3 (2004): 335–51.

Kanno, Y., and B. Norton. "Imagined Communities and Educational Possibilities: Introduction." *Journal of Language, Identity, and Education* 2, no. 4 (2003): 241–49.

Kaplan, Arie. *From Krakow to Krypton: Jews and Comic Books*. Philadelphia: Jewish Publication Society, 2008.

Karmen, Andrew. *Crime Victims: An Introduction to Victimology*. Independence, KY: Cengage Learning, 2009.

Katz, Jack. "What Makes Crime News?" *Media, Culture, and Society* 9 (1987): 47–75.

Kaveney, Roz. *Superheroes! Capes and Crusaders in Comics and Films*. London: Tauris, 2008.

Keyes, C. "Comic Book Publisher Praised for Reflecting 'Tolerance of Islam.'" *CNN.com*, April 27, 2010. www.cnn.com.

Keys, Karl. "State Capital Cases Relief Denied: *State v. Timmendequas* (NJ)." *Capital Defense Weekly*, January 2, 2005. http://capitaldefenseweekly.com/archives/010205.htm.

Keys, L. "Drawing Peace in the Middle East: Super Men Replace Superman as the Israeli-Palestinian Conflict Invades Comics." *Forward*, April 11, 2003. www.forward.com/issues/2003/03.04.11/arts1.html.

Khan, A. "Middle East Heroes: Drawn to a Fair Future." *New Statesmen*, January 15, 2007.

Khouri, Andy. "Generation WildStorm: Growing Up in Jim Lee's Universe." *Comics Alliance*, September 22, 2010. http://www.comicsalliance.com/2010/09/22/wildstorm-history-jim-lee.

Kirkorian, Greg. "5 Lacking Parts of the Wonder Mythos and How JMS's Run May Fix Them." *Comixology*, August 17, 2010. http://blog.comixology.com/2010/08/17/5-lacking-parts-of-the-wonder-mythos-and-how-jms%E2%80%99s-run-may-fix-them.

Klavan, Andrew. "Opinion: What Bush and Batman Have in Common." *Wall Street Journal*, July 25, 2008, sec. Commentary (U.S.). http://online.wsj.com/article/SB121694247343482821.html.

Kleiman, Mark A. R. *When Brute Force Fails: How to Have Less Crime and Less Punishment*. Princeton, NJ: Princeton University Press, 2010.

Knowles, Chris. *Our Gods Wear Spandex: The Secret History of Comic Book Heroes*. Newbury Port, MA: Weiser Books, 2007.

Kraftl, Peter. "Utopia, Performativity, and the Unhomely." *Environment and Planning D: Society and Space* 25, no. 1 (2007): 120–43.

Kurtz, Josh. "New Growth in a Captive Market." *New York Times*, December 31, 1989. http://www.nytimes.com/1989/12/31/business/new-growth-in-a-captive-market.html.

Lackner, Michael. "Hate America 'Superhero'?" *Front Page Mag*, May 12, 2004. http://97.74.65.51/readArticle.aspx?ARTID=13067.

Lang, Jeffrey S., and Patrick Trimble. "Whatever Happened to the Man of Tomorrow? An Examination of the American Monomyth and the Comic Book Superhero." *Journal of Popular Culture* 22, no. 3 (1988): 157–73.

Lawrence, John Shelton, and Robert Jewett. *The Myth of the American Superhero*. Grand Rapids, MI: Eerdmans, 2002.

Lee, R. "Superheroes with a Muslim Message: 99 Islamic Superheroes Find Success on Newsstands." *ABC News*, May 16, 2007. http://abcnews.go.com/WN/story?id=3181105.

Lendrum, Bob. "The Super Black Macho, One Baaad Mutha: Black Superhero Masculinity in 1970s Mainstream Comic Books." *Extrapolation: Journal of Science Fiction and Fantasy* 46, no. 3 (2005): 360–72.

Lifton, Robert Jay. *Destroying the World to Save It: Aum Shinrikyo, Apocalyptic Violence, and the New Global Terrorism*. New York: Picador, 2000.

Lockhart, Ross E. "The Transcendent Image: Jaime Hernandez's *The Death of Speedy*." *Hares Rock Lots*, 2007. http://www.haresrocklots.com/essays/speedy.html.

Lombroso, Cesare. *Criminal Man*. Translated by Mary Gibson and Nicole Rafter. Durham, NC: Duke University Press, 2006.

Lonely Gods. "No Place for a Girl: Batman Comics of the 1950s." *Lonely Gods*. http://www.lonelygods.com/w/bat2.html.

Lopes, Paul Douglas. *Demanding Respect: The Evolution of the American Comic Book*. Kindle ed. Philadelphia: Temple University Press, 2009.

Lord Darkseid. "Blackfolk: Black Superheroes," *LiveJournal*, May 30, 2010. http://community.livejournal.com/blackfolk/8063556.html.

Lovell, Jared. "Step Aside Superman: This Is a Job for [Captain] America! Comic Books and Superheroes Post September 11." In *Media Representations of September 11*, 161–73. Westport, CT: Praeger, 2003.

Lynch, Michael J., Raymond J. Michalowski, and W. Byron Groves. *The New Primer in Radical Criminology: Critical Perspectives on Crime, Power, and Identity*. Third ed. St. Louis, MO: Willow Tree Press, 2000.

MacDonald, Heidi, and Calvin Reid. "Fans Wild for New York Comic Con 2010." *Publishers Weekly.com*, October 12, 2010. http://www.publishersweekly.com/pw/by-topic/industry-news/trade-shows-events/article/44806-fans-wild-for-new-york-comic-con-2010.html.

Madrid, Mike. *The Supergirls: Fashion, Feminism, Fantasy, and the History of Comic Book Heroines*. Minneapolis, MN: Exterminating Angel Press, 2009.

Magnus, Beta. "Nerd Rage #1: Cassandra Cain as Batgirl." *Beta Is Dead*, June 30, 2010. http://betaisdead.blogspot.com/2010/06/nerd-rage-1-cassandra-cain-as-batgirl.html.

Mann, Coramae Richey, Marjorie S. Zatz, and Nancy Rodriguez. *Images of Color, Images of Crime: Readings*. Third ed. New York: Oxford University Press, 2006.

Manuel, F. "Toward a Psychological History of Utopias." *Daedalus* 94 (1965): 319.

Martin, Susan Ehrlich, and Nancy Jurik. *Doing Justice, Doing Gender: Women in Law and Criminal Justice Occupations*. Thousand Oaks, CA: Sage Publications, 1996.

Martinson, Robert. "What Works? Questions and Answers about Prison Reform." *Public Interest* 35 (1974): 22–54.

Maruna, Shadd. *Making Good: How Ex-Convicts Reform and Rebuild Their Lives.* Washington, DC: American Psychological Association, 2001.

Marvel. "Take 10: Power Couples." *Marvel.com,* February 22, 2010. http://marvel.com/news/story/11420/take_10_power_couples.

Mastro, Dana E., and Amanda L. Robinson. "Cops and Crooks: Images of Minorities on Primetime Television." *Journal of Criminal Justice* 28, no. 5 (2000): 385–96.

McAllister, M. P., E. H. Sewell, and I. Gordon. *Comics and Ideology.* New York: Peter Lang, 2001.

McCloud, Scott. *Reinventing Comics: How Imagination and Technology Are Revolutionizing an Art Form.* New York: Perennial Paperbacks, 2000.

McDuffie, Dwayne. "Another Black Superhero Is Now Dead." *Dwayne McDuffie Forums,* July 3, 2009. http://dwaynemcduffie.com.lamphost.net/forums/viewtopic.php?p=5499&sid=08df5e80b9ffocb3c59d325ed610eea1.

McFarlane, Todd. *Spawn Origins Volume 1.* New York: Image, 2009. http://www.amazon.com/Spawn-Origins-1-Todd-McFarlane/dp/160706071X/ref=sr_1_1?ie=UTF8&qid=1329246293&sr=8-1.

McGrath, Karen. "Gender, Race, and Latina Identity: An Examination of Marvel Comics' Amazing Fantasy and Arana." *Atlantic Journal of Communication* 15, no. 4 (2007): 268–83.

McIntyre, John S., and American Psychiatric Assocation. *Quick Reference to the Diagnostic Criteria from DSM-IV.* Washington, DC: American Psychiatric Association, 1994.

Media Matters. "Beck Ties New 'Half-Black Half-Hispanic Gay Spider-Man' to Michelle Obama Saying That 'We're Gonna Have to Change Our Traditions.'" *Mediamatters.org,* August 3, 2011. http://mediamatters.org/mmtv/201108030013.

———. "Mission Accomplished: A Look Back at the Media's Fawning Coverage of Bush's Premature Declaration of Victory in Iraq." *Mediamatters.org,* April 27, 2006. http://mediamatters.org/research/200604270005.

Medved, Michael. "Captain America, Traitor?" *National Review,* April 4, 2003. http://article.nationalreview.com/268435/captain-america-traitor/michael-medved.

Meet the Press. "Meet the Press Transcript Sunday September 14, 2003." *MSNBC,* September 14, 2003. http://webcache.googleusercontent.com/search?q=cache:SHZK8fxtuEwJ:www.msnbc.msn.com/id/3080244/+9/11+everything+changed&cd=7&hl=en&ct=clnk&gl=us&client=firefox-a.

Meloy, J. Reid. *The Psychopathic Mind: Origins, Dynamics, and Treatment.* Northvale, NJ: Jason Aronson, 1988.

Messerschmidt, James. *Capitalism, Patriarchy, and Crime.* Rowman & Littlefield, Inc., 1986.

———. *Masculinities and Crime.* Lanham, MD: Rowman & Littlefield, 1993.

———. *Crime as Structured Action: Gender, Race, Class, and Crime in the Making.* Thousand Oaks, CA: Sage Publications, 1997.

Miranda v. Arizona. 384 U.S. 436 (1966).

Misiroglu, Gina. *Supervillain Book: The Evil Side of Comics and Hollywood.* Detroit, MI: Visible Ink Press, 2006.

———. *The Superhero Book.* Detroit, MI: Visible Ink Press, 2004.

Moore, Matt. "At DC Comics, Readers' Letters to Make a Return." *Washington Post,* January 3, 2011. http://www.washingtonpost.com/wp-dyn/content/article/2011/01/03/AR2011010303437.html.

Morrison, Wayne. "Lombroso and the Birth of Criminological Positivism: Scientific Mastery or Cultural Artifice?" In *Cultural Criminology Unleashed*, edited by Jeff Ferrell, Keith Hayward, Wayne Morrison, and Mike Presdee, 67–80. London: Glasshouse Press, 2004.

Movieweb. "All Time Top 100 Grossing Films." *Movieweb*, 2011. http://www.movieweb.com/movie.boxoffice.alltime/php.

Mozzocco, Caleb. "Every Day Is Like Wednesday: Cry for Justice Continues to Make Me Laugh . . . and Cry, Alternately, Depending on the Page." *Every Day Is Like Wednesday*, August 31, 2009. http://everydayislikewednesday.blogspot.com/2009/08/cry-for-justice-continues-to-make-me.html.

MSNBC. "Video Sales Overtaking Music." *MSNBC*, June 26, 2007. http://articles.moneycentral.msn.com/Investing/Extra/VideoGameSalesOvertakingMusic.aspx.

Mulholland, James. "Teaching and Learning the 9/11 Novel." *Mark Athitakis's American Fiction Notes*, May 4, 2009. http://americanfiction.wordpress.com/2009/05/10/teaching-and-learning-the-911-novel.

Mulvey, Laura. "Visual Pleasure and Narrative Cinema." In *Film Theory and Criticism: Introductory Readings*, edited by Leo Brady and Marshall Cohen, 833–44. New York: Oxford University Press, 1999.

Murphy, Graham J. "Gotham (K)Nights: Utopianism, American Mythology, and Frank Miller's Bat(-topia)." *ImageTexT: Interdisciplinary Comics Studies* 4, no. 2 (2008). http://www.english.ufl.edu/imagetext/archives/v4_2/murphy.

Nama, Adilifu. *Super Black: American Pop Culture and Black Superheroes*. Kindle. Austin: University of Texas Press, 2011.

Newman, Graeme. "Batman and Justice: The True Story." *Humanity and Society* 17, no. 3 (1993): 297–320.

niggaz4life. "Nick Fury Is Black OMG." *DeviantART*, n.d. http://niggaz4life.deviantart.com/art/Nick-Fury-is-black-omg-281776417.

9/11 Emergency Relief. Alternative Comics, 2002.

Nyberg, Amy Kiste. "Comic Books and Juvenile Delinquency: An Historical Perspective." In *Popular Culture, Crime, and Justice*, edited by Frankie and Donna Hale, 61–70. Belmont, CA: West, 1998.

———. "Of Heroes and Superheroes." In *Media Representations of September 11*, 175–85. Westport, CT: Praeger, 2003.

———. *Seal of Approval: The History of the Comics Code*. Jackson: University Press of Mississippi, 1998.

Offenberger, Rik. "Getting Down with Cully Hamner." *Comics Bulletin*, n.d. http://www.comicsbulletin.com/features/112569591736650.htm.

Ollie. "San Diego's Superhero." *San Diego Reader*, April 15, 2010. http://www.sandiegoreader.com/news/2009/apr/15/cover/.

"One Million Moms." *One Million Moms*, n.d. http://onemillionmoms.com/about.

paime77. "STAG for Urbanity2002." *DeviantART*, September 24, 2006. http://paime77.deviantart.com/art/STAG-for-Urbanity2002-40302645?q=&qo=.

Palmer-Mehta, V., and K. Hay. "A Superhero for Gays? Gay Masculinity and Green Lantern." *Journal of Popular Culture* 28, no. 4 (2005): 390-404.

Pat. "Batman and Guns." *Silver Age Comics*, August 15, 2005. http://sacomics.blogspot.com/2005/08/batman-and-guns.html.

Patterson, Brett. "No Man's Land: Social Order in Gotham City and New Orleans." In *Batman and Philosophy: The Dark Knight of the Soul.*, edited by M. Arp and R. White. Hoboken, NJ: Wiley, 2008.

Percora, Norma. "Superman/Superboys/Supermen: The Comic Books Hero as Socializing Agent. In *Men, Masculinity, and the Media*, edited by Steve Craig, 61–77. Newbury Park, CA: Sage Publications, 1992.

Perez-Rivas, Manuel. "Bush Vows to Rid the World of 'Evil-doers.'" *CNN*, September 16, 2001. http://archives.cnn.com/2001/US/09/16/gen.bush.terrorism.

Phillips, Nickie. "The Dark Knight: Constructing Images of Good vs. Evil in an Age of Anxiety." *Popular Culture, Crime, and Social Control* 14 (2010): 25–44.

Phillips, Nickie, and Natasha Frost. "Crime in Prime Time." In *Race, Crime, and the Media*, edited by Robert Bing. New York: McGraw-Hill Humanities/Social Sciences/Languages, 2010.

Phillips, Nickie, and Staci Strobl. "Cultural Criminology and Kryptonite: Constructions of Crime and Justice in Comic Books in America." *Crime, Media, Culture* 2, no. 3 (2006): 304–31.

Plowright, Frank. *The Slings and Arrows Comic Guide: A Critical Assessment.* N.p.: Slings & Arrows, 2003.

Potter, Gary W., and Victor E. Kappeler. *Constructing Crime: Perspective on Making News and Social Problems.* Second ed. Long Grove, IL: Waveland Press, 2006.

Presdee, Mike. *Cultural Criminology and the Carnival of Crime.* New York: Routledge, 2001.

Pruitt, Dwain C. "Adding Color to a Four-Color World: Recent Scholarship on Race and Ethnicity in Comic Books." *Review of New Books* 37, no. 2 (2009): 45–47.

Pustz, Matthew J. *Comic Book Culture: Fanboys and True Believers.* Jackson: University Press of Mississippi, 2000.

Quinney, Richard. "The Way of Peace: On Crime, Suffering, and Service." In *Criminology as Peacemaking*, 3–13. Bloomington: Indiana University Press, 1991.

Rafter, Nicole. "Crime, Film, and Criminology." *Theoretical Criminology* 11, no. 3 (2007): 403–20.

———. *The Criminal Brain: Understanding Biological Theories of Crime.* New York: New York University Press, 2008.

Reid, Calvin. "Soldout in San Diego: Another Booming Comic-Con." *Publisher's Weekly*, July 27, 2009. http://www.publishersweekly.com/article/401634-Soldout_in_San_Diego_Another_Booming_Comic_Con.php.

Reiman, Jeffrey. *The Rich Get Richer and the Poor Get Prison.* Second ed. New York: Wiley, 1984.

review2akill. "The Devil's Dare." *review2akill.com*, July 14, 2010. http://review2akill.com/2010/07/14/the-devils-dare.

Reyns, Bradford, and Billy Henson. "Superhero Justice: The Depiction of Crime and Justice in Modern-Age Comic Books and Graphic Novels." In *Popular Culture, Crime, and Social Control* 14 (2010): 45–66.

Roberts, Garyn. "Understanding the Sequential Art of Comic Strips and Comic Books and Their Descendants in the Early Years of the New Millennium." *Journal of American Culture* 27, no. 2 (June 2004): 210–17.

Rockler, Naomi R. "Race, Whiteness, 'Lightness,' and Relevance: African American and European American Interpretations of *Jumpstart* and *The Boondocks.*" *Critical Studies in Media Communication* 19, no. 4 (2002): 398–418.

Rogers, Alan. "Legendary Comics Writer Alan Moore on Superheroes, the League, and Making Magic." *Wired*, February 23, 2009. http://www.wired.com/entertainment/hollywood/magazine/17-03/ff_moore_qa?currentPage=all.

Rogers, Vaneta. "Jason Aaron: Sticking with 'Scalped.'" *Newsarama*, October 17, 2008. http://www.newsarama.com/comics/100817-Jason-Aaron.html.

Ross, Brian, and Richard Esposito. "CIA's Harsh Interrogation Techniques Described." *ABC News*, November 18, 2005. http://abcnews.go.com/Blotter/Investigation/story?id=1322866#.T3H8G46BHdU.

Rozier, William. "'Scalped': Not an Everyday Crime Story." *Indian Country Today*, July 1, 2010. http://www.indiancountrytoday.com/living/97302829.html.

Russell-Brown, Katheryn. *The Color of Crime: Racial Hoaxes, White Fear, Black Protectionism, Police Harassment, and Other Macroaggressions*. New York: New York University Press, 1999.

Saenz, Arlette. "Death Penalty: Applause for Rick Perry's 'Ultimate Justice' at Republican Debate." *ABC News*, September 8, 2011. http://abcnews.go.com/blogs/politics/2011/09/death-penalty-applause-for-rick-perrys-ultimate-justice-at-republican-debate.

Said, Edward. "Homage to Joe Sacco." In *Palestine*. Seattle, WA: Fantagraphics Books, 2001.

Sampson, Robert J., and William Julius Wilson. "Toward a Theory of Race, Crime, and Urban Inequality." In *Crime and Inequality*, 36–54. Stanford, CA: Stanford University Press, 1995.

Sanchez, Julian. "The Revolt of the Comic Books." *American Prospect*, November 9, 2007. http://www.prospect.org/cs/articles?article=the_revolt_of_the_comic_boooks.

Sanders, Clinton, and Eleanor Lyon. "Repetitive Retribution: Media Images and the Cultural Construction of Criminal Justice." In *Cultural Criminology*, edited by Jeff Ferrell and Clinton Sanders, 25–44. Boston: Northeastern University Press, 1995.

Schlam, Helena Frankil. "Contemporary Scribes: Jewish American Cartoonists." *Shofar: An Interdisciplinary Journal of Jewish Studies* 20, no. 1 (2001): 101.

Schlesinger, Louis. "The Potential Sex Murderer: Ominous Signs, Risk Assessment." *Journal of Threat Assessment* 1 (2001): 47–74.

Sellin, Thorsten. *Culture, Conflict, and Crime*. Brooklyn, NY: Social Science Research Council, 1938.

Senior, Jennifer. "The Firemen's Friar." *New York Magazine*, November 12, 2001. http://nymag.com/nymetro/news/sept11/features/5372.

Shaheen, Jack G. "Arab Images in American Comic Books." *Journal of Popular Culture* 28, no. 1 (1994): 23–33.

Signorelli, Nancy. *Violence in the Media*. Santa Barbara, CA: ABC-CLIO, 2005.

Silver2467. "Wonder Woman Maxwell Lord." *Comic Vine*, May 22, 2010. http://www.comicvine.com/wonder-woman/29-2048/wonder-woman-maxwell-lord/92-547211.

Simone, Gail. "Women in Refrigerators." *Unheardtaunts*, 1999. http://www.unheardtaunts.com/wir/index.html.

Simpson, Paul, Helen Rodiss, and Michaela Bushell. *The Rough Guide to Superheroes*. N.p.: Rough Guides Reference, 2004.

Singer, Marc. "'Black Skins' and White Masks: Comic Books and the Secret of Race." *African American Review* 35, no. 1 (2002): 107–19. http://findarticles.com/p/articles/mi_m2838/is_1_36/ai_85185720.

Skoble, Aeon. "Superhero Revisionism in *Watchmen* and *The Dark Knight Returns*." In *Superheroes and Philosophy*, edited by Tom Morris and Matt Morris, 13:29–41. Popular Culture and Philosophy. Chicago: Open Court, 2005.

Smelik, Anneke. "Lara Croft, Kill Bill, and the Battle for Theory in Feminist Film Studies." In *Doing Gender in Media Art and Culture*, edited by Rosemarie Buikema and Iris Van der Tuin, 178–192. New York: Routledge, 2009.

Smith, Graham. "Self-Proclaimed Superhero 'Shadow Hare' Declares War on Crime . . . Although at 5ft 7ins Tall He Might Need a Little Help." *Daily Mail*, May 2, 2009. http://www.dailymail.co.uk/news/worldnews/article-1176031.

Snetiker, Marc. "Avengers Files: Nick Fury." *Entertainment Weekly*, April 30, 2012. http://popwatch.ew.com/2012/04/30/avengers-files-nick-fury.

Sontag, Susan. *Illness as Metaphor and AIDS and Its Metaphors*. New York: Picador, 2001.

Spivak, Gayatri Chakravorty. "World Systems and the Creole." *Narrative* 14, no. 1 (2006): 102–12.

Stamp, Jimmy. "On Influence: Batman, Gotham City, and an Overzealous Architecture Historian with a Working Knowledge of Explosives." *Life without Buildings*, June 1, 2009. http://lifewithoutbuildings.net/2009/06.

Stein, Abbie. *Prologue to Violence: Child Abuse, Dissociation, and Crime*. Mahwah, NJ: Analytic Press, 2007.

Stillman, Sarah. "'The Missing White Girl Syndrome': Disappeared Women and Media Activism." *Gender & Development* 15, no. 3 (2007): 491–502.

Storey, John. *Cultural Theory and Popular Culture: An Introduction*. Fifth ed. London: Longman, 2009.

Strinati, Dominic. "The Big Nothing? Contemporary Culture and the Emergence of Postmodernism." *European Journal of Social Sciences* 6, no. 3 (1993): 359–75.

Subcommittee to Investigate Juvenile Delinquency. "Hearings before the Subcommittee to Investigate Juvenile Delinquency of the Committee on the Judiciary United States Eighty-third Congress Second Session Pursuant to S. 190." Washington, DC: United States Government Printing Office, June 21, 1954. http://www.thecomicbooks.com/front-page.html.

Surette, Ray. *Media, Crime, and Criminal Justice: Images, Realities, and Policies*. Third ed. Independence, KY: Wadsworth, 2006.

———. "The Media, the Public, and Criminal Justice Policy." *Journal of the Institute of Justice and International Studies* (2003): 39–52.

Suskind, Ron. "Faith, Certainty, and the Presidency of George W. Bush." *New York Times*, October 17, 2004, sec. Magazine. http://www.nytimes.com/2004/10/17/magazine/17BUSH.html.

Tallon, F., and A. Walls. "Superman and Kingdom Come: The Surprise of Philosophical Theology." In *Superheroes and Philosophy: Truth, Justice, and the Socratic Way*, edited by Tom Morris and Matt Morris, 207–20. Chicago: Open Court, 2005.

Taylor, Ian, Paul Walton, and Jock Young. *The New Criminology: For a Social Theory of Deviance*. New York: Routledge, 1973.

"The Comics Code Authority (as Adopted in 1954)." *Comicartville Library*, January 12, 2010. http://www.comicartville.com/comicscode.htm.

"The Negative Zone Gulag." *What Were They Thinking?* February 9, 2008. http://luchins.com/what-were-they-thinking/the-negative-zone-gulag.

The Sentencing Project and Marc Mauer. *Race to Incarcerate*. Revised and updated ed. New York: New Press, 2006.

Thrasher, Frederic. "The Comics and Delinquency: Cause of Scapegoat." *Journal of Educational Sociology* 23, no. 4 (1949): 195–205.

Toh, Justine. "The Tools and Toys of (the) War (on Terror): Consumer Desire, Military Fetish, and Regime Change in Batman Begins." In *Reframing 9/11: Film, Popular Culture, and the "War on Terror,"* edited by Jeff Birkenstein, Anna Froula, and Karen Randell, 2026–2219. Kindle for iPad. New York: Continuum, 2010.

Trechak, Brad. "DC Comics Is Now DC Entertainment." *Huffpost TV,* September 10, 2009. http://www.aoltv.com/2009/09/10/dc-comics-is-now-dc-entertainment.

Truitt, Brian. "Half-Black, Half-Hispanic Spider-Man Revealed." *USA Today,* August 2, 2011. http://www.usatoday.com/life/comics/2011-08-01-black-spider-man_n.htm.

Tunnell, Kenneth D. "Socially Disorganized Rural Communities." *Crime, Media, Culture* 2, no. 3 (2006): 332–37.

U.S. Congress. Senate. Committee on the Judiciary. Juvenile Deliquency. "Comic Books and Juvenile Delinquency," 1955-56. Library of Congress Catalogue Card Number 77-90720. http://www.thecomicbooks.com/old/kefauver.html.

Vaid, Urvashi. *Virtual Equality: The Mainstreaming of Gay and Lesbian Liberation.* New York: Anchor Books, 1996.

Varnum, Robin, and Christina T. Gibbons. *The Language of Comics: Word and Image.* Jackson: University Press of Mississippi, 2007.

Versluys, Kristaan. "Art Spiegelman's *In the Shadow of No Towers*: 9/11 and the Representation of Trauma." *Modern Fiction Studies* 52, no. 4 (2006): 980–1001.

Vollum, Scott, and Cary Adkinson. "The Portrayal of Crime and Justice in the Comic Book Superhero Mythos." *Journal of Criminal Justice and Popular Culture* 10, no. 2 (2003): 96–108.

von Hirsch, Andrew. *Doing Justice: The Choice of Punishments: Report of the Committee for the Study of Incarceration.* New York: Hill and Wang, 1976.

Wahlund, Katarina, and Marianne Kristiansson. "Aggression, Psychopathy and Brain Imaging: Review and Future Recommendations." *International Journal of Law and Psychiatry* 32, no. 4 (May 5, 2009): 266–71.

Waid, Mark. "Mark Waid Talks 'Irredeemable.'" *Comic Book Resources,* February 2, 2009. http://www.comicbookresources.com/?page=article&id=19801.

Walker, David. "Why Aren't There More Black Superheroes?" *MSN Movies,* 2009. http://paralleluniverse.msn.com/comic-con/black-superheroes/story/feature/?GT1=28140.

Walker, Samuel. *Sense and Nonsense about Crime, Drugs, and Communities.* Independence, KY: Cengage Learning, 2010.

Wanzo, Rebecca. "Wearing Hero-Face: Black Citizens and Melancholic Patriotism in *Truth: Red, White, and Black.*" *Journal of Popular Culture* 42, no. 2 (April 2009): 339–62.

Weiland, Jonah. "'Coup D'etat: Sleeper' and 'Afterword' Sold Out at DC." *Comic Book Resources,* March 23, 2004. http://www.comicbookresources.com/?page=article&id=3306.

Weinstein, Simcha. *Up, Up, and Oy Vey: How Jewish History, Culture, and Values Shaped the Comic Book Superhero.* Fort Lee, NJ: Barricade Books, 2009.

Weisberg, Robert. "The Death Penalty Meets Social Science: Deterrence and Jury Behavior under New Scrutiny." *Annual Review of Law and Social Science* 1, no. 1 (December 2005): 151–70.

Welch, Kelly. "Black Criminal Stereotypes and Racial Profiling." *Journal of Contemporary Criminal Justice* 23 (2007): 276–88.

Wenger, Etienne. *Communities of Practice: Learning, Memory, and Identity.* Cambridge, UK: Cambridge University Press, 1998.

Wertham, Fredric. *Seduction of the Innocent.* New York: Rinehart, 1954.

Wheeler, Andrew. "No More Mutants by Andrew Wheeler #3: The Secret Asians." *Bleeding Cool*, September 25, 2010. http://www.bleedingcool.com/2010/09/25/no-more-mutants-by-andrew-wheeler-3-the-secret-asians.

Whitt, Tony. "Nick Fury: Does It Matter If He's Black or White?" *Mania.com*, September 10, 2003. http://www.mania.com/comicscape-september-10-2003_article_39611.html.

Wight, Emily, and Genevieve Roberts. "Online Anger Erupts over Blockbuster's 'Racelifting.'" *The Independent*, n.d. http://www.independent.co.uk/arts-entertainment/films/news/online-anger-erupts-over-blockbusters-racelifting-7626976.html.

Williams, D. "Arab Superheroes Leap Pyramids in a Single Bound." *Washington Post Foreign Service*, February 16, 2005.

Williams, Jeff. "Comics: A Tool of Subversion?" In *Interrogating Popular Culture: Deviance, Justice, and Social Order*, edited by S. E. Anderson and G. J. Howard, 97–115. Guilderland, NY: Harrow and Heston, 1998.

Wilson, James Q. *Thinking about Crime*. New York: Basic Books, 1975.

Winick, Judd. *Green Lantern: Brother's Keeper*. New York: DC Comics, 2003.

Wolf-Meyer, Matthew. "The World Ozymandias Made: Utopias in the Superhero Comic, Subculture, and the Conservation of Difference." *Journal of Popular Culture* 36, no. 3 (2003): 497–517.

Wolk, Douglas. *Reading Comics: How Graphic Novels Work and What They Mean*. Cambridge, MA: Da Capo Press, 2007.

Woods, S. "Graphic Violence." *Rolling Stone*, April 20, 2006.

Wright, Bradford W. *Comic Book Nation: The Transformation of Youth Culture in America*. Baltimore, MD: Johns Hopkins University Press, 2003.

Yang, Jeff, Parry Shen, Keith Chow, and Jerry Ma. *Secret Identities: The Asian-American Superhero Anthology*. New York: New Press, 2009.

Young, Jock. "Constructing the Paradigm of Violence: Mass Media, Violence, and Youth." *malcolmread.co.uk*, January 2003. www.malcolmread.co.uk/JockYoung/constructing_jan_2003.pdf.

———. "Moral Panic: Its Origins in Resistance, Ressentiment, and the Translation of Fantasy into Reality." *British Journal of Criminology* 49, no. 1 (2009): 4–16.

———. "Radical Criminology in Britain: The Emergence of a Competing Paradigm." *British Journal of Criminology* 28 (1988): 159–83.

———. *The Exclusive Society: Social Exclusion, Crime, and Difference in Late Modernity*. London: Sage Publications, 1999.

Zimring, Franklin E., and Gordon Hawkins. *Incapacitation: Penal Confinement and the Restraint of Crime*. New York: Oxford University Press, 1997.

INDEX

ABOUT THE AUTHORS

Nickie D. Phillips is Associate Professor in the Department of Sociology and Criminal Justice at St. Francis College.

Staci Strobl is Associate Professor in the Department of Law, Police Science, and Criminal Justice Administration at John Jay College of Criminal Justice, City University of New York.

Made in the USA
Lexington, KY
13 June 2018